D1246661

EVOLUTION AND ETHICS

✦ THE BARNES & NOBLE LIBRARY OF ESSENTIAL READING ✦

EVOLUTION AND ETHICS
And Other Essays

THOMAS H. HUXLEY

INTRODUCTION BY SHERRIE LYONS

BARNES & NOBLE

NEW YORK

THE BARNES & NOBLE
LIBRARY OF ESSENTIAL READING

Introduction and Suggested Reading © 2006
by Barnes & Noble, Inc.

Originally published in 1893

This 2006 edition published by Barnes & Noble, Inc.

All rights reserved. No part of this publication may be reproduced, stored
in a retrieval system, or transmitted, in any form or by any
means, electronic, mechanical, photocopying, recording, or
otherwise, without prior written permission from the publisher.

ISBN-13: 978-0-7607-8337-5
ISBN-10: 0-7607-8337-3

Printed and bound in the United States of America

1 3 5 7 9 10 8 6 4 2

Contents

INTRODUCTION

ALTHOUGH THOMAS HUXLEY DUBBED HIMSELF "DARWIN'S BULLDOG" and said he was prepared to go to the stake if necessary to defend Darwin's theory of evolution, he did not think the doctrine of evolution could give us the ethics to put into practice. In spite of the vast amount of literature on evolutionary ethics that has accumulated since Huxley wrote *Evolution and Ethics*, his book still provides one of the clearest articulations on the subject. Huxley argued that even if one accepts that evolution has produced creatures such as ourselves with a moral sense, it does not follow that we can look to evolution to define the content of what we call moral. Controversial in Huxley's time, evolutionary ethics remains a hotly debated topic today. Evolutionary theory has and continues to provide tremendous insight on our quest to understand the brain and behavior. Moral systems are a universal characteristic of human societies; therefore the tendency to develop them must be an integral part of human nature. Any evolutionary account of our origins must take morality quite seriously, and we must build it into our theories about human behavior. However, the attempt to build a naturalistic ethics grounded in evolutionary theory remains problematic, and Huxley's writings are as relevant today as when he first penned them. His style is sharp and lucid, and *Evolution and Ethics* displays Huxley's far-reaching knowledge of a vast array of topics, from Buddhism to the nature of consciousness, and provides guidance in navigating the land mines that infuse the field of evolutionary ethics.

Thomas H. Huxley was born in 1825 in the English country village of Ealing. He was the youngest of seven children of George and Rachel Withers Huxley. His father was a schoolteacher, but Huxley received little regular schooling and was largely self-taught. Even as a young boy he had interests in a staggering array of subjects. From James Hutton, he learned about geology. From reading Sir William Hamilton's "The Philosophy of the Unconditioned," he came to embrace the skepticism that typified his mature thought. Although he attended church regularly, as he grew older he realized that he was one of those skeptics or infidels of whom preachers spoke with horror. Often called an atheist or a materialist, Huxley later coined the term "agnostic" to describe his own philosophical system of belief after finding that none of the various other "isms" properly described his views. From Thomas Carlyle, he developed a sympathy for the poor that was later reinforced by his exposure to the squalor and poverty he saw in the East End of London.

Huxley showed an affinity for anatomy and received a scholarship to the medical school attached to London's Charing Cross Hospital when he was only fifteen. Except for physiology, most of the medical curriculum bored him. Nevertheless, he won first prize for chemistry, also taking honors in anatomy and physiology. He later won a gold medal in those subjects in the Bachelor of Medicine exam, but he was too young to qualify for a license to practice medicine. Like many others who made their mark in the natural sciences, Huxley took a voyage around the world, serving as the assistant surgeon on the HMS *Rattlesnake* from 1846 to 1850. In Australia he met his future wife, Henrietta Anne Heathorn. They married in 1855 and had a long and happy marriage and seven children.

Huxley's life was one of incessant activity. He lectured at the School of Mines and continued to do research in physiology and biology. Evenings were often spent speaking before working men or learned societies. In 1862, he served as president of the biology section of the British Association for Advancement of Science (BAAS), and he became president of the association in 1870. In 1869 and 1870, he was president of both the Geological Society and the Ethnological Society.

Huxley's voyage on the *Rattlesnake* resulted in some of his most important scientific work and established his reputation within the scientific community. However, it was his defense of Darwinism that brought him into the public spotlight in a famous encounter with Bishop Samuel Wilberforce at the 1860 Oxford meeting of the BAAS. Wilberforce, who had been coached by Richard Owen in his attack on evolution, asked Huxley whether "it was on his grandfather's or his grandmother's side that the ape ancestry comes in." Huxley replied:

> . . . a man has no reason to be ashamed of having an ape for his grandfather. If there were an ancestor whom I should feel shame in recalling it would rather be a man of restless and versatile intellect—who, not content with an equivocal success in his own sphere of activity, plunges into scientific questions with which he has no real acquaintance, only to obscure them by an aimless rhetoric, and distract the attention of his hearers from the real point at issue by eloquent digressions and skilled appeals to religious prejudice.

Huxley's reply created pandemonium. According to one account, ladies fainted.

Huxley correctly perceived that the most threatening aspect of Darwin's theory was its significance for human origins. This resulted in his most famous work, *Man's Place in Nature,* which was published in 1863, eight years before Darwin's *Descent of Man.* In it, Huxley argued powerfully and eloquently that humans were no exception to the theory of evolution. However, Huxley wrote several hundred scientific monographs and pursued a research program in developmental morphology that was quite distinct from the ideas espoused in *The Origin of Species.* Nevertheless, he is best remembered as a popularizer and defender of Darwinism and for his popular essays on a staggering array of subjects, from geology to education to religion. *Evolution and Ethics* is the final volume of a nine-volume set culled from hundreds of these essays.

Evolution and Ethics contains several essays, but the most frequently cited are the "Romanes Lecture" and the longer "Prolegomena." George Romanes was a biologist and psychologist and a close colleague

of both Darwin and Huxley. He founded the Romanes Lecture in 1892 as an annual free public lecture at Oxford University to be given by leading intellectuals. Romanes invited Huxley to give the second lecture in 1893, following William Gladstone, four-time prime minister of England and someone with whom Huxley had often crossed swords over political, religious, and scientific issues. However, the Romanes Foundation stated that the lecturer "shall abstain from treating either Religion or Politics."

Huxley had long been thinking about the relationship of ethical and evolutionary theory in the history of philosophy. But he pointed out that "Ethical Science was, on all sides, so entangled with Religion and Politics" that he needed all the "dexterity of an egg-dancer." Fortunately, the prohibition against addressing religion and politics in the Romanes Lecture no longer holds. Princeton University President Shirley M. Tilghman began the 2005 Romanes Lecture, "Strange Bedfellows: Science, Politics and Religion," by pointing out that she "by necessity will be walking on Huxley's metaphorical eggshells."[1]

Darwin's ideas had led many thoughtful people to ask whether it was possible to create a system of ethics based on evolutionary theory. At first glance it appears that Huxley has answered this question with a resounding no.

> The propounders of what are called the "ethics of evolution," when the "evolution of ethics" would usually better express the object of their speculations, adduce a number of more or less interesting facts and more or less sound arguments in favor of the origin of the moral sentiments . . . by a process of evolution. . . . But as the immoral sentiments have no less been evolved, there is so far, as much natural sanction for the one as the other. The thief and the murderer follow nature just as much as the philanthropist. Cosmic evolution may teach us how the good and the evil tendencies of man may have come about; but, in itself, it is incompetent to furnish any better reason why what we call good is preferable to what we call evil than we had before. [2]

However, the "Prolegomena" and the "Romanes Lecture" must be situated in their historical context to fully understand why Huxley wrote what he did. Examining Huxley's entire corpus of work demonstrates that his view of nature was not as harsh at it appears in these essays.

Huxley was optimistic about the insights that evolution could provide for human society. In the 1860s, he believed that the key to successfully playing the game of life was learning the rules of the game, and those rules were the laws of nature. The game of life was infinitely more difficult and complicated than chess, and the other player was hidden from us, although his play was always "fair, just, and patient." To learn the rules one must turn to the teacher, who was Nature herself. If people directed their affections and wills "into an earnest and loving desire to move in harmony with [Nature's] laws," this would lead to a just and fair society.[3]

By the time of the "Romanes Lecture," however, Huxley's views had changed considerably. Herbert Spencer had articulated the advantages of applying evolutionary theory to social behavior, espousing an ethic that became known as Social Darwinism. In 1864, Spencer coined the phrase "survival of the fittest," which Darwin later adopted to describe the ongoing struggle for existence that resulted in natural selection. Spencer and his followers argued that one's moral obligations should be to promote this struggle for existence in the social realm. Thus he was against any sort of social safety net such as the so-called poor laws and other forms of public assistance to provide relief for the poor because they only contributed to the survival of the least fit.[4] In a similar vein in the 1880s, William Sumner maintained that struggle and competition were the law of nature. "Nature is entirely neutral: she submits to him who most energetically and resolutely assails her. She grants her rewards to the fittest."[5] If we try to redistribute those rewards, we may lessen the inequalities, but we are rewarding and promoting the survival of the unfit, which will result in the deterioration of society. Here was a social program, an ethic that grounded its validity in Darwin's theory.

Needless to say, many people could not abide an ethic that was counter to all common decency, that claimed the state had no obligation to the less-fortunate members of society. Huxley responded to the harsh extreme individualism of Spencer in the "Romanes Lecture," claiming that:

> Laws and moral precepts are directed to the end of curbing the cosmic process and reminding the individual of his duty to the community. . . . Let us understand, once and for all that the ethical progress of society depends, not on imitating the cosmic process, still less in running away from it, but in combating it.

Huxley, like many later critics such as G. E. Moore, attacked evolutionary ethics on the grounds that it committed the naturalistic fallacy. Just because nature *is* a certain way does not mean nature *ought* to be that way. However, Huxley's critique actually goes far deeper than this.

Implicit in the various versions of evolutionary ethics was the idea that nature was progressive. Huxley denied this. In earlier writings, he had argued that one of the great strengths of Darwin's theory was that in addition to explaining how organisms change and progress, it also explained how many organisms do not progress, and some even become simpler.[6] Thus we cannot assume that applying the principles of evolution to the social realm would result in the progress and improvement of society. Huxley realized that "fittest" had a connotation of "best," but as he correctly pointed out, if the environment suddenly became much cooler, the survival of the fittest would most likely bring about in the plant world a population of more and more stunted and humbler organisms. In such an environment, the lichen and diatoms might be the most fit. Furthermore, the strict definition of Darwinian fitness is reproductive success. However, surely no one would label a serial rapist who successfully impregnates hundreds of women the "best" member of society.

The key to reproductive success is adaptation. Adaptation is at the core of Darwin's theory: the mechanism of natural selection did not just explain how organisms changed, but how they changed adaptively. Although this idea of adaptation has been evolutionary theory's greatest strength, it has also been its greatest weakness because we can tell an endless number of adaptive stories. Which one should we believe? Particularly in explaining human evolution, cultural biases have strongly influenced the types of stories that have been told. Huxley himself was responding to a particular story that was being told in his time.

Critics on both sides misconstrued Huxley's lecture. Free thinkers accused him of abandoning them while conservatives welcomed him as a convert to orthodoxy. Neither assumption was true. Because of the injunction to avoid any discussion of theology in the lecture, Huxley had to leave much unsaid. To clarify his views, the following year he wrote the "Prolegomena," prefacing the reissue of the lecture.

Countering Huxley's harsh view of nature, Peter Kropotkin in *Mutual Aid* (1902) claimed that natural selection promoted group characteristics and sentiments, and that we have a natural sentiment to help each other: "The fittest are the most sociable animals and sociability appears as the chief factor of evolution. . . . Those mammals, which stand at the very top of the animal world and most approach man by their structure and intelligence are eminently sociable."[7] Kropotkin's ideas about how to improve society were diametrically opposed to those of Spencer, yet both men claimed that their ethics came directly out of evolutionary theory. It seems more accurate to say that they read their own social/political views into evolutionary theory. This problem continues to plague evolutionary ethics to the present day as is evidenced by the contentious literature of sociobiology and evolutionary psychology.

In light of recent work on group selection, altruism, and extensive studies on non-human primates, particularly the work of Franz de Waal, the possibility of building an ethics rooted in biology seems more promising. De Waal has argued that we can see the origins of right and wrong in primate behavior. Chimpanzees exhibit such traits as attachment, nurturance, empathy, and special treatment of the disabled or injured. Chimpanzee society has its own set of rules that are internalized and will result in punishment if broken. They have concepts of giving, trading, and revenge. They exhibit peacemaking behavior and moralistic aggression against violations of reciprocity.

Primate behavior not only demonstrates the evolution of ethics, but also shows that the ethics of evolution is not contrary to our own ethical sensibilities. In *Man's Place in Nature*, Huxley also suggests such a possibility as he comments on the commonality of traits between man and beast. He asks, "Is mother-love vile because a hen shows it, or fidelity base because dogs possess it?"[8] Nature is not just red in tooth and claw. Humans are not fundamentally brutish or noble. We are both, just like our primate cousins and our ancestors, and just as Huxley claimed.

Evolution teaches us that behaviors have evolved to enhance survival, and therefore ethical premises are products of the particular history of our species. They are deeply rooted, and while human behavior is very flexible, it has strong genetic underpinnings. In that sense, it is possible to change ethical laws at the deepest level in the ongoing struggle to stay adapted to an ever-changing environment. One of the implications of evolutionary ethics is that there can be no absolute, objective standard of morality that is eternal. Our species might eventually evolve rules that we would presently consider morally abhorrent. Current research in both evolution and neurobiology suggests that this does not mean we are doomed to a moral relativity.

Unselfish behavior towards one's offspring has undoubtedly been naturally selected. Those who look after their children will generally be more successful in having their genes passed on to future generations than those who don't. Building on J. B. S. Haldane's work from the 1930s, W. D. Hamilton in the 1960s provided a rigorous mathematical account of how altruistic behavior could have evolved, which John Maynard Smith dubbed "kin selection." Cooperation turns out to be a good survival strategy, just as Kropotkin argued. Many socio-biologists argue that altruism is selfish, merely another way of getting one's genes into the next generation. When someone gives up her life to save her child, evolutionarily this could be described as a selfish act, but at the level of intentions or motivation, it is an unselfish act. Thus, describing it as a genuine altruistic act is appropriate, even if ultimately the origins of why people behave this way is rooted in kin selection. Furthermore, people often save non-kin and act unselfishly with no thought of reciprocity or reward. Research by neurobiologist Antonio Damasio on the role of empathy in rational decision-making and the discovery of mirror neurons, sometimes referred to as empathy or Dali Lama neurons, suggest that empathy and kindness are an essential part of our nature and can provide a basis for building a moral code. This suggests the possibility of an evolutionary ethics that may finally break free of the many problems that have plagued it.

If Huxley were alive today, he would be thrilled with these new findings. Committed to empirical investigation, he maintained that one must "follow humbly wherever and to whatever abysses nature leads."[9] Modern research suggests a way out of the abyss of the dark side of human nature, validating Huxley's earlier views that learning and abiding by nature's rules would result in a just and fair society. But not only must nature be interpreted, every human act results from a complex interaction of nature and culture. In this regard, Huxley's fundamental message in *Evolution and Ethics* is not historically contingent. It is an eloquent and compelling reminder that great caution must be exercised in evaluating any ethical system.

Sherrie Lyons holds a Ph.D. in the history of science from the University of Chicago. She is the author of *Thomas Henry Huxley, The Evolution of a Scientist,* and numerous articles on various aspects of nineteenth- and twentieth-century evolutionary biology. She teaches at Empire State College, New York.

PREFACE

THE DISCOURSE ON *EVOLUTION AND ETHICS*, REPRINTED IN THE FIRST half of the present volume, was delivered before the University of Oxford, as the second of the annual lectures founded by Mr. Romanes: whose name I may not write without deploring the untimely death, in the flower of his age, of a friend endeared to me, as to so many others, by his kindly nature; and justly valued by all his colleagues for his powers of investigation and his zeal for the advancement of knowledge. I well remember, when Mr. Romanes' early work came into my hands, as one of the secretaries of the Royal Society, how much I rejoiced in the accession to the ranks of the little army of workers in science of a recruit so well qualified to take a high place among us.

It was at my friend's urgent request that I agreed to undertake the lecture, should I be honored with an official proposal to give it, though I confess not without misgivings, if only on account of the serious fatigue and hoarseness which public speaking has for some years caused me; while I knew that it would be my fate to follow the most accomplished and facile orator of our time, whose indomitable youth is in no matter, more manifest than in his penetrating and musical voice. A certain saying about comparisons intruded itself somewhat importunately.

And even if I disregarded the weakness of my body in the matter of voice, and that of my mind in the matter of vanity, there remained a third difficulty. For several reasons, my attention, during a number of years, has been much directed to the bearing of modern scientific thought on the problems of morals and of politics, and I did not care to be diverted from that topic. Moreover, I thought it the most important and the worthiest which, at the present time, could engage the attention even of an ancient and renowned University.

But it is a condition of the Romanes foundation that the lecturer shall abstain from treating of either Religion or Politics; and it appeared to me that, more than most, perhaps, I was bound to act, not merely up to the letter, but in the spirit, of that prohibition. Yet Ethical Science is, on all sides, so entangled with Religion and Politics, that the lecturer who essays to touch the former without coming into contact with either of the latter, needs all the dexterity of an egg-dancer; and may even discover that his sense of clearness and his sense of propriety come into conflict, by no means to the advantage of the former.

I had little notion of the real magnitude of these difficulties when I set about my task; but I am consoled for my pains and anxiety by observing that none of the multitudinous criticisms with which I have been favored and, often, instructed, find fault with me on the score of having strayed out of bounds.

Among my critics there are not a few to whom I feel deeply indebted for the careful attention which they have given to the exposition thus hampered; and further weakened, I am afraid, by my forgetfulness of a maxim touching lectures of a popular character, which has descended to me from that prince of lecturers, Mr. Faraday. He was once asked by a beginner, called upon to address a highly select and cultivated audience, what he might suppose his hearers to know already. Whereupon the past master of the art of exposition emphatically replied "Nothing!"

To my shame as a retired veteran, who has all his life profited by this great precept of lecturing strategy, I forgot all about it just when it would have been most useful. I was fatuous enough to imagine that a number of propositions, which I thought established, and which, in fact, I had advanced without challenge on former occasions, needed no repetition.

I have endeavored to repair my error by prefacing the lecture with some matter—chiefly elementary or recapitulatory—to which I have given the title of "Prolegomena." I wish I could have hit upon a heading of less pedantic aspect which would have served my purpose; and if it be urged that the new building looks over large for the edifice to which it is added, I can only plead the precedent of the ancient architects, who always made the adytum the smallest part of the temple.

If I had attempted to reply in full to the criticisms to which I have referred, I know not what extent of ground would have been covered by my *pronaos*. All I have endeavored to do, at present, is to remove that which seems to have proved a stumbling-block to many—namely, the apparent paradox that ethical nature, while born of cosmic nature, is necessarily at enmity with its parent. Unless the arguments set forth in the Prolegomena, in the simplest language at my command, have some flaw which I am unable to discern, this seeming paradox is a truth, as great as it is plain, the recognition of which is fundamental for the ethical philosopher.

We cannot do without our inheritance from the forefathers who were the puppets of the cosmic process; the society which renounces it must be destroyed from without. Still less can we do with too much of it; the society in which it dominates must be destroyed from within.

The motive of the drama of human life is the necessity, laid upon every man who comes into the world, of discovering the mean between self-assertion and self-restraint suited to his character and his circumstances. And the eternally tragic aspect of the drama lies in this: that the problem set before us is one the elements of which can be but imperfectly known, and of which even an approximately right solution rarely presents itself, until that stern critic, aged experience, has been furnished with ample justification for venting his sarcastic humor upon the irreparable blunders we have already made.

I have reprinted the letters on the *Darkest England* scheme, published in the *Times* of December 1890 and January 1891; and subsequently issued, with additions, as a pamphlet, under the title of *Social Diseases and Worse Remedies*; because, although the clever attempt to rush the country on behalf of that scheme has been balked, Mr. Booth's standing army remains afoot, retaining all the capacities for mischief which are inherent in its constitution. I am desirous that this fact should be kept steadily in view; and that the moderation of the clamor of the drums and trumpets should not lead us to forget the existence of a force, which, in bad hands, may, at anytime, be used for bad purposes.

In 1892, a Committee was "formed for the purpose of investigating the manner in which the moneys, subscribed in response to the appeal made in the book entitled *In Darkest England and the Way out*, have been expended." The members of this body were gentlemen in whose competency and equity everyone must have complete confidence; and in December 1892 they published a report in which they declare that, "with the exception of the sums expended on the 'barracks' at Hadleigh," the moneys in question have been "devoted only to the objects and expended in the methods set out in that appeal, and to and in no others."

Nevertheless, their final conclusion runs as follows:

> (4) That whilst the invested property, real and personal, resulting from such Appeal is so vested and controlled by the Trust of the Deed of January 30th, 1891, that any application of it to purposes other than those declared in the deed by any "General" of the Salvation Army would amount to a breach of trust, and would subject him to the proceedings of a civil and criminal character, before mentioned in the Report, *adequate legal safeguards do not at present exist to prevent the misapplication of such property.*

The passage I have italicised forms part of a document dated December 19th, 1892. It follows, that, even after the Deed of January 30th, 1891, was executed, "adequate legal safeguards" "to prevent the misapplication of the property" did not exist. What then was the state of things, up to a week earlier, that is on January 22nd, 1891, when my twelfth and last letter appeared in the *Times*? A better justification for what I have said about the want of adequate security for the proper administration of the funds intrusted to Mr. Booth could not be desired, unless it be that which is to be found in the following passages of the Report (pp. 21 and 22):

"It is possible that a 'General' may be forgetful of his duty, and sell property and appropriate the proceeds to his own use, or to meeting the general liabilities of the Salvation Army. As matters now stand, he, and he alone, would have control over such a sale. Against such possibilities it appears to the Committee to be reasonable that some check should be imposed."

Once more let it be remembered that this opinion, given under the hand of Sir Henry James, was expressed by the Committee, with the Trust Deed of 1891, which has been so sedulously flaunted before the public, in full view.

The Committee made a suggestion for the improvement of this very unsatisfactory state of things; but the exact value set upon it by the suggestors should be carefully considered (p. 22).

"The Committee are fully aware that if the views thus expressed are carried out, the safeguards and checks created will not be sufficient for all purposes absolutely to prevent possible dealing with the property and moneys, inconsistent with the purposes to which they are intended to be devoted."

In fact, they are content to express the very modest hope that "if the suggestion made be acted upon, some hindrance will thereby be placed in the way of anyone acting dishonestly in respect of the disposal of the property and moneys referred to."

I do not know, and, under the circumstances, I cannot say I much care, whether the suggestions of the Committee have, or have not, been acted upon. Whether or not, the fact remains, that an unscrupulous "General" will have a pretty free hand, notwithstanding "some" hindrance.

Thus, the judgment of the highly authoritative, and certainly not hostile, Committee of 1892, upon the issues with which they concerned themselves is hardly such as to inspire enthusiastic confidence. And it is further to be borne in mind that they carefully excluded from their duties "any examination of the principles, government, teaching, or methods of the Salvation Army as a religious organization, or of its affairs" except so far as they related to the administration of the moneys collected by the *Darkest England* appeal.

Consequently, the most important questions discussed in my letters were not in anyway touched by the Committee. Even if their report had been far more favorable to the *Darkest England* scheme than it is; if it had really assured the contributors that the funds raised were fully secured against malversation; the objections, on social and political grounds, to Mr. Booth's despotic organization, with its thousands of docile satellites pledged to blind obedience, set forth in the letters, would be in no degree weakened. The "sixpennyworth of good" would still he outweighed by the "shilling'sworth of harm"; if indeed the relative worth, or unworth, of the latter should not be rated in pounds rather than in shillings.

What would one not give for the opinion of the financial members of the Committee about the famous Bank; and that of the legal experts about the proposed "tribunes of the people"?

HODESLEA, EASTBOURNE,
July 1894

CHAPTER ONE

EVOLUTION AND ETHICS

Prolegomena

[1894]

I

IT MAY BE SAFELY ASSUMED THAT, TWO THOUSAND YEARS AGO, BEFORE Cæsar set foot in southern Britain, the whole countryside visible from the windows of the room in which I write, was in what is called "the state of nature." Except, it may be, by raising a few sepulchral mounds, such as those which still, here and there, break the flowing contours of the downs, man's hands had made no mark upon it; and the thin veil of vegetation which overspread the broad-backed heights and the shelving sides of the coombs was unaffected by his industry. The native grasses and weeds, the scattered patches of gorse, contended with one another for the possession of the scanty surface soil; they fought against the droughts of summer, the frosts of winter, and the furious gales which swept, with unbroken force, now from the Atlantic, and now from the North Sea, at all times of the year; they filled up, as they best might, the gaps made in their ranks by all sorts of underground and overground animal ravagers. One year with another, an average population, the floating balance of the unceasing struggle for existence among the indigenous plants, maintained itself. It is as little to be doubted, that an essentially similar state of nature prevailed, in this region, for many thousand years before the coming of Cæsar; and there is no assignable reason for denying that it might continue to exist through an equally prolonged futurity, except for the intervention of man.

Reckoned by our customary standards of duration, the native vegetation, like the "everlasting hills" which it clothes, seems a type of permanence. The little Amarella Gentians, which abound in some places today, are the descendants of those that were trodden underfoot by the prehistoric savages who have left their flint tools about, here and there; and they followed ancestors which, in the climate of the glacial epoch, probably flourished better than they do now. Compared with the long past of this humble plant, all the history of civilized men is but an episode.

Yet nothing is more certain than that, measured by the liberal scale of timekeeping of the universe, this present state of nature, however it may seem to have gone and to go on forever, is but a fleeting phase of her infinite variety; merely the last of the series of changes which the earth's surface has undergone in the course of the millions of years of its existence. Turn back a square foot of the thin turf, and the solid foundation of the land, exposed in cliffs of chalk five hundred feet high on the adjacent shore, yields full assurance of a time when the sea covered the site of the "everlasting hills"; and when the vegetation of what land lay nearest, was as different from the present Flora of the Sussex downs, as that of Central Africa now is.[1] No less certain is it that, between the time during which the chalk was formed and that at which the original turf came into existence, thousands of centuries elapsed, in the course of which, the state of nature of the ages during which the chalk was deposited, passed into that which now is, by changes so slow that, in the coming and going of the generations of men, had such witnessed them, the contemporary conditions would have seemed to be unchanging and unchangeable.

But it is also certain that, before the deposition of the chalk, a vastly longer period had elapsed, throughout which it is easy to follow the traces of the same process of ceaseless modification and of the internecine struggle for existence of living things; and that even when we can get no further back, it is not because there is any reason to think we have reached the beginning, but because the trail of the most ancient life remains hidden, or has become obliterated.

Thus that state of nature of the world of plants, which we began by considering, is far from possessing the attribute of permanence. Rather its very essence is impermanence. It may have lasted twenty or thirty thousand years, it may last for twenty or thirty thousand years more, without obvious change; but, as surely as it has followed upon a very different state, so it will be followed by an equally different condition. That which endures is not one or another association of living forms, but the process of which the cosmos is the product, and of which these are among the transitory expressions. And in the living world, one of the most characteristic features of this cosmic process is the struggle for existence, the competition of each with all, the result of which is the selection, that is to say, the survival of those forms which, on the whole, are best adapted to the conditions which at any period obtain; and which are, therefore, in that respect, and only in that respect, the fittest.[2] The acme reached by the cosmic process in the vegetation of the downs is seen in the turf, with its weeds and gorse. Under the conditions, they have come out of the struggle victorious; and, by surviving, have proved that they are the fittest to survive.

That the state of nature, at anytime, is a temporary phase of a process of incessant change, which has been going on for innumerable ages, appears to me to be a proposition as well established as any in modern history. Paleontology assures us, in addition, that the ancient philosophers who, with less reason, held the same doctrine, erred in supposing that the phases formed a cycle, exactly repeating the past, exactly foreshadowing the future, in their rotations. On the contrary, it furnishes us with conclusive reasons for thinking that, if every link in the ancestry of these humble indigenous plants had been preserved and were accessible to us, the whole would present a converging series of forms of gradually diminishing complexity, until, at some period in the history of the earth, far more remote than any of which organic remains have yet been discovered, they would merge in those low groups among which the boundaries between animal and vegetable life become effaced.[3]

The word "evolution," now generally applied to the cosmic process, has had a singular history, and is used in various senses.[4]

Taken in its popular signification it means progressive development, that is, gradual change from a condition of relative uniformity to one of relative complexity; but its connotation has been widened to include the phenomena of retrogressive metamorphosis, that is, of progress from a condition of relative complexity to one of relative uniformity.

As a natural process, of the same character as the development of a tree from its seed, or of a fowl from its egg, evolution excludes creation and all other kinds of supernatural intervention. As the expression of a fixed order, every stage of which is the effect of causes operating according to definite rules, the conception of evolution no less excludes that of chance. It is very desirable to remember that evolution is not an explanation of the cosmic process, but merely a generalized statement of the method and results of that process. And, further, that, if there is proof that the cosmic process was set going by any agent, then that agent will be the creator of it and of all its products, although supernatural intervention may remain strictly excluded from its further course.

So far as that limited revelation of the nature of things, which we call scientific knowledge, has yet gone, it tends, with constantly increasing emphasis, to the belief that, not merely the world of plants, but that of animals; not merely living things, but the whole fabric of the earth; not merely our planet, but the whole solar system; not merely our star and its satellites, but the millions of similar bodies which bear witness to the order which pervades boundless space, and has endured through boundless time; are all working out their predestined courses of evolution.

With none of these have I anything to do, at present, except with that exhibited by the forms of life which tenant the earth. All plants and animals exhibit the tendency to vary, the causes of which have yet to be ascertained; it is the tendency of the conditions of life, at any given time, while favoring the existence of the variations best adapted to them, to oppose that of the rest and thus to exercise selection; and all living things tend to multiply without limit, while the means of support are limited; the obvious cause of which is the production of offspring more numerous than their progenitors, but with equal expectation of life in the actuarial sense. Without the first tendency there could be no evolution. Without the second, there would be no good reason why one variation should disappear and another take its place; that is to say there would be no selection. Without the third, the struggle for existence, the agent of the selective process in the state of nature, would vanish.[5]

Granting the existence of these tendencies, all the known facts of the history of plants and of animals may be brought into rational correlation. And this is more than can be said for any other hypothesis that I know of. Such hypotheses, for example, as that of the existence of a primitive, orderless chaos; of a passive and sluggish eternal matter molded, with but partial success, by archetypal ideas; of a brand-new world-stuff suddenly created and swiftly shaped by a supernatural power; receive no encouragement, but the contrary, from our present knowledge. That our earth may once have formed part of a nebulous cosmic magma is certainly possible, indeed seems highly probable; but there is no reason to doubt that order reigned there, as completely as amidst what we regard as the most finished works of nature or of man.[6] The faith which is born of knowledge, finds its object in an eternal order, bringing forth ceaseless change, through endless time, in endless space; the manifestations of the cosmic energy alternating between phases of potentiality and phases of explication. It may be that, as Kant suggests,[7] every cosmic magma predestined to evolve into a new world, has been the no less predestined end of a vanished predecessor.

II

Three or four years have elapsed since the state of nature, to which I have referred, was brought to an end, so far as a small patch of the soil is concerned, by the intervention of man. The patch was cut off from the rest by a wall; within the area thus protected, the native vegetation was, as far as possible, extirpated; while a colony of strange plants was imported and set down in its place. In short, it was made into a garden. At the present time, this artificially treated area presents an aspect extraordinarily different from that of so much of the land as remains in the state of nature, outside the wall. Trees, shrubs, and herbs, many of them appertaining to the state of nature of remote parts of the globe, abound and flourish. Moreover, considerable quantities of vegetables, fruits, and flowers are produced, of kinds which neither now exist, nor have ever existed, except under conditions such as obtain in the garden; and which, therefore, are as much works of the art of man as the frames and glass-houses in which some of them are raised. That the "state of Art," thus created in the state of nature by man, is sustained by and dependent on him, would at once become apparent, if the watchful supervision of the gardener were withdrawn, and the antagonistic influences of the general cosmic process were no longer sedulously warded off, or counteracted. The walls and gates would decay; quadrupedal and bipedal intruders would devour and tread down the useful and beautiful plants; birds, insects, blight, and mildew would work their will; the seeds of the native plants, carried by winds or other agencies, would immigrate, and in virtue of their long-earned special adaptation to the local conditions, these despised native weeds would soon choke their choice exotic rivals. A century or two hence, little beyond the foundations of the wall and of the houses and frames would be left, in evidence of the victory of the cosmic powers at work in the state of nature, over the temporary obstacles to their supremacy, set up by the art of the horticulturist.

It will be admitted that the garden is as much a work of art,[8] or artifice, as anything that can be mentioned. The energy localized in certain human bodies, directed by similarly localized intellects, has produced a collocation of other material bodies which could not be brought about in the state of nature. The same proposition is true of all the works of man's hands, from a flint implement to a cathedral or a chronometer; and it is because it is true, that we call these things artificial, term them works of art, or artifice, by way of distinguishing them from the products of the cosmic process, working outside man, which we call natural, or works of nature. The distinction thus drawn between the works of nature and those of man, is universally recognized; and it is, as I conceive, both useful and justifiable.

III

No doubt, it may be properly urged that the operation of human energy and intelligence, which has brought into existence and maintains the garden, by what I have called "the horticultural process," is, strictly speaking, part and parcel of the cosmic process. And no one could more readily agree to that proposition than I. In fact, I do not know that anyone has taken more pains than I have, during the last thirty years, to insist upon the doctrine, so much reviled in the early part of that period, that man, physical, intellectual, and moral, is as much a part of nature, as purely a product of the cosmic process, as the humblest weed.[9]

But if, following up this admission, it is urged that, such being the case, the cosmic process cannot be in antagonism with that horticultural process which is part of itself—I can only reply, that if the conclusion that the two are antagonistic is logically absurd, I am sorry for logic, because, as we have seen, the fact is so. The garden is in the same position as every other work of man's art; it is a result of the cosmic process working through and by human energy and intelligence; and, as is the case with every other artificial thing set up in the state of nature, the influences of the latter are constantly tending to break it down and destroy it. No doubt, the Forth bridge and an ironclad in the offing are, in ultimate resort, products of the cosmic process; as much so as the river which flows under the one, or the seawater on which the other floats. Nevertheless, every breeze strains the bridge a little, every tide does something to weaken its foundations; every change of temperature alters the adjustment of its parts, produces friction and consequent wear and tear. From time to time, the bridge must be repaired, just as the ironclad must go into dock; simply because nature is always tending to reclaim that which her child, man, has borrowed from her and has arranged in combinations which are not those favored by the general cosmic process.

Thus, it is not only true that the cosmic energy, working through man upon a portion of the plant world, opposes the same energy as it works through the state of nature, but a similar antagonism is everywhere manifest between the artificial and the natural. Even in the state of nature itself, what is the struggle for existence but the antagonism of the results of the cosmic process in the region of life, one to another?[10]

IV

Not only is the state of nature hostile to the state of art of the garden; but the principle of the horticultural process, by which the latter is created and maintained, is antithetic to that of the cosmic process. The characteristic feature of the latter is the intense and unceasing competition of the struggle for existence. The characteristic of the former is the elimination of that struggle, by the removal of the conditions which give rise to it. The tendency of the cosmic process is to bring about the adjustment of the forms of plant life to the current conditions; the tendency of the horticultural process is the adjustment of the conditions to the needs of the forms of plant life which the gardener desires to raise.

The cosmic process uses unrestricted multiplication as the means whereby hundreds compete for the place and nourishment adequate for one; it employs frost and drought to cut off the weak and unfortunate; to survive, there is need not only of strength, but of flexibility and of good fortune.

The gardener, on the other hand, restricts multiplication; provides that each plant shall have sufficient space and nourishment; protects from frost and drought; and, in every other way attempts to modify the conditions, in such a manner as to bring about the survival of those forms which most nearly approach the standard of the useful, or the beautiful, which he has in his mind.

If the fruits and the tubers, the foliage and the flowers thus obtained, reach, or sufficiently approach, that ideal, there is no reason why the *status quo* attained should not be indefinitely prolonged. So long as the state of nature remains approximately the same, so long will the energy and intelligence which created the garden suffice to maintain it. However, the limits within which this mastery of man over nature can be maintained are narrow. If the conditions of the cretaceous epoch returned, I fear the most skillful of gardeners would have to give up the cultivation of apples and gooseberries; while, if those of the glacial period once again obtained, open asparagus beds would be superfluous, and the training of fruit trees against the most favorable of south walls, a waste of time and trouble.

But it is extremely important to note that, the state of nature remaining the same, if the produce does not satisfy the gardener, it may be made to approach his ideal more closely. Although, the struggle for existence may be at end, the possibility of progress remains. In discussions on these topics, it is often strangely forgotten that the essential conditions of the modification, or evolution, of living things are variation and hereditary transmission. Selection is the means by which certain variations are favored and their progeny preserved. But the struggle for existence is only one of the means by which selection may be effected. The endless varieties of cultivated flowers, fruits, roots, tubers, and bulbs are not products of selection by means of the struggle for existence, but of direct selection, in view of an ideal of utility or beauty. Amidst a multitude of plants, occupying the same station and subjected to the same conditions, in the garden, varieties arise. The varieties tending in a given direction are preserved, and the rest are destroyed. And the same process takes place among the varieties until, for example, the wild kale becomes a cabbage, or the wild *Viola tricolor* a prize pansy.

V

The process of colonization presents analogies to the formation of a garden which are highly instructive. Suppose a shipload of English colonists sent to form a settlement, in such a country as Tasmania was in the middle of the last century. On landing, they find themselves in the midst of a state of nature, widely different from that left behind them in everything but the most general physical conditions. The common plants, the common birds and quadrupeds, are as totally distinct as the men from anything to be seen on the side of the globe from which they come. The colonists proceed to put an end to this state of things over as large an area as they desire to occupy. They clear away the native vegetation, extirpate or drive out the animal population, so far as may be necessary, and take measures to defend themselves from the re-immigration of either. In their place, they introduce English grain and fruit trees; English dogs, sheep, cattle, horses; and English men; in fact, they set up a new Flora and Fauna and a new variety of mankind, within the old state of nature. Their farms and pastures represent a garden on a great scale, and themselves the gardeners who have to keep it up, in watchful antagonism to the old *régime*. Considered as a whole, the colony is a composite unit introduced into the old state of nature; and, thenceforward, a competitor in the struggle for existence, to conquer or be vanquished.

Under the conditions supposed, there is no doubt of the result, if the work of the colonists be carried out energetically and with intelligent combination of all their forces. On the other hand, if they are slothful, stupid, and careless; or if they waste their energies in contests with one another, the chances are that the old state of nature will have the best of it. The native savage will destroy the immigrant civilized man; of the English animals and plants some will be extirpated by their indigenous rivals, others will pass into the feral state and themselves become components of the state of nature. In a few decades, all other traces of the settlement will have vanished.

VI

Let us now imagine that some administrative authority, as far superior in power and intelligence to men, as men are to their cattle, is set over the colony, charged to deal with its human elements in such a manner as to assure the victory of the settlement over the antagonistic influences of the state of nature in which it is set down. He would proceed in the same fashion as that in which the gardener dealt with his garden. In the first place, he would, as far as possible, put a stop to the influence of external competition by thoroughly extirpating and excluding the native rivals, whether men, beasts, or plants. And our administrator would select his human agents, with a view to his ideal of a successful colony, just as the gardener selects his plants with a view to his ideal of useful or beautiful products.

In the second place, in order that no struggle for the means of existence between these human agents should weaken the efficiency of the corporate whole in the battle with the state of nature, he would make arrangements by which each would be provided with those means; and would be relieved from the fear of being deprived of them by his stronger or more cunning fellows. Laws, sanctioned by the combined force of the colony, would restrain the self-assertion of each man within the limits required for the maintenance of peace. In other words, the cosmic struggle for existence, as between man and man, would be rigorously suppressed; and selection, by its means, would be as completely excluded as it is from the garden.

At the same time, the obstacles to the full development of the capacities of the colonists by other conditions of the state of nature than those already mentioned, would be removed by the creation of artificial conditions of existence of a more favorable character. Protection against extremes of heat and cold would be afforded by houses and clothing; drainage and irrigation works would antagonize the effects of excessive rain and excessive drought; roads, bridges, canals, carriages, and ships would overcome the natural obstacles to locomotion and transport; mechanical engines would supplement the natural strength of men and of their draught animals; hygienic precautions would check, or remove, the natural causes of disease. With every step of this progress in civilization, the colonists would become more and more independent of the state of nature; more and more, their lives would be conditioned by a state of art. In order to attain his ends, the administrator would have to avail himself of the courage, industry, and cooperative intelligence of the settlers; and it is plain that the interest of the community would be best served by increasing the proportion of persons who possess such qualities, and diminishing that of persons devoid of them. In other words, by selection directed towards an ideal.

Thus the administrator might look to the establishment of an earthly paradise, a true garden of Eden, in which all things should work together towards the well-being of the gardeners: within which the cosmic process, the coarse struggle for existence of the state of nature, should be abolished; in which that state should be replaced by a state of art; where every plant and every lower animal should be adapted to human wants, and would perish if human supervision and protection were withdrawn; where men themselves should have been selected, with a view to their efficiency as organs for the performance of the functions of a perfected society. And this ideal polity would have been brought about, not by gradually adjusting the men to the conditions around them, but by creating artificial conditions for them; not by allowing the free play of the struggle for existence, but by excluding that struggle; and by substituting selection directed towards the administrator's ideal for the selection it exercises.

VII

But the Eden would have its serpent, and a very subtle beast too. Man shares with the rest of the living world the mighty instinct of reproduction and its consequence, the tendency to multiply with great rapidity. The better the measures of the administrator achieved their object, the more completely the destructive agencies of the state of nature were defeated, the less would that multiplication be checked.

On the other hand, within the colony, the enforcement of peace, which deprives every man of the power to take away the means of existence from another, simply because he is the stronger, would have put an end to the struggle for existence between the colonists, and the competition for the commodities of existence, which would alone remain, is no check upon population.

Thus, as soon as the colonists began to multiply, the administrator would have to face the tendency to the reintroduction of the cosmic struggle into his artificial fabric, in consequence of the competition, not merely for the commodities, but for the means of existence. When the colony reached the limit of possible expansion, the surplus population must be disposed of somehow; or the fierce struggle for existence must recommence and destroy that peace, which is the fundamental condition of the maintenance of the state of art against the state of nature.

Supposing the administrator to be guided by purely scientific considerations, he would, like the gardener, meet this most serious difficulty by systematic extirpation, or exclusion, of the superfluous. The hopelessly diseased, the infirm aged, the weak or deformed in body or in mind, the excess of infants born, would be put away, as the gardener pulls up defective and superfluous plants, or the breeder destroys undesirable cattle. Only the strong and the healthy, carefully matched, with a view to the progeny best adapted to the purposes of the administrator, would be permitted to perpetuate their kind.

VIII

Of the more thoroughgoing of the multitudinous attempts to apply the principles of cosmic evolution, or what are supposed to be such, to social and political problems, which have appeared of late years, a considerable proportion appear to me to be based upon the notion that human society is competent to furnish, from its own resources, an administrator of the kind I have imagined. The pigeons, in short, are to be their own Sir John Sebright.[11] A despotic government, whether individual or collective, is to be endowed with the preternatural intelligence, and with what, I am afraid, many will consider the preternatural ruthlessness, required for the purpose of carrying out the principle of improvement by selection, with the somewhat drastic thoroughness upon which the success of the method depends. Experience certainly does not justify us in limiting the ruthlessness of individual "saviors of society"; and, on the well-known grounds of the aphorism which denies both body and soul to corporations, it seems probable (indeed the belief is not without support in history) that a collective despotism, a mob got to believe in its own divine right by demagogic missionaries, would be capable of more thorough work in this direction than any single tyrant, puffed up with the same illusion, has ever achieved. But intelligence is another affair. The fact that "saviors of society" take to that trade is evidence enough that they have none to spare. And such as they possess is generally sold to the capitalists of physical force on whose resources they depend. However, I doubt whether even the keenest judge of character, if he had before him a hundred boys and girls under fourteen, could pick out, with the least chance of success, those who should be kept, as certain to be serviceable members of the polity, and those who should be chloroformed, as equally sure to be stupid, idle, or vicious. The "points" of a good or of a bad citizen are really far harder to discern than those of a puppy or a short-horn calf; many do not show themselves before the practical difficulties of life stimulate manhood to full exertion. And by that time the mischief is done. The evil stock, if it be one, has had time to multiply, and selection is nullified.

IX

I have other reasons for fearing that this logical ideal of evolutionary regimentation—this pigeon-fanciers' polity—is unattainable. In the absence of any such a severely scientific administrator as we have been dreaming of, human society is kept together by bonds of such a singular character, that the attempt to perfect society after his fashion would run serious risk of loosening them.

Social organization is not peculiar to men. Other societies, such as those constituted by bees and ants, have also arisen out of the advantage of cooperation in the struggle for existence; and their resemblances to, and their differences from, human society are alike instructive. The society formed by the hive bee fulfills the ideal of the communistic aphorism "to each according to his needs, from each according to his capacity." Within it, the struggle for existence is strictly limited. Queen, drones, and workers have each their allotted sufficiency of food; each performs the function assigned to it in the economy of the hive, and all contribute to the success of the whole cooperative society in its competition with rival collectors of nectar and pollen and with other enemies, in the state of nature without. In the same sense as the garden, or the colony, is a work of human art, the bee polity is a work of apiarian art, brought about by the cosmic process, working through the organization of the hymenopterous type.

Now this society is the direct product of an organic necessity, impelling every member of it to a course of action which tends to the good of the whole. Each bee has its duty and none has any rights. Whether bees are susceptible of feeling and capable of thought is a question which cannot be dogmatically answered. As a pious opinion, I am disposed to deny them more than the merest rudiments of consciousness.[12] But it is curious to reflect that a thoughtful drone (workers and queens would have no leisure for speculation) with a turn for ethical philosophy, must needs profess himself an intuitive moralist of the purest water. He would point out, with perfect justice, that the devotion of the workers to a life of ceaseless toil for a mere subsistence wage, cannot be accounted for either by enlightened selfishness, or by any other sort of utilitarian motives; since these bees begin to work, without experience or reflection, as they emerge from the cell in which they are hatched. Plainly, an eternal and immutable principle, innate in each bee, can alone account for the phenomena. On the other hand, the biologist, who traces out all the extant stages of gradation between solitary and hive bees, as clearly sees in the latter, simply the perfection of an automatic mechanism, hammered out by the blows of the struggle for existence upon the progeny of the former, during long ages of constant variation.

X

I see no reason to doubt that, at its origin, human society was as much a product of organic necessity as that of the bees.[13] The human family, to begin with, rested upon exactly the same conditions as those which gave rise to similar associations among animals lower in the scale. Further, it is easy to see that every increase in the duration of the family ties, with the resulting cooperation of a larger and larger number of descendants for protection and defense, would give the families in which such modification took place a distinct advantage over the others. And, as in the hive, the progressive limitation of the struggle for existence between the members of the family would involve increasing efficiency as regards outside competition.

But there is this vast and fundamental difference between bee society and human society. In the former, the members of the society are each organically predestined to the performance of one particular class of functions only. If they were endowed with desires, each could desire to perform none but those offices for which its organization specially fits it; and which, in view of the good of the whole, it is proper it should do. So long as a new queen does not make her appearance, rivalries and competition are absent from the bee polity.

Among mankind, on the contrary, there is no such predestination to a sharply defined place in the social organism. However much men may differ in the quality of their intellects, the intensity of their passions, and the delicacy of their sensations, it cannot be said that one is fitted by his organization to be an agricultural laborer and nothing else, and another to be a landowner and nothing else. Moreover, with all their enormous differences in natural endowment, men agree in one thing, and that is their innate desire to enjoy the pleasures and to escape the pains of life; and, in short, to do nothing but that which it pleases them to do, without the least reference to the welfare of the society into which they are born. That is their inheritance (the reality at the bottom of the doctrine of original sin) from the long series of ancestors, human and semi-human and brutal, in whom the strength of this innate tendency to self-assertion was the condition of victory in the struggle for existence. That is the reason of the *aviditas vitæ*[14]—the insatiable hunger for enjoyment—of all mankind, which is one of the essential conditions of success in the war with the state of nature outside; and yet the sure agent of the destruction of society if allowed free play within.

The check upon this free play of self-assertion, or natural liberty, which is the necessary condition for the origin of human society, is the product of organic necessities of a different kind from those upon which the constitution of the hive depends. One of these is the mutual affection of parent and offspring, intensified by the long infancy of the human species. But the most important is the tendency, so strongly developed in man, to reproduce in himself actions and feelings similar to, or correlated with, those of other men. Man is the most consummate of all mimics in the animal world; none but himself can draw or model; none comes near him in the scope, variety, and exactness of vocal imitation; none is such a master of gesture; while he seems to be impelled thus to imitate for the pure pleasure of it. And there is no such another emotional chameleon. By a purely reflex operation of the mind, we take the hue of passion of those who are about us, or, it may be, the complementary color. It is not by any conscious "putting one's self in the place" of a joyful or a suffering person that the state of mind we call sympathy usually arises;[15] indeed, it is often contrary to one's sense of right, and in spite of one's will, that "fellow-feeling makes us wondrous kind," or the reverse. However complete may be the indifference to public opinion, in a cool, intellectual view, of the traditional sage, it has not yet been my fortune to meet with any actual sage who took its hostile manifestations with entire equanimity. Indeed, I doubt if the philosopher lives, or ever has lived, who could know himself to be heartily despised by a street boy without some irritation. And, though one cannot justify Haman for wishing to hang Mordecai on such a very high gibbet, yet, really, the consciousness of the Vizier of Ahasuerus, as he went in and out of the gate, that this obscure Jew had no respect for him, must have been very annoying.[16]

It is needful only to look around us, to see that the greatest restrainer of the anti-social tendencies of men is fear, not of the law, but of the opinion of their fellows. The conventions of honor bind men who break legal, moral, and religious bonds; and, while people endure the extremity of physical pain rather than part with life, shame drives the weakest to suicide.

Every forward step of social progress brings men into closer relations with their fellows, and increases the importance of the pleasures and pains derived from sympathy. We judge the acts of others by our own sympathies, and we judge our own acts by the sympathies of others, everyday and all day long, from childhood upwards, until associations, as indissoluble as those of language, are formed between certain acts and the feelings of approbation or disapprobation. It becomes impossible to imagine some acts without disapprobation, or others without approbation of the actor, whether he be one's self, or anyone else. We come to think in the acquired dialect of morals. An artificial personality, the "man within," as Adam Smith[17] calls conscience, is built up beside the natural personality. He is the watchman of society, charged to restrain the anti-social tendencies of the natural man within the limits required by social welfare.

XI

I have termed this evolution of the feelings out of which the primitive bonds of human society are so largely forged, into the organized and personified sympathy we call conscience, the ethical process.[18] So far as it tends to make any human society more efficient in the struggle for existence with the state of nature, or with other societies, it works in harmonious contrast with the cosmic process. But it is nonetheless true that, since law and morals are restraints upon the struggle for existence between men in society, the ethical process is in opposition to the principle of the cosmic process, and tends to the suppression of the qualities best fitted for success in that struggle.[19]

It is further to be observed that, just as the self-assertion, necessary to the maintenance of society against the state of nature, will destroy that society if it is allowed free operation within; so the self-restraint, the essence of the ethical process, which is no less an essential condition of the existence of every polity, may, by excess, become ruinous to it.

Moralists of all ages and of all faiths, attending only to the relations of men towards one another in an ideal society, have agreed upon the "golden rule," "Do as you would be done by." In other words, let sympathy be your guide; put yourself in the place of the man towards whom your action is directed; and do to him what you would like to have done to yourself under the circumstances. However much one may admire the generosity of such a rule of conduct; however confident one may be that average men may be thoroughly depended upon not to carry it out to its full logical consequences; it is nevertheless desirable to recognize the fact that these consequences are incompatible with the existence of a civil state, under any circumstances of this world which have obtained, or, so far as one can see, are, likely to come to pass.

For I imagine there can be no doubt that the great desire of every wrongdoer is to escape from the painful consequences of his actions. If I put myself in the place of the man who has robbed me, I find that I am possessed by an exceeding desire not to be fined or imprisoned; if in that of the man who has smitten me on one cheek, I contemplate with satisfaction the absence of any worse result than the turning of the other cheek for like treatment. Strictly observed, the "golden rule" involves the negation of law by the refusal to put it in motion against law-breakers; and, as regards the external relations of a polity, it is the refusal to continue the struggle for existence. It can be obeyed, even partially, only under the protection of a society which repudiates it. Without such shelter, the followers of the "golden rule" may indulge in hopes of heaven, but they must reckon with the certainty that other people will be masters of the earth.

What would become of the garden if the gardener treated all the weeds and slugs and birds and trespassers as he would like to be treated, if he were in their place?

XII

Under the preceding heads, I have endeavored to represent in broad, but I hope faithful, outlines the essential features of the state of nature and of that cosmic process of which it is the outcome, so far as was needful for my argument; I have contrasted with the state of nature the state of art, produced by human intelligence and energy, as it is exemplified by a garden; and I have shown that the state of art, here and elsewhere, can be maintained only by the constant counteraction of the hostile influences of the state of nature. Further, I have pointed out that the "horticultural process" which thus sets itself against the "cosmic process" is opposed to the latter in principle, in so far as it tends to arrest the struggle for existence, by restraining the multiplication which is one of the chief causes of that struggle, and by creating artificial conditions of life, better adapted to the cultivated plants than are the conditions of the state of nature. And I have dwelt upon the fact that, though the progressive modification, which is the consequence of the struggle for existence in the state of nature, is at an end, such modification may still be effected by that selection, in view of an ideal of usefulness, or of pleasantness, to man, of which the state of nature knows nothing.

I have proceeded to show that a colony, set down in a country in the state of nature, presents close analogies with a garden; and I have indicated the course of action which an administrator, able and willing to carry out horticultural principles, would adopt, in order to secure the success of such a newly formed polity, supposing it to be capable of indefinite expansion. In the contrary case, I have shown that difficulties must arise; that the unlimited increase of the population over a limited area must, sooner or later, reintroduce into the colony that struggle for the means of existence between the colonists, which it was the primary object of the administrator to exclude, insomuch as it is fatal to the mutual peace which is the prime condition of the union of men in society.

I have briefly described the nature of the only radical cure, known to me, for the disease which would thus threaten the existence of the colony; and, however regretfully, I have been obliged to admit that this rigorously scientific method of applying the principles of evolution to human society hardly comes within the region of practical politics; not for want of will on the part of a great many people; but because, for one reason, there is no hope that mere human beings will ever possess enough intelligence to select the fittest. And I have adduced other grounds for arriving at the same conclusion.

I have pointed out that human society took its rise in the organic necessities expressed by imitation and by the sympathetic emotions; and that, in the struggle for existence with the state of nature and with other societies, as part of it, those in which men were thus led to close cooperation had a great advantage.[20] But, since each man retained more or less of the faculties common to all the rest, and especially a full share of the desire for unlimited self-gratification, the struggle for existence within society could only be gradually eliminated. So long as any of it remained, society continued to be an imperfect instrument of the struggle for existence and, consequently, was improvable by the selective influence of that struggle.

Other things being alike, the tribe of savages in which order was best maintained; in which there was most security within the tribe and the most loyal mutual support outside it, would be the survivors.

I have termed this gradual strengthening of the social bond, which, though it arrests the struggle for existence inside society, up to a certain point improves the chances of society, as a corporate whole, in the cosmic struggle—the ethical process. I have endeavored to show that, when the ethical process has advanced so far as to secure every member of the society in the possession of the means of existence, the struggle for existence, as between man and man, within that society is, *ipso facto,* at an end. And, as it is undeniable that the most highly civilized societies have substantially reached this position, it follows that, so far as they are concerned, the struggle for existence can play no important part within them.[21] In other words, the kind of evolution which is brought about in the state of nature cannot take place.

I have further shown cause for the belief that direct selection, after the fashion of the horticulturist and the breeder, neither has played, nor can play, any important part in the evolution of society; apart from other reasons, because I do not see how such selection could be practiced without a serious weakening, it may be the destruction, of the bonds which hold society together. It strikes me that men who are accustomed to contemplate the active or passive extirpation of the weak, the unfortunate, and the superfluous; who justify that conduct on the ground that it has the sanction of the cosmic process, and is the only way of ensuring the progress of the race; who, if they are consistent, must rank medicine among the black arts and count the physician a mischievous preserver of the unfit; on whose matrimonial undertakings the principles of the stud have the chief influence; whose whole lives, therefore, are an education in the noble art of suppressing natural affection and sympathy, are not likely to have any large stock of these commodities left. But, without them, there is no conscience, nor any restraint on the conduct of men, except the calculation of self-interest, the balancing of certain present gratifications against doubtful future pains; and experience tells us how much that is worth. Everyday, we see firm believers in the hell of the theologians commit acts by which, as they believe when cool, they risk eternal punishment; while they hold back from those which are opposed to the sympathies of their associates.

XIII

That progressive modification of civilization which passes by the name of the "evolution of society," is, in fact, a process of an essentially different character, both from that which brings about the evolution of species, in the state of nature, and from that which gives rise to the evolution of varieties, in the state of art.

There can be no doubt that vast changes have taken place in English civilization since the reign of the Tudors. But I am not aware of a particle of evidence in favor of the conclusion that this evolutionary process has been accompanied by any modification of the physical, or the mental, characters of the men who have been the subjects of it. I have not met with any grounds for suspecting that the average Englishmen of today are sensibly different from those that Shakspere knew and drew. We look into his magic mirror of the Elizabethan age, and behold, nowise darkly, the presentment of ourselves.

During these three centuries, from the reign of Elizabeth to that of Victoria, the struggle for existence between man and man has been so largely restrained among the great mass of the population (except for one or two short intervals of civil war), that it can have had little, or no, selective operation. As to anything comparable to direct selection, it has been practiced on so small a scale that it may also be neglected. The criminal law, in so far as by putting to death, or by subjecting to long periods of imprisonment, those who infringe its provisions, it prevents the propagation of hereditary criminal tendencies; and the poor-law, in so far as it separates married couples, whose destitution arises from hereditary defects of character, are doubtless selective agents operating in favor of the non-criminal and the more effective members of society. But the proportion of the population which they influence is very small; and, generally, the hereditary criminal and the hereditary pauper have propagated their kind before the law affects them. In a large proportion of cases, crime and pauperism have nothing to do with heredity; but are the consequence, partly, of circumstances and, partly, of the possession of qualities, which, under different conditions of life, might have excited esteem and even admiration. It was a shrewd man of the world who, in discussing sewage problems, remarked that dirt is riches in the wrong place; and that sound aphorism has moral applications. The benevolence and open-handed generosity which adorn a rich man, may make a pauper of a poor one; the energy and courage to which the successful soldier owes his rise, the cool and daring subtlety to which the great financier owes his fortune, may very easily, under unfavorable conditions, lead their possessors to the gallows, or to the hulks. Moreover, it is fairly probable that the children of a "failure" will receive from their other parent just that little modification of character which makes all the difference. I sometimes wonder whether people, who talk so freely about extirpating the unfit, ever dispassionately consider their own history. Surely, one must be very "fit," indeed, not to know of an occasion, or perhaps two, in one's life, when it would have been only too easy to qualify for a place among the "unfit."

In my belief the innate qualities, physical, intellectual, and moral, of our nation have remained substantially the same for the last four or five centuries. If the struggle for existence has affected us to any serious extent (and I doubt it) it has been, indirectly, through our military and industrial wars with other nations.

XIV

What is often called the struggle for existence in society (I plead guilty to having used the term too loosely myself), is a contest, not for the means of existence, but for the means of enjoyment. Those who occupy the first places in this practical competitive examination are the rich and the influential; those who fail, more or less, occupy the lower places, down to the squalid obscurity of the pauper and the criminal. Upon the most liberal estimate, I suppose the former group will not amount to two percent of the population. I doubt if the latter exceeds another two percent; but let it be supposed, for the sake of argument, that it is as great as five percent.[22]

As it is only in the latter group that anything comparable to the struggle for existence in the state of nature can take place; as it is only among this twentieth, of the whole people that numerous men, women, and children die of rapid or slow starvation, or of the diseases incidental to permanently bad conditions of life; and as there is nothing to prevent their multiplication before they are killed off, while, in spite of greater infant mortality, they increase faster than the rich; it seems clear that the struggle for existence in this class can have no appreciable selective influence upon the other 95 percent of the population.

What sort of a sheep breeder would he be who should content himself with picking out the worst fifty out of a thousand, leaving them on a barren common till the weakest starved, and then letting the survivors go back to mix with the rest? And the parallel is too favorable; since in a large number of cases, the actual poor and the convicted criminals are neither the weakest nor the worst.

In the struggle for the means of enjoyment, the qualities which ensure success are energy, industry, intellectual capacity, tenacity of purpose, and, at least as much sympathy as is necessary to make a man understand the feelings of his fellows. Were there none of those artificial arrangements by which fools and knaves are kept at the top of society instead of sinking to their natural place at the bottom,[23] the struggle for the means of enjoyment would ensure a constant circulation of the human units of the social compound, from the bottom to the top and from the top to the bottom. The survivors of the contest, those who continued to form the great bulk of the polity, would not be those "fittest" who got to the very top, but the great body of the moderately "fit," whose numbers and superior propagative power, enable them always to swamp the exceptionally endowed minority.

I think it must be obvious to everyone, that, whether we consider the internal or the external interests of society, it is desirable they should be in the hands of those who are endowed with the largest share of energy, of industry, of intellectual capacity, of tenacity of purpose, while they are not devoid of sympathetic humanity; and, in so far as the struggle for the means of enjoyment tends to place such men in possession of wealth and influence, it is a process which tends to the good of society. But the process, as we have seen, has no real resemblance to that which adapts living beings to current conditions in the state of nature; nor any to the artificial selection of the horticulturist.

XV

To return, once more, to the parallel of horticulture. In the modern world, the gardening of men by themselves is practically restricted to the performance, not of selection, but of that other function of the gardener, the creation of conditions more favorable than those of the state of nature; to the end of facilitating the free expansion of the innate faculties of the citizen, so far as it is consistent with the general good. And the business of the moral and political philosopher appears to me to be the ascertainment, by the same method of observation, experiment, and ratiocination, as is practiced in other kinds of scientific work, of the course of conduct which will best conduce to that end.

But, supposing this course of conduct to be scientifically determined and carefully followed out, it cannot put an end to the struggle for existence in the state of nature; and it will not so much as tend, in anyway, to the adaptation of man to that state. Even should the whole human race be absorbed in one vast polity, within which "absolute political justice" reigns, the struggle for existence "with the state of nature outside it, and the tendency to the return of the struggle within, in consequence of over-multiplication, will remain; and, unless men's inheritance from the ancestors who fought a good fight in the state of nature, their dose of original sin, is rooted out by some method at present unrevealed, at any rate to disbelievers in supernaturalism, every child born into the world will still bring with him the instinct of unlimited self-assertion. He will have to learn the lesson of self-restraint and renunciation. But the practice of self-restraint and renunciation is not happiness, though it may be something much better.

That man, as a "political animal," is susceptible of a vast amount of improvement, by education, by instruction, and by the application of his intelligence to the adaptation of the conditions of life to his higher needs, I entertain not the slightest doubt. But, so long as he remains liable to error, intellectual or moral; so long as he is compelled to be perpetually on guard against the cosmic forces, whose ends are not his ends, without and within himself; so long as he is haunted by inexpugnable memories and hopeless aspirations; so long as the recognition of his intellectual limitations forces him to acknowledge his incapacity to penetrate the mystery of existence; the prospect of attaining untroubled happiness, or of a state which can, even remotely, deserve the title of perfection, appears to me to be as misleading an illusion as ever was dangled before the eyes of poor humanity. And there have been many of them.

That which lies before the human race is a constant struggle to maintain and improve, in opposition to the State of Nature, the State of Art of an organized polity; in which, and by "which, man may develop a worthy civilization, capable of maintaining and constantly improving itself, until the evolution of our globe shall have entered so far upon its downward course that the cosmic process resumes its sway; and, once more, the State of Nature prevails over the surface of our planet.

Note (see p. 18). It seems the fashion nowadays to ignore Hartley; though, a century and a half ago, he not only laid the foundations but built up much of the superstructure of a true theory of the Evolution of the intellectual and moral facilities. He speaks of what I have termed the ethical process as "our Progress from Self-interest to Self-annihilation." *Observations on Slaw* (1749), vol. ii. p. 281.

CHAPTER TWO

EVOLUTION AND ETHICS

[The Romanes Lecture, 1893]

Soleo enim et in aliena castra transire, non tanquam transfuga sed tanquam explorator. (L. ANNÆI SENECÆ EPIST. II. 4)

THERE IS A DELIGHTFUL CHILD'S STORY, KNOWN BY THE TITLE OF *Jack and the Beanstalk*, with which my contemporaries who are present will be familiar. But so many of our grave and reverend juniors have been brought up on severer intellectual diet, and, perhaps, have become acquainted with fairyland only through primers of comparative mythology, that it may be needful to give an outline of the tale. It is a legend of a bean-plant, which grows and grows until it reaches the high heavens and there spreads out into a vast canopy of foliage. The hero, being moved to climb the stalk, discovers that the leafy expanse supports a world composed of the same elements as that below, but yet strangely new; and his adventures there, on which I may not dwell, must have completely changed his views of the nature of things; though the story, not having been composed by, or for, philosophers, has nothing to say about views.

My present enterprise has a certain analogy to that of the daring adventurer. I beg you to accompany me in an attempt to reach a world which, to many, is probably strange, by the help of a bean. It is, as you know, a simple, inert-looking thing. Yet, if planted under proper conditions, of which sufficient warmth is one of the most important, it manifests active powers of a very remarkable kind. A small green seedling emerges, rises to the surface of the soil, rapidly increases in size and, at the same time, undergoes a series of metamorphoses which do not excite our wonder as much as those which meet us in legendary history, merely because they are to be seen everyday and all day long.

By insensible steps, the plant builds itself up into a large and various fabric of root, stem, leaves, flowers, and fruit, everyone molded within and without in accordance with an extremely complex but, at the same time, minutely defined pattern. In each of these complicated structures, as in their smallest constituents, there is an immanent energy which, in harmony with that resident in all the others, incessantly works towards the maintenance of the whole and the efficient performance of the part which it has to play in the economy of nature.

But no sooner has the edifice, reared with such exact elaboration, attained completeness, than it begins to crumble. By degrees, the plant withers and disappears from view, leaving behind more or fewer apparently inert and simple bodies, just like the bean from which it sprang; and, like it, endowed with the potentiality of giving rise to a similar cycle of manifestations.

Neither the poetic nor the scientific imagination is put to much strain in the search after analogies with this process of going forth and, as it were, returning to the starting-point. It may be likened to the ascent and descent of a slung stone, or the course of an arrow along its trajectory. Or we may say that the living energy takes first an upward and then a downward road. Or it may seem preferable to compare the expansion of the germ into the full-grown plant, to the unfolding of a fan, or to the rolling forth and widening of a stream; and thus to arrive at the conception of "development," or "evolution." Here as elsewhere, names are "noise and smoke"; the important point is to have a clear and adequate conception of the fact signified by a name. And, in this case, the fact is the Sisyphæan process, in the course of which, the living and growing plant passes from the relative simplicity and latent potentiality of the seed to the full epiphany of a highly differentiated type, thence to fall back to simplicity and potentiality.

The value of a strong intellectual grasp of the nature of this process lies in the circumstance that what is true of the bean is true of living things in general. From very low forms up to the highest—in the animal no less than in the vegetable kingdom—the process of life presents the same appearance[1] of cyclical evolution. Nay, we have but to cast our eyes over the rest of the world and cyclical change presents itself on all sides. It meets us in the water that flows to the sea and returns to the springs; in the heavenly bodies that wax and wane, go and return to their places; in the inexorable sequence of the ages of man's life; in that successive rise, apogee, and fall of dynasties and of states which is the most prominent topic of civil history.

As no man fording a swift stream can dip his foot twice into the same water, so no man can, with exactness, affirm of anything in the sensible world that it is.[2] As he utters the words, nay, as he thinks them, the predicate ceases to be applicable; the present has become the past; the "is" should be "was." And the more we learn of the nature of things, the more evident is it that what we call rest is only unperceived activity; that seeming peace is silent but strenuous battle. In every part, at every moment, the state of the cosmos is the expression of a transitory adjustment of contending forces; a scene of strife, in which all the combatants fall in turn. What is true of each part, is true of the whole. Natural knowledge tends more and more to the conclusion that "all the choir of heaven and furniture of the earth" are the transitory forms of parcels of cosmic substance wending along the road of evolution, from nebulous potentiality, through endless growths of sun and planet and satellite; through all varieties of matter; through infinite diversities of life and thought; possibly, through modes of being of which we neither have a conception, nor are competent to form any, back to the indefinable latency from which they arose. Thus the most obvious attribute of the cosmos is its impermanence. It assumes the aspect not so much of a permanent entity as of a changeful process, in which naught endures save the flow of energy and the rational order which pervades it.

We have climbed our bean-stalk and have reached a wonderland in which the common and the familiar become things new and strange. In the exploration of the cosmic process thus typified, the highest intelligence of man finds inexhaustible employment; giants are subdued to our service; and the spiritual affections of the contemplative philosopher are engaged by beauties worthy of eternal constancy.

But there is another aspect of the cosmic process, so perfect as a mechanism, so beautiful as a work of art. Where the cosmopoietic energy works through sentient beings, there arises, among its other manifestations, that which we call pain or suffering. This baleful product of evolution increases in quantity and in intensity, with advancing grades of animal organization, until it attains its highest level in man. Further, the consummation is not reached in man, the mere animal; nor in man, the whole or half savage; but only in man, the member of an organized polity. And it is a necessary consequence of his attempt to live in this way; that is, under those conditions which are essential to the full development of his noblest powers.

Man, the animal, in fact, has worked his way to the headship of the sentient world, and has become the superb animal which he is, in virtue of his success in the struggle for existence. The conditions having been of a certain order, man's organization has adjusted itself to them better than that of his competitors in the cosmic strife. In the case of mankind, the self-assertion, the unscrupulous seizing upon all that can be grasped, the tenacious holding of all that can be kept, which constitute the essence of the struggle for existence, have answered. For his successful progress, throughout the savage state, man has been largely indebted to those qualities which he shares with the ape and the tiger; his exceptional physical organization; his cunning, his sociability, his curiosity, and his imitativeness; his ruthless and ferocious destructiveness when his anger is roused by opposition.

But, in proportion as men have passed from anarchy to social organization, and in proportion as civilization has grown in worth, these deeply ingrained serviceable qualities have become defects. After the manner of successful persons, civilized man would gladly kick down the ladder by which he has climbed. He would be only too pleased to see "the ape and tiger die." But they decline to suit his convenience; and the unwelcome intrusion of these boon companions of his hot youth into the ranged existence of civil life adds pains and griefs, innumerable and immeasurably great, to those which the cosmic process necessarily brings on the mere animal. In fact, civilized man brands all these ape and tiger promptings with the name of sins; he punishes many of the acts which flow from them as crimes; and, in extreme cases, he does his best to put an end to the survival of the fittest of former days by axe and rope.

I have said that civilized man has reached this point; the assertion is perhaps too broad and general; I had better put it that ethical man has attained thereto. The science of ethics professes to furnish us with a reasoned rule of life; to tell us what is right action and why it is so. Whatever differences of opinion may exist among experts, there is a general consensus that the ape and tiger methods of the struggle for existence are not reconcilable with sound ethical principles.

The hero of our story descended the bean-stalk, and came back to the common world, where fare and work were alike hard; where ugly competitors were much commoner than beautiful princesses; and where the everlasting battle with self was much less sure to be crowned with victory than a turn-to with a giant. We have done the like. Thousands upon thousands of our fellows, thousands of years ago, have preceded us in finding themselves face to face with the same dread problem of evil. They also have seen that the cosmic process is evolution; that it is full of wonder, full of beauty, and, at the same time, full of pain. They have sought to discover the bearing of these great facts on ethics; to find out whether there is, or is not, a sanction for morality in the ways of the cosmos.

Theories of the universe, in which the conception of evolution plays a leading part, were extant at least six centuries before our era. Certain knowledge of them, in the fifth century, reaches us from localities as distant as the valley of the Ganges and the Asiatic coasts of the Ægean. To the early philosophers of Hindostan, no less than to those of Ionia, the salient and characteristic feature of the phenomenal world was its changefulness; the unresting flow of all things, through birth to visible being and thence to not being, in which they could discern no sign of a beginning and for which they saw no prospect of an ending. It was no less plain to some of these antique forerunners of modern philosophy that suffering is the badge of all the tribe of sentient things; that it is no accidental accompaniment, but an essential constituent of the cosmic process. The energetic Greek might find fierce joys in a world in which "strife is father and king"; but the old Aryan spirit was subdued to quietism in the Indian sage; the mist of suffering which spread over humanity hid everything else from his view; to him life was one with suffering and suffering with life.

In Hindostan, as in Ionia, a period of relatively high and tolerably stable civilization had succeeded long ages of semi-barbarism and struggle. Out of wealth and security had come leisure and refinement, and, close at their heels, had followed the malady of thought. To the struggle for bare existence, which never ends, though it may be alleviated and partially disguised for a fortunate few, succeeded the struggle to make existence intelligible and to bring the order of things into harmony with the moral sense of man, which also never ends, but, for the thinking few, becomes keener with every increase of knowledge and with every step towards the realization of a worthy ideal of life.

Two thousand five hundred years ago, the value of civilization was as apparent as it is now; then, as now, it was obvious that only in the garden of an orderly polity can the finest fruits humanity is capable of bearing be produced. But it had also become evident that the blessings of culture were not unmixed. The garden was apt to turn into a hothouse. The stimulation of the senses, the pampering of the emotions, endlessly multiplied the sources of pleasure. The constant widening of the intellectual field indefinitely extended the range of that especially human faculty of looking before and after, which adds to the fleeting present those old and new worlds of the past and the future, wherein men dwell the more the higher their culture. But that very sharpening of the sense and that subtle refinement of emotion, which brought such a wealth of pleasures, were fatally attended by a proportional enlargement of the capacity for suffering; and the divine faculty of imagination, while it created new heavens and new earths, provided them with the corresponding hells of futile regret for the past and morbid anxiety for the future.[3] Finally, the inevitable penalty of over-stimulation, exhaustion, opened the gates of civilization to its great enemy, ennui; the stale and flat weariness when man delights not, nor woman neither; when all things are vanity and vexation; and life seems not worth living except to escape the bore of dying.

Even purely intellectual progress brings about its revenges. Problems settled in a rough and ready way by rude men, absorbed in action, demand renewed attention and show themselves to be still unread riddles when men have time to think. The beneficent demon, doubt, whose name is Legion and who dwells amongst the tombs of old faiths, enters into mankind and thenceforth refuses to be cast out. Sacred customs, venerable dooms of ancestral wisdom, hallowed by tradition and professing to hold good for all time, are put to the question. Cultured reflection asks for their credentials; judges them by its own standards; finally, gathers those of which it approves into ethical systems, in which the reasoning is rarely much more than a decent pretext for the adoption of foregone conclusions.

One of the oldest and most important elements in such systems is the conception of justice. Society is impossible unless those who are associated agree to observe certain rules of conduct towards one another; its stability depends on the steadiness with which they abide by that agreement; and, so far as they waver, that mutual trust which is the bond of society is weakened or destroyed. Wolves could not hunt in packs except for the real, though unexpressed, understanding that they should not attack one another during the chase. The most rudimentary polity is a pack of men living under the like tacit, or expressed, understanding; and having made the very important advance upon wolf society, that they agree to use the force of the whole body against individuals who violate it and in favor of those who observe it. This observance of a common understanding, with the consequent distribution of punishments and rewards according to accepted rules, received the name of justice, while the contrary was called injustice. Early ethics did not take much note of the animus of the violator of the rules. But civilization could not advance far, without the establishment of a capital distinction between the case of involuntary and that of wilful misdeed; between a merely wrong action and a guilty one. And, with increasing refinement of moral appreciation, the problem of desert, which arises out of this distinction, acquired more and more theoretical and practical importance. If life must be given for life, yet it was recognized that the unintentional slayer did not altogether deserve death; and, by a sort of compromise between the public and the private conception, of justice, a sanctuary was provided in which he might take refuge from the avenger of blood.

The idea of justice thus underwent a gradual sublimation from punishment and reward according to acts, to punishment and reward according to desert; or, in other words, according to motive. Righteousness, that is, action from right motive, not only became synonymous with justice, but the positive constituent of innocence and the very heart of goodness.

Now when the ancient sage, whether Indian or Greek, who had attained to this conception of goodness, looked the world, and especially human life, in the face, he found it as hard as we do to bring the course of evolution into harmony with even the elementary requirements of the ethical ideal of the just and the good.

If there is one thing plainer than another, it is that neither the pleasures nor the pains of life, in the merely animal world, are distributed according to desert; for it is admittedly impossible for the lower orders of sentient beings to deserve either the one or the other. If there is a generalization from the facts of human life which has the assent of thoughtful men in every age and country, it is that the violator of ethical rules constantly escapes the punishment which he deserves; that the wicked flourishes like a green bay tree, while the righteous begs his bread; that the sins of the fathers are visited upon the children; that, in the realm of nature, ignorance is punished just as severely as wilful wrong; and that thousands upon thousands of innocent beings suffer for the crime, or the unintentional trespass of one.

Greek and Semite and Indian are agreed upon this subject. The book of Job is at one with the *Works and Days* and the Buddhist Sutras; the Psalmist and the Preacher of Israel, with the Tragic Poets of Greece. What is a more common motive of the ancient tragedy in fact, than the unfathomable injustice of the nature of things; what is more deeply felt to be true than its presentation of the destruction of the blameless by the work of his own hands, or by the fatal operation of the sins of others? Surely Oedipus was pure of heart; it was the natural sequence of events—the cosmic process—which drove him, in all innocence, to slay his father and become the husband of his mother, to the desolation of his people and his own headlong ruin. Or to step, for a moment, beyond the chronological limits I have set myself, what constitutes the sempiternal attraction of Hamlet but the appeal to deepest experience of that history of a no less blameless dreamer, dragged, in spite of himself, into a world out of joint; involved in a tangle of crime and misery, created by one of the prime agents of the cosmic process as it works in and through man?

Thus, brought before the tribunal of ethics, the cosmos might well seem to stand condemned. The conscience of man revolted against the moral indifference of nature, and the microcosmic atom should have found the illimitable macrocosm guilty. But few, or none, ventured to record that verdict.

In the great Semitic trial of this issue, Job takes refuge in silence and submission; the Indian and the Greek, less wise perhaps, attempt to reconcile the irreconcilable and plead for the defendant. To this end, the Greeks invented Theodicies; while the Indians devised what, in its ultimate form, must rather be termed a Cosmodicy. For, though Buddhism recognizes gods many and lords many, they are products of the cosmic process; and transitory, however long enduring, manifestations of its eternal activity. In the doctrine of transmigration, whatever its origin, Brahminical and Buddhist speculation found, ready to hand,[4] the means of constructing a plausible vindication of the ways of the cosmos to man. If this world is full of pain and sorrow; if grief and evil fall, like the rain, upon both the just and the unjust; it is because, like the rain, they are links in the endless chain of natural causation by which past, present, and future are indissolubly connected; and there is no more injustice in the one case than in the other. Every sentient being is reaping as it has sown; if not in this life, then in one or other of the infinite series of antecedent existences of which it is the latest term. The present distribution of good and evil is, therefore, the algebraical sum of accumulated positive and negative deserts; or, rather, it depends on the floating balance of the account. For it was not thought necessary that a complete settlement should ever take place. Arrears might stand over as a sort of "hanging gale"; a period of celestial happiness just earned might be succeeded by ages of torment in a hideous nether world, the balance still overdue for some remote ancestral error.[5]

Whether the cosmic process looks anymore moral than at first, after such a vindication, may perhaps be questioned. Yet this plea of justification is not less plausible than others; and none but very hasty thinkers will reject it on the ground of inherent absurdity. Like the doctrine of evolution itself, that of transmigration has its roots in the world of reality; and it may claim such support as the great argument from analogy is capable of supplying.

Everyday experience familiarizes us with the facts which are grouped under the name of heredity. Everyone of us bears upon him obvious marks of his parentage, perhaps of remoter relationships. More particularly, the sum of tendencies to act in a certain way, which we call "character," is often to be traced through a long series of progenitors and collaterals. So we may justly say that this "character"—this moral and intellectual essence of a man—does veritably pass over from one fleshly tabernacle to another, and does really transmigrate from generation to generation. In the newborn infant, the character of the stock lies latent, and the Ego is little more than a bundle of potentialities. But, very early, these become actualities; from childhood to age they manifest themselves in dulness or brightness, weakness or strength, viciousness or uprightness; and with each feature modified by confluence with another character, if by nothing else, the character passes on to its incarnation in new bodies.

The Indian philosophers called character, as thus defined, "karma."[6] It is this karma which passed from life to life and linked them in the chain of transmigrations; and they held that it is modified in each life, not merely by confluence of parentage, but by its own acts. They were, in fact, strong believers in the theory, so much disputed just at present of the hereditary transmission of acquired characters. That the manifestation of the tendencies of a character may be greatly facilitated, or impeded, by conditions, of which self-discipline, or the absence of it, are among the most important, is indubitable; but that the character itself is modified in this way is by no means so certain; it is not so sure that the transmitted character of an evil liver is worse, or that of a righteous man better, than that which he received. Indian philosophy, however, did not admit of any doubt on this subject; the belief in the influence of conditions, notably of self-discipline, on the karma was not merely a necessary postulate of its theory of retribution, but it presented the only way of escape from the endless round of transmigrations.

The earlier forms of Indian philosophy agreed with those prevalent in our own times, in supposing the existence of a permanent reality, or "substance," beneath the shifting series of phenomena, whether of matter or of mind. The substance of the cosmos was "Brahma," that of the individual man "Atman"; and the latter was separated from the former only, if I may so speak, by its phenomenal envelope, by the casing of sensations, thoughts and desires, pleasures and pains, which make up the illusive phantasmagoria of life. This the ignorant take for reality; their "Atman" therefore remains eternally imprisoned in delusions, bound by the fetters of desire and scourged by the whip of misery. But the man who has attained enlightenment sees that the apparent reality is mere illusion, or, as was said a couple of thousand years later, that there is nothing good nor bad but thinking makes it so. If the cosmos "is just and of our pleasant vices makes instruments to scourge us," it would seem that the only way to escape from our heritage of evil is to destroy that fountain of desire whence our vices flow; to refuse any longer to be the instruments of the evolutionary process, and withdraw from the struggle for existence. If the karma is modifiable by self-discipline, if its coarser desires, one after another, can be extinguished, the ultimate fundamental desire of self-assertion, or the desire to be, may also be destroyed.[7] Then the bubble of illusion will burst, and the freed individual "Atman" will lose itself in the universal "Brahma."

Such seems to have been the pre-Buddhistic conception of salvation, and of the way to be followed by those who would attain thereto. No more thorough mortification of the flesh has ever been attempted than that achieved by the Indian ascetic anchorite; no later monachism has so nearly succeeded in reducing the human mind to that condition of impassive quasi-somnambulism, which, but for its acknowledged holiness, might run the risk of being confounded with idiocy.

And this salvation, it will be observed, was to be attained through knowledge, and by action based on that knowledge; just as the experimenter, who would obtain a certain physical or chemical result, must have a knowledge of the natural laws involved and the persistent disciplined will adequate to carry out all the various operations required. The supernatural, in our sense of the term, was entirely excluded. There was no external power which could affect the sequence of cause and effect which gives rise to karma; none but the will of the subject of the karma which could put an end to it.

Only one rule of conduct could be based upon the remarkable theory of which I have endeavored to give a reasoned outline. It was folly to continue to exist when an overplus of pain was certain; and the probabilities in favor of the increase of misery with the prolongation of existence, were so overwhelming. Slaying the body only made matters worse; there was nothing for it but to slay the soul by the voluntary arrest of all its activities. Property, social ties, family affections, common companionship, must be abandoned; the most natural appetites, even that for food, must be suppressed, or at least minimized; until all that remained of a man was the impassive, extenuated, mendicant monk, self-hypnotized into cataleptic trances, which the deluded mystic took for foretastes of the final union with Brahma.

The founder of Buddhism accepted the chief postulates demanded by his predecessors. But he was not satisfied with the practical annihilation involved in merging the individual existence in the unconditioned—the Atman in Brahma. It would seem that the admission of the existence of any substance whatever—even of the tenuity of that which has neither quality nor energy and of which no predicate whatever can be asserted—appeared to him to be a danger and a snare. Though reduced to a hypostatized negation, Brahma was not to be trusted; so long as entity was there, it might conceivably resume the weary round of evolution, with all its train of immeasurable miseries. Gautama got rid of even that shade of a shadow of permanent existence by a metaphysical *tour de force* of great interest to the student of philosophy, seeing that it supplies the wanting half of Bishop Berkeley's well-known idealistic argument.

Granting the premises, I am not aware of any escape from Berkeley's conclusion, that the "substance" of matter is a metaphysical unknown quantity, of the existence of which there is no proof. What Berkeley does not seem to have so clearly perceived is that the non-existence of a substance of mind is equally arguable; and that the result of the impartial applications of his reasonings is the reduction of the All to co-existences and sequences of phenomena, beneath and beyond which there is nothing cognoscible. It is a remarkable indication of the subtlety of Indian speculation that Gautama should have seen deeper than the greatest of modern idealists; though it must be admitted that, if some of Berkeley's reasonings respecting the nature of spirit are pushed home, they reach pretty much the same conclusion.[8]

Accepting the prevalent Brahminical doctrine that the whole cosmos, celestial, terrestrial, and infernal, with its population of gods and other celestial beings, of sentient animals, of Mara and his devils, is incessantly shifting through recurring cycles of production and destruction, in each of which every human being has his transmigratory representative, Gautama proceeded to eliminate substance altogether; and to reduce the cosmos to a mere flow of sensations, emotions, volitions, and thoughts, devoid of any substratum. As, on the surface of a stream of water, we see ripples and whirlpools, which last for a while and then vanish with the causes that gave rise to them, so what seem individual existences are mere temporary associations of phenomena circling round a center, "like a dog tied to a post." In the whole universe there is nothing permanent, no eternal substance either of mind or of matter. Personality is a metaphysical fancy; and in very truth, not only we, but all things, in the worlds without end of the cosmic phantasmagoria, are such stuff as dreams are made of.

What then becomes of karma? Karma remains untouched. As the peculiar form of energy we call magnetism may be transmitted from a loadstone to a piece of steel, from the steel to a piece of nickel, as it may be strengthened or weakened by the conditions to which it is subjected while resident in each piece, so it seems to have been conceived that karma might be transmitted from one phenomenal association to another by a sort of induction. However this may be, Gautama doubtless had a better guarantee for the abolition of transmigration, when no wrack of substance, either of Atman or of Brahma, was left behind; when, in short, a man had but to dream that he willed not to dream, to put an end to all dreaming.

This end of life's dream is Nirvana. What Nirvana is the learned do not agree. But, since the best original authorities tell us there is neither desire nor activity, nor any possibility of phenomenal reappearance for the sage who has entered Nirvana, it may be safely said of this acme of Buddhistic philosophy—"the rest is silence."[9]

Thus there is no very great practical disagreement between Gautama and his predecessors with respect to the end of action; but it is otherwise as regards the means to that end. With just insight into human nature, Gautama declared extreme ascetic practices to be useless and indeed harmful. The appetites and the passions are not to be abolished by mere mortification of the body; they must, in addition, be attacked on their own ground and conquered by steady cultivation of the mental habits which oppose them; by universal benevolence; by the return of good for evil; by humility; by abstinence from evil thought; in short, by total renunciation of that self-assertion which is the essence of the cosmic process.

Doubtless, it is to these ethical qualities that Buddhism owes its marvelous success.[10] A system which knows no God in the western sense; which denies a soul to man; which counts the belief in immortality a blunder and the hope of it a sin; which refuses any efficacy to prayer and sacrifice; which bids men look to nothing but their own efforts for salvation; which, in its original purity, knew nothing of vows of obedience, abhorred intolerance, and never sought the aid of the secular arm; yet spread over a considerable moiety of the Old World with marvelous rapidity, and is still, with whatever base admixture of foreign superstitions, the dominant creed of a large fraction of mankind.

Let us now set our faces westwards, towards Asia Minor and Greece and Italy, to view the rise and progress of another philosophy, apparently independent, but no less pervaded by the conception of evolution.[11]

The sages of Miletus were pronounced evolutionists; and, however dark may be some of the sayings of Heracleitus of Ephesus, who was probably a contemporary of Gautama, no better expressions of the essence of the modern doctrine of evolution can be found than are presented by some of his pithy aphorisms and striking metaphors.[12] Indeed, many of my present auditors must have observed that, more than once, I have borrowed from him in the brief exposition of the theory of evolution with which this discourse commenced.

But when the focus of Greek intellectual activity shifted to Athens, the leading minds concentrated their attention upon ethical problems. Forsaking the study of the macrocosm for that of the microcosm, they lost the key to the thought of the great Ephesian, which, I imagine, is more intelligible to us than it was to Socrates, or to Plato. Socrates, more especially, set the fashion of a kind of inverse agnosticism, by teaching that the problems of physics lie beyond the reach of the human intellect; that the attempt to solve them is essentially vain; that the one worthy object of investigation is the problem of ethical life; and his example was followed by the Cynics and the later Stoics. Even the comprehensive knowledge and the penetrating intellect of Aristotle failed to suggest to him that in holding the eternity of the world, within its present range of mutation, he was making a retrogressive step. The scientific heritage of Heracleitus passed into the hands neither of Plato nor of Aristotle, but into those of Democritus. But the world was not yet ready to receive the great conceptions of the philosopher of Abdera. It was reserved for the Stoics to return to the track marked out by the earlier philosophers; and, professing themselves disciples of Heracleitus, to develop the idea of evolution systematically. In doing this, they not only omitted some characteristic features of their master's teaching, but they made additions altogether foreign to it. One of the most influential of these importations was the transcendental theism which had come into vogue. The restless, fiery energy, operating according to law, out of which all things emerge and into which they return, in the endless successive cycles of the great year; which creates and destroys worlds as a wanton child builds up, and anon levels, sand castles on the seashore; was metamorphosed into a material world-soul and decked out with all the attributes of ideal Divinity; not merely with infinite power and transcendent wisdom, but with absolute goodness.

The consequences of this step were momentous. For if the cosmos is the effect of an immanent, omnipotent, and infinitely beneficent cause, the existence in it of real evil, still less of necessarily inherent evil, is plainly inadmissible.[13] Yet the universal experience of mankind testified then, as now, that, whether we look within us or without us, evil stares us in the face on all sides; that if anything is real, pain and sorrow and wrong are realities.

It would be a new thing in history if à priori philosophers were daunted by the factious opposition of experience; and the Stoics were the last men to allow themselves to be beaten by mere facts. "Give me a doctrine and I will find the reasons for it," said Chrysippus. So they perfected, if they did not invent, that ingenious and plausible form of pleading, the Theodicy; for the purpose of showing firstly, that there is no such thing as evil; secondly, that if there is, it is the necessary correlate of good; and, moreover, that it is either due to our own fault, or inflicted for our benefit. Theodicies have been very popular in their time, and I believe that a numerous, though somewhat dwarfed, progeny of them still survives. So far as I know, they are all variations of the theme set forth in those famous six lines of the *Essay on Man*, in which Pope sums up Bolingbroke's reminiscences of stoical and other speculations of this kind—

> All nature is but art, unknown to thee;
> All chance, direction which thou canst not see;
> All discord, harmony not understood;
> All partial evil, universal good;
> And spite of pride, in erring reason's spite,
> One truth is clear: whatever is is right.

Yet, surely, if there are few more important truths than those enunciated in the first triad, the second is open to very grave objections. That there is a "soul of good in things evil" is unquestionable; nor will any wise man deny the disciplinary value of pain and sorrow. But these considerations do not help us to see why the immense multitude of irresponsible sentient beings, which cannot profit by such discipline, should suffer; nor why, among the endless possibilities open to omnipotence—that of sinless, happy existence among the rest—the actuality in which sin and misery abound should be that selected. Surely it is mere cheap rhetoric to call arguments which have never yet been answered by even the meekest and the least rational of Optimists, suggestions of the pride of reason. As to the concluding aphorism, its fittest place would be as an inscription in letters of mud over the portal of some "stye of Epicurus";[14] for that is where the logical application of it to practice would land men, with every aspiration stifled and every effort paralyzed. Why try to set right what is right already? Why strive to improve the best of all possible worlds? Let us eat and drink, for as today all is right, so tomorrow all will be.

But the attempt of the Stoics to blind themselves to the reality of evil, as a necessary concomitant of the cosmic process, had less success than that of the Indian philosophers to exclude the reality of good from their purview. Unfortunately, it is much easier to shut one's eyes to good than to evil. Pain and sorrow knock at our doors more loudly than pleasure and happiness; and the prints of their heavy footsteps are less easily effaced. Before the grim realities of practical life the pleasant fictions of optimism vanished. If this were the best of all possible worlds, it nevertheless proved itself a very inconvenient habitation for the ideal sage.

The stoical summary of the whole duty of man, "Live according to nature," would seem to imply that the cosmic process is an exemplar for human conduct. Ethics would thus become applied Natural History. In fact, a confused employment of the maxim, in this sense, has done immeasurable mischief in later times. It has furnished an axiomatic foundation for the philosophy of philosophasters and for the moralizing of sentimentalists. But the Stoics were, at bottom, not merely noble, but sane, men; and if we look closely into what they really meant by this ill-used phrase, it will be found to present no justification for the mischievous conclusions that have been deduced from it.

In the language of the Stoa, "Nature" was a word of many meanings. There was the "Nature" of the cosmos and the "Nature" of man. In the latter, the animal "nature," which man shares with a moiety of the living part of the cosmos, was distinguished from a higher "nature." Even in this higher nature there were grades of rank. The logical faculty is an instrument which may be turned to account for any purpose. The passions and the emotions are so closely tied to the lower nature that they may be considered to be pathological, rather than normal, phenomena. The one supreme, hegemonic, faculty, which constitutes the essential "nature" of man, is most nearly represented by that which, in the language of a later philosophy, has been called the pure reason. It is this "nature" which holds up the ideal of the supreme good and demands absolute submission of the will to its behests. It is this which commands all men to love one another, to return good for evil, to regard one another as fellow-citizens of one great state. Indeed, seeing that the progress towards perfection of a civilized state, or polity, depends on the obedience of its members to these commands, the Stoics sometimes termed the pure reason the "political" nature. Unfortunately, the sense of the adjective has undergone so much modification, that the application of it to that which commands the sacrifice of self to the common good would now sound almost grotesque.[15]

But what part is played by the theory of evolution in this view of ethics? So far as I can discern, the ethical system of the Stoics, which is essentially intuitive, and reverences the categorical imperative as strongly as that of any later moralists, might have been just what it was if they had held any other theory; whether that of special creation, on the one side, or that of the eternal existence of the present order, on the other.[16] To the Stoic, the cosmos had no importance for the conscience, except in so far as he chose to think it a pedagogue to virtue. The pertinacious optimism of our philosophers hid from them the actual state of the case. It prevented them from seeing that cosmic nature is no school of virtue, but the headquarters of the enemy of ethical nature. The logic of facts was necessary to convince them that the cosmos works through the lower nature of man, not for righteousness, but against it. And it finally drove them to confess that the existence of their ideal "wise man" was incompatible with the nature of things; that even a passable approximation to that ideal was to be attained only at the cost of renunciation of the world and mortification, not merely of the flesh, but of all human affections. The state of perfection was that "apatheia"[17] in which desire, though it may still be felt, is powerless to move the will, reduced to the sole function of executing the commands of pure reason. Even this residuum of activity was to be regarded as a temporary loan, as an efflux of the divine world-pervading spirit, chafing at its imprisonment in the flesh, until such time as death enabled it to return to its source in the all-pervading logos.

I find it difficult to discover any very great difference between Apatheia and Nirvana, except that stoical speculation agrees with pre-Buddhistic philosophy, rather than with the teachings of Gautama, in so far as it postulates a permanent substance equivalent to "Brahma" and "Atman"; and that, in stoical practice, the adoption of the life of the mendicant cynic was held to be more a counsel of perfection than an indispensable condition of the higher life.

Thus the extremes touch. Greek thought and Indian thought set out from ground common to both, diverge widely, develop under very different physical and moral conditions, and finally converge to practically the same end.

The Vedas and the Homeric epos set before us a world of rich and vigorous life, full of joyous fighting men

> That ever with a frolic welcome took
> The thunder and the sunshine. . . .

and who were ready to brave the very Gods themselves when their blood was up. A few centuries pass away, and under the influence of civilization the descendants of these men are "sicklied o'er with the pale cast of thought"—frank pessimists, or, at best, make-believe optimists. The courage of the warlike stock may be as hardly tried as before, perhaps more hardly, but the enemy is self. The hero has become a monk. The man of action is replaced by the quietist, whose highest aspiration is to be the passive instrument of the divine Reason. By the Tiber, as by the Ganges, ethical man admits that the cosmos is too strong for him; and, destroying every bond which ties him to it by ascetic discipline, he seeks salvation in absolute renunciation.[18]

Modern thought is making a fresh start from the base whence Indian and Greek philosophy set out; and, the human mind being very much what it was six-and-twenty centuries ago, there is no ground for wonder if it presents indications of a tendency to move along the old lines to the same results.

We are more than sufficiently familiar with modern pessimism, at least as a speculation; for I cannot call to mind that any of its present votaries have sealed their faith by assuming the rags and the bowl of the mendicant Bhikku, or the cloak and the wallet of the Cynic. The obstacles placed in the way of sturdy vagrancy by an unphilosophical police have, perhaps, proved too formidable for philosophical consistency. We also know modern speculative optimism, with its perfectibility of the species, reign of peace, and lion and lamb transformation scenes; but one does not hear so much of it as one did forty years ago; indeed, I imagine it is to be met with more commonly at the tables of the healthy and wealthy, than in the congregations of the wise. The majority of us, I apprehend, profess neither pessimism nor optimism. We hold that the world is neither so good, nor so bad, as it conceivably might be; and, as most of us have reason, now and again, to discover that it can be. Those who have failed to experience the joys that make life worth living are, probably, in as small a minority as those who have never known the griefs that rob existence of its savor and turn its richest fruits into mere dust and ashes.

Further, I think I do not err in assuming that, however diverse their views on philosophical and religious matters, most men are agreed that the proportion of good and evil in life may be very sensibly affected by human action. I never heard anybody doubt that the evil may be thus increased, or diminished; and it would seem to follow that good must be similarly susceptible of addition or subtraction. Finally, to my knowledge, nobody professes to doubt that, so far forth as we possess a power of bettering things, it is our paramount duty to use it and to train all our intellect and energy to this supreme service of our kind.

Hence the pressing interest of the question, to what extent modern progress in natural knowledge, and, more especially, the general outcome of that progress in the doctrine of evolution, is competent to help us in the great work of helping one another?

The propounders of what are called the "ethics of evolution," when the "evolution of ethics" would usually better express the object of their speculations, adduce a number of more or less interesting facts and more or less sound arguments, in favor of the origin of the moral sentiments, in the same way as other natural phenomena, by a process of evolution. I have little doubt, for my own part, that they are on the right track; but as the immoral sentiments have no less been evolved, there is, so far, as much natural sanction for the one as the other. The thief and the murderer follow nature just as much as the philanthropist. Cosmic evolution may teach us how the good and the evil tendencies of man may have come about; but, in itself, it is incompetent to furnish any better reason why what we call good is preferable to what we call evil than we had before. Someday, I doubt not, we shall arrive at an understanding of the evolution of the æsthetic faculty; but all the understanding in the world will neither increase nor diminish the force of the intuition that this is beautiful and that is ugly.

There is another fallacy which appears to me to pervade the so-called "ethics of evolution." It is the notion that because, on the whole, animals and plants have advanced in perfection of organization by means of the struggle for existence and the consequent "survival of the fittest"; therefore men in society, men as ethical beings, must look to the same process to help them towards perfection. I suspect that this fallacy has arisen out of the unfortunate ambiguity of the phrase "survival of the fittest." "Fittest" has a connotation of "best"; and about "best" there hangs a moral flavor. In cosmic nature, however, what is "fittest" depends upon the conditions. Long since,[19] I ventured to point out that if our hemisphere were to cool again, the survival of the fittest might bring about, in the vegetable kingdom, a population of more and more stunted and humbler and humbler organisms, until the "fittest" that survived might be nothing but lichens, diatoms, and such microscopic organisms as those which give red snow its color; while, if it became hotter, the pleasant valleys of the Thames and Isis might be uninhabitable by any animated beings save those that flourish in a tropical jungle. They, as the fittest, the best adapted to the changed conditions, would survive.

Men in society are undoubtedly subject to the cosmic process. As among other animals, multiplication goes on without cessation, and involves severe competition for the means of support. The struggle for existence tends to eliminate those less fitted to adapt themselves to the circumstances of their existence. The strongest, the most self-assertive, tend to tread down the weaker. But the influence of the cosmic process on the evolution of society is the greater the more rudimentary its civilization. Social progress means a checking of the cosmic process at every step and the substitution for it of another, which may be called the ethical process; the end of which is not the survival of those who may happen to be the fittest, in respect of the whole of the conditions which obtain, but of those who are ethically the best.[20]

As I have already urged, the practice of that which is ethically best—what we call goodness or virtue—involves a course of conduct which, in all respects, is opposed to that which leads to success in the cosmic struggle for existence. In place of ruthless self-assertion it demands self-restraint; in place of thrusting aside, or treading down, all competitors, it requires that the individual shall not merely respect, but shall help his fellows; its influence is directed, not so much to the survival of the fittest, as to the fitting of as many as possible to survive. It repudiates the gladiatorial theory of existence. It demands that each man who enters into the enjoyment of the advantages of a polity shall be mindful of his debt to those who have laboriously constructed it; and shall take heed that no act of his weakens the fabric in which he has been permitted to live. Laws and moral precepts are directed to the end of curbing the cosmic process and reminding the individual of his duty to the community, to the protection and influence of which he owes, if not existence itself, at least the life of something better than a brutal savage.

It is from neglect of these plain considerations that the fanatical individualism[21] of our time attempts to apply the analogy of cosmic nature to society. Once more we have a misapplication of the stoical injunction to follow nature; the duties of the individual to the state are forgotten, and his tendencies to self-assertion are dignified by the name of rights. It is seriously debated whether the members of a community are justified in using their combined strength to constrain one of their number to contribute his share to the maintenance of it; or even to prevent him from doing his best to destroy it. The straggle for existence, which has done such admirable work in cosmic nature, must, it appears, be equally beneficent in the ethical sphere. Yet if that which I have insisted upon is true; if the cosmic process has no sort of relation to moral ends; if the imitation of it by man is inconsistent with the first principles of ethics; what becomes of this surprising theory?

Let us understand, once for all, that the ethical progress of society depends, not on imitating the cosmic process, still less in running away from it, but in combating it. It may seem an audacious proposal thus to pit the microcosm against the macrocosm and to set man to subdue nature to his higher ends; but I venture to think that the great intellectual difference between the ancient times with which we have been occupied and our day, lies in the solid foundation we have acquired for the hope that such an enterprise may meet with a certain measure of success.

The history of civilization details the steps by which men have succeeded in building up an artificial world within the cosmos. Fragile reed as he may be, man, as Pascal says, is a thinking reed:[22] there lies within him a fund of energy, operating intelligently and so far akin to that which pervades the universe, that it is competent to influence and modify the cosmic process. In virtue of his intelligence, the dwarf bends the Titan to his will. In every family, in every polity that has been established, the cosmic process in man has been restrained and otherwise modified by law and custom; in surrounding nature, it has been similarly influenced by the art of the shepherd, the agriculturist, the artisan. As civilization has advanced, so has the extent of this interference increased; until the organized and highly developed sciences and arts of the present day have endowed man with a command over the course of non-human nature greater than that once attributed to the magicians. The most impressive, I might say startling, of these changes have been brought about in the course of the last two centuries; while a right comprehension of the process of life and of the means of influencing its manifestations is only just dawning upon us. We do not yet see our way beyond generalities; and we are befogged by the obtrusion of false analogies and crude anticipations. But Astronomy, Physics, Chemistry, have all had to pass through similar phases, before they reached the stage at which their influence became an important factor in human affairs. Physiology, Psychology, Ethics, Political Science, must submit to the same ordeal. Yet it seems to me irrational to doubt that, at no distant period, they will work as great a revolution in the sphere of practice.

The theory of evolution encourages no millennial anticipations. If, for millions of years, our globe has taken the upward road, yet, some time, the summit will be reached and the downward route will be commenced. The most daring imagination will hardly venture upon the suggestion that the power and the intelligence of man can ever arrest the procession of the great year.

Moreover, the cosmic nature born with us and, to a large extent, necessary for our maintenance, is the outcome of millions of years of severe training, and it would be folly to imagine that a few centuries will suffice to subdue its masterfulness to purely ethical ends. Ethical nature may count upon having to reckon with a tenacious and powerful enemy as long as the world lasts. But, on the other hand, I see no limit to the extent to which intelligence and will, guided by sound principles of investigation, and organized in common effort, may modify the conditions of existence, for a period longer than that now covered by history. And much may be done to change the nature of man himself.[23] The intelligence which has converted the brother of the wolf into the faithful guardian of the flock ought to be able to do something towards curbing the instincts of savagery in civilized men.

But if we may permit ourselves a larger hope of abatement of the essential evil of the world than was possible to those who, in the infancy of exact knowledge, faced the problem of existence more than a score of centuries ago, I deem it an essential condition of the realization of that hope that we should cast aside the notion that the escape from pain and sorrow is the proper object of life.

We have long since emerged from the heroic childhood of our race, when good and evil could be met with the same "frolic welcome"; the attempts to escape from evil, whether Indian or Greek, have ended in flight from the battlefield; it remains to us to throw aside the youthful over-confidence and the no less youthful discouragement of nonage. We are grown men, and must play the man

> strong in will
> To strive, to seek, to find, and not to yield,

cherishing the good that falls in our way, and bearing the evil, in and around us, with stout hearts set on diminishing it. So far, we all may strive in one faith towards one hope:

> It may be that the gulfs will wash us down,
> It may be we shall touch the Happy Isles,
>
> . . . . but something ere the end,
> Some work of noble note may yet be done. (^{24})

NOTES

Note 1 (p. 29)

I HAVE BEEN CAREFUL TO SPEAK OF THE "APPEARANCE" OF CYCLICAL evolution presented by living things; for, on critical examination, it will be found that the course of vegetable and of animal life is not exactly represented by the figure of a cycle which returns into itself. What actually happens, in all but the lowest organisms, is that one part of the growing germ (A) gives rise to tissues and organs; while another part (B) remains in its primitive condition, or is but slightly modified. The moiety A becomes the body of the adult and, sooner or later, perishes, while portions of the moiety B are detached and, as offspring, continue the life of the species. Thus, if we trace back an organism along the direct line of descent from its remotest ancestor, B, as a whole, has never suffered death; portions of it, only, have been cast off and died in each individual offspring.

Everybody is familiar with the way in which the "suckers" of a strawberry plant behave. A thin cylinder of living tissue keeps on growing at its free end, until it attains a considerable length. At successive intervals, it develops buds which grow into strawberry plants; and these become independent by the death of the parts of the sucker which connect them. The rest of the sucker, however, may go on living and growing indefinitely, and, circumstances remaining favorable, there is no obvious reason why it should ever die. The living substance *B,* in a manner, answers to the sucker. If we could restore the continuity which was once possessed by the portions of *B,* contained in all the individuals of a direct line of descent, they would form a sucker, or *stolon,* on which these individuals would be strung, and which would never have wholly died.

A species remains unchanged so long as the potentiality of development resident in *B* remains unaltered; so long, e.g., as the buds of the strawberry sucker tend to become typical strawberry plants. In the case of the progressive evolution of a species, the developmental potentiality of *B* becomes of a higher and higher order. In retrogressive evolution, the contrary would be the case. The phenomena of atavism seem to show that retrogressive evolution, that is, the return of a species to one or other of its earlier forms, is a possibility to be reckoned with. The simplification of structure, which is so common in the parasitic members of a group, however, does not properly come under this head. The worm-like, limbless *Lernæa* has no resemblance to any of the stages of development of the many-limbed active animals of the group to which it belongs.

Note 2 (p. 29)

Heracleitus says, Ποταμῷ γὰρ οὐκ ἔστι δὶς ἐμβῆναι τῷ αὐτῷ; but, to be strictly accurate, the river remains, though the water of which it is composed changes—just as a man retains his identity though the whole substance of his body is constantly shifting.

This is put very well by Seneca (Ep. lvii. i. 20, Ed. Ruhkopf): *"Corpora nostra rapiuntur fluminum more, quidquid vides currit cum tempore; nihil ex his quæ videmus manet. Ego ipse dum loquor mutari ista, mutatus sum. Hoc est quod ait Heraclitus 'In idem flumen bis non descendimus.' Manet idem fluminis nomen, aqua transmissa est. Hoc in amne manifestius est quam in homine, sed nos quoque non minus velox cursus prætervehit."*

Note 3 (p. 32)

"Multa bona nostra nobis nocent, timoris enim tormentum memoria reducit, providentia anticipat. Nemo tantum præsentibus miser est." (Seneca, Ed. v. 7.)

Among the many wise and weighty aphorisms of the Roman Bacon, few sound the realities of life more deeply than "*Multa bona nostra nobis nocent.*" If there is a soul of good in things evil, it is at least equally true that there is a soul of evil in things good: for things, like men, have "*les défauts de leurs qualités.*" It is one of the last lessons one learns from experience, but not the least important, that a heavy tax is levied upon all forms of success; and that failure is one of the commonest disguises assumed by blessings.

Note 4 (p. 35)

There is within the body of every man a soul which, at the death of the body, flies away from it like a bird out of a cage, and enters upon a new life . . . either in one of the heavens or one of the hells or on this earth. The only exception is the rare case of a man having in this life acquired a true knowledge of God. According to the pre-Buddhistic theory, the soul of such a man goes along the path of the Gods to God, and, being united with Him, enters upon an immortal life in which his individuality is not extinguished. In the latter theory, his soul is directly absorbed into the Great Soul, is lost in it, and has no longer any independent existence. The souls of all other men enter, after the death of the body, upon a new existence in one or other of the many different modes of being. If in heaven or hell, the soul itself becomes a god or demon without entering a body; all superhuman beings, save the great gods, being looked upon as not eternal, but merely temporary creatures. If the soul returns to earth it may or may not enter a new body; and this either of a human being, an animal, a plant, or even a material object. For all these are possessed of souls, and there is no essential difference between these souls and the souls of men—all being alike mere sparks of the Great Spirit, who is the only real existence. (Rhys Davids, *Hibbert Lectures,* 1881, p. 83.)

For what I have said about Indian Philosophy, I am particularly indebted to the luminous exposition of primitive Buddhism and its relations to earlier Hindu thought, which is given by Prof. Rhys Davids in his remarkable *Hibbert Lectures* for 1881, and *Buddhism* (1890). The only apology I can offer for the freedom with which I have borrowed from him in these notes, is my desire to leave no doubt as to my indebtedness. I have also found Dr. Oldenberg's *Buddha* (Ed. 2, 1890) very helpful. The origin of the theory of transmigration stated in the above extract is an unsolved problem. That it differs widely from the Egyptian metempsychosis is clear. In fact, since men usually people the other world with phantoms of this, the Egyptian doctrine would seem to presuppose the Indian as a more archaic belief.

Prof. Rhys Davids has fully insisted upon the ethical importance of the transmigration theory. "One of the latest speculations now being put forward among ourselves would seek to explain each man's character, and even his outward condition in life, by the character he inherited from his ancestors, a character gradually formed during a practically endless series of past existences, modified only by the conditions into which he was born, those very conditions being also, in like manner, the last result of a practically endless series of past causes. Gotama's speculation might be stated in the same words. But it attempted also to explain, in a way different from that which would be adopted by the exponents of the modern theory, that strange problem which it is also the motive of the wonderful drama of the book of Job to explain—the fact that the actual distribution here of good fortune, or misery, is entirely independent of the moral qualities which men call good or bad. We cannot wonder that a teacher, whose whole system was so essentially an ethical reformation, should have felt it incumbent upon him to seek an explanation of this apparent injustice. And all the more so, since the belief he had inherited, the theory of the transmigration of souls, had provided a solution perfectly sufficient to anyone who could accept that belief." (*Hibbert Lectures,* p. 93.) I should venture to suggest the substitution of "largely" for "entirely" in the foregoing passage. Whether a ship makes a good or a bad voyage is largely independent of the conduct of the captain, but it is largely affected by that conduct. Though powerless before a hurricane he may weather many a bad gale.

Note 5 (p. 36)

The outward condition of the soul is, in each new birth, determined by its actions in a previous birth; but by each action in succession, and not by the balance struck after the evil has been reckoned off against the good. A good man who has once uttered a slander may spend a hundred thousand years as a god, in consequence of his goodness, and when the power of his good actions is exhausted, may be born as a dumb man on account of his transgression; and a robber who has once done an act of mercy, may come to life in a king's body as the result of his virtue, and then suffer torments for ages in hell or as a ghost without a body, or be re-born many times as a slave or an outcast, in consequence of his evil life.

There is no escape, according to this theory, from the result of any act; though it is only the consequences of its own acts that each soul has to endure. The force has been set in motion by itself and can never stop; and its effect can never be foretold. If evil, it can never be modified or prevented, for it depends on a cause already completed, that is now forever beyond the soul's control. There is even no continuing consciousness, no memory of the past that could guide the soul to any knowledge of its fate. The only advantage open to it is to add in this life to the sum of its good actions, that it may bear fruit with the rest. And even this can only happen in some future life under essentially the same conditions as the present one: subject, like the present one, to old age, decay, and death; and affording opportunity, like the present one, for the commission of errors, ignorances, or sins, which in their turn must inevitably produce their due effect of sickness, disability, or woe. Thus is the soul tossed about from life to life, from billow to billow in the great ocean of transmigration. And there is no escape save for the very few, who, during their birth as men, attain to a right knowledge of the Great Spirit: and thus enter into immortality, or, as the later philosophers taught, are absorbed into the Divine Essence. (Rhys Davids, *Hibbert Lectures*, pp. 85, 86.)

The state after death thus imagined by the Hindu philosophers has a certain analogy to the purgatory of the Roman Church; except that escape from it is dependent, not on a divine decree modified, it may be, by sacerdotal or saintly intercession, but by the acts of the individual himself; and that while ultimate emergence into heavenly bliss of the good, or well-prayed for, Catholic is professedly assured, the chances in favor of the attainment of absorption, or of Nirvana, by any individual Hindu are extremely small.

Note 6 (p. 36)

"That part of the then prevalent transmigration theory which could not be proved false seemed to meet a deeply felt necessity, seemed to supply a moral cause which would explain the unequal distribution here of happinesss or woe, so utterly inconsistent with the present characters of men." Gautama "still therefore talked of men's previous existence, but by no means in the way that he is generally represented to have done." What he taught was "the transmigration of character." He held that after the death of any being, whether human or not, there survived nothing at all but that being's "Karma," the result, that is, of its mental and bodily actions. Every individual, whether human or divine, was the last inheritor and the last result of the Karma of a long series of past individuals—"a series so long that its beginning is beyond the reach of calculation, and its end will be coincident with the destruction of the world." (Rhys Davids, *Hibbert Lectures*, p. 92.)

In the theory of evolution, the tendency of a germ to develop according to a certain specific type. e.g., of the kidney bean seed to grow into a plant having all the characters of *Phaseolus vulgaris,* is its "Karma." It is the "last inheritor and the last result" of all the conditions that have affected a line of ancestry which goes back for many millions of years to the time when life first appeared on the earth. The moiety *B* of the substance of the bean plant (see *Note* 1) is the last link in a once continuous chain extending from the primitive living substance: and the characters of the successive species to which it has given rise are the manifestations of its gradually modified Karma. As Prof. Rhys Davids aptly says, the snowdrop "is a snowdrop and not an oak, and just that kind of snowdrop, because it is the outcome of the Karma of an endless series of past existences." (*Hibbert Lectures,* p. 114.)

Note 7 (p. 37)

It is interesting to notice that the very point which is the weakness of the theory—the supposed concentration of the effect of the Karma in one new being—presented itself to the early Buddhists themselves as a difficulty. They avoided it, partly by explaining that it was a particular thirst in the creature dying (a craving, Tanhā, which plays otherwise a great part in the Buddhist theory) which actually caused the birth of the new individual who was to inherit the Karma of the former one. But, how this took place, how the craving desire produced this effect, was acknowledged to be a mystery patent only to a Buddha. (Rhys Davids, *Hibbert Lectures,* p. 95.)

Among the many parallelisms of Stoicism and Buddhism, it is curious to find one for this Tanhā, "thirst," or "craving desire" for life. Seneca writes (Epist. lxxvi. 18): "*Si enim ullum aliud est bonum quam honestum, sequetur nos aviditas vitæ aviditas rerum vitam instruentium: quod est intolerabile infinitum, vagum.*"

Note 8 (p. 39)

The distinguishing characteristic of Buddhism was that it started a new line, that it looked upon the deepest questions men have to solve from an entirely different standpoint. It swept away from the field of its vision the whole of the great soul-theory which had hitherto so completely filled and dominated the minds of the superstitious and the thoughtful alike. For the first time in the history of the world, it proclaimed a salvation which each man could gain for himself and by himself, in this world, during this life, without any the least reference to God, or to Gods, either great or small. Like the Upanishads, it placed the first importance on knowledge; but it was no longer a knowledge of God, it was a clear perception of the real nature, as they supposed it to be, of men and things. And it added to the necessity of knowledge, the necessity of purity, of courtesy, of uprightness, of peace and of a universal love far reaching, grown great and beyond measure. (Rhys Davids, *Hibbert Lectures* p. 29.)

The contemporary Greek philosophy takes an analogous direction. According to Heracleitus, the universe was made neither by Gods nor men; but, from all eternity, has been, and to all eternity, will be, immortal fire, glowing and fading in due measure. (Mullach, *Heracliti fragmenta,* 27.) And the part assigned by his successors, the Stoics, to the knowledge and the volition of the "wise man" made their Divinity (for logical thinkers) a subject for compliments, rather than a power to be reckoned with. In Hindu speculation the "Arahat," still more the "Buddha," becomes the superior of Brahma; the stoical "wise man" is, at least, the equal of Zeus.

Berkeley affirms over and over again that no idea can be formed of a soul or spirit—"If any man shall doubt of the truth of what is here delivered, let him but reflect and try if he can form any idea of power or active being; and whether he hath ideas of two principal powers marked by the names of *will* and *understanding* distinct from each other, as well as from a third idea of substance or being in general, with a relative notion of its supporting or being the subject of the aforesaid power, which is signified by the name *soul* or *spirit.* This is what some hold: but, so far as I can see, the words *will, soul, spirit,* do not stand for different ideas or, in truth, for any idea at all, but for something which is very different from ideas, and which, being an agent, cannot be like unto or represented by any idea whatever [though it must be owned at the same time, that we have some notion of soul, spirit, and the operations of the mind, such as willing, loving, hating, inasmuch as we know or understand the meaning of these words"]. (*The Principles of Human Knowledge,* lxxvi. See also §§ lxxxix., cxxxv., cxlv.)

It is open to discussion. I think, whether it is possible to have "some notion" of that of which we can form no "idea."

Berkeley attaches several predicates to the "perceiving active being mind, spirit, soul or myself" (Parts I, II). It is said, for example, to be "indivisible, incorporeal, unextended, and incorruptible." The predicate indivisible, though negative in form, has highly positive consequences. For, if "perceiving active being" is strictly indivisible, man's soul must be one with the Divine spirit: which is good Hindu or Stoical doctrine, but hardly orthodox Christian philosophy. If, on the other hand, the "substance" of active perceiving "being" is actually divided into the one Divine and innumerable human entities, how can the predicate "indivisible" be rigorously applicable to it?

Taking the words cited, as they stand, they amount to the denial of the possibility of any knowledge of substance. "Matter" having been resolved into mere affections of "spirit," "spirit" melts away into an admittedly inconceivable and unknowable hypostasis of thought and power—consequently the existence of anything in the universe beyond a flow of phenomena is a purely hypothetical assumption. Indeed a pyrrhonist might raise the objection that if "*esse*" is "*percipi*" spirit itself can have no existence except as a perception, hypostatized into a "self," or as a perception of some other spirit. In the former case, objective reality vanishes; in the latter, there would seem to be the need of an infinite series of spirits each perceiving the others.

It is curious to observe how very closely the phraseology of Berkeley sometimes approaches that of the Stoics: thus (cxlviii.) "It seems to be a *general pretence of the unthinking* herd *that they cannot see God.* . . . But, alas, we need only open our eyes to see the Sovereign Lord of all things with a more full and clear view, than we do any of our fellow-creatures . . . we do at all times and in all places perceive manifest tokens of the Divinity: everything we see, hear, feel, or any wise perceive by sense, being a sign or effect of the power of God" . . . (cxlix.) "It is therefore plain, that *nothing can be more evident* to anyone that is capable of the least reflection, *than the existence of God,* or a spirit who is intimately present to our minds, producing in them all that variety of ideas or sensations which continually affect us, on whom we have an absolute and entire dependence, in short, *in whom we live and move and have our being.*" (cl.) [But you will say hath Nature no share in the production of natural things, and must they be all ascribed to the immediate and sole operation of God? . . . if by *Nature* is meant some being distinct from God, as well as from the laws of nature and things perceived by sense, I must confess that word is to me an empty sound, without any intelligible meaning annexed to it.] Nature in this acceptation is a vain *Chimæra* introduced by those heathens, who had not just notions of the omnipresence and infinite perfection of God."

Compare Seneca (*De Beneficiis,* iv. 7):

"*Natura, inquit, hæc mihi præstat. Non intelligis te, quum hoc dicis, mutare Nomen Deo? Quid enim est aliud Natura quam Deus, et divina ratio, toti mundo et partibus ejus inserta? Quoties voles tibi licet aliter hunc auctorem rerum nostrarum compellare, et Jovem illum optimum et maximum rite dices, et tonantem, et statorem: qui non, ut historici tradiderunt, ex eo quod post votum susceptum acies Romanorum fugientum stetit, sed quod stant beneficio ejus omnia, stator, stabilitorque est: hunc eundem et fatum si dixeris, non mentieris, nam quum fatum nihil aliud est, quam series implexa causarum, ille est prima omnium causa, ea qua cæteræ pendent.*" It would appear, therefore, that the good Bishop is somewhat hard upon the "heathen," of whose words his own might be a paraphrase.

There is yet another direction in which Berkeley's philosophy, I will not say agrees with Gautama's, but at any rate helps to make a fundamental dogma of Buddhism intelligible.

> I find I can excite ideas in my mind at pleasure, and vary and shift the scene as often as I think fit. It is no more than willing, and straightway this or that idea arises in my fancy: and by the same power, it is obliterated, and makes way for another. This making and unmaking of ideas doth very properly denominate the mind active. This much is certain and grounded on experience. . . . (*Principles,* xxviii.)

A good many of us, I fancy, have reason to think that experience tells them very much the contrary; and are painfully familiar with the obsession of the mind by ideas which cannot be obliterated by any effort of the will and steadily refuse to make way for others. But what I desire to point out is that if Gautama was equally confident that he could "make and unmake" ideas—then, since he had resolved self into a group of ideal phantoms—the possibility of abolishing self by volition naturally followed.

Note 9 (p. 40)

According to Buddhism, the relation of one life to the next is merely that borne by the flame of one lamp to the flame of another lamp which is set alight by it. To the "Arahat" or adept "no outward form, no compound thing, no creature, no creator, no existence of any kind, must appear to be other than a temporary collocation of its component parts, fated inevitably to be dissolved."—(Rhys Davids, *Hibbert Lectures,* p. 211.)

The self is nothing but a group of phenomena held together by the desire of life; when that desire shall have ceased, "the Karma of that particular chain of lives will cease to influence any longer any distinct individual, and there will be no more birth; for birth, decay, and death, grief, lamentation, and despair will have come, so far as regards that chain of lives, forever to an end."

The state of mind of the Arahat in which the desire of life has ceased is Nirvana. Dr. Oldenberg has very acutely and patiently considered the various interpretations which have been attached to "Nirvana" in the work to which I have referred (pp. 285 *et seq.*). The result of his and other discussions of the question may I think be briefly stated thus:

1. Logical deduction from the predicates attached to the term "Nirvana" strips it of all reality, conceivability, or perceivability, whether by Gods or men. For all practical purposes, therefore, it comes to exactly the same thing as annihilation.
2. But it is not annihilation in the ordinary sense, inasmuch as it could take place in the living Arahat or Buddha.
3. And, since, for the faithful Buddhist, that which was abolished in the Arahat was the possibility of further pain, sorrow, or sin; and that which was attained was perfect peace; his mind directed itself exclusively to this joyful consummation, and personified the negation of all conceivable existence and of all pain into a positive bliss. This was all the more easy, as Gautama refused to give any dogmatic definition of Nirvana. There is something analogous in the way in which people commonly talk of the "happy release" of a man who has been long suffering from mortal disease. According to their own views, it must always be extremely doubtful whether the man will be any happier after the "release" than before. But they do not choose to look at the matter in this light.

The popular notion that, with practical, if not metaphysical, annihilation in view, Buddhism must needs be a sad and gloomy faith seems to be inconsistent with fact; on the contrary, the prospect of Nirvana fills the true believer, not merely with cheerfulness, but with an ecstatic desire to reach it.

Note 10 (p. 68)

The influence of the picture of the personal qualities of Gautama, afforded by the legendary anecdotes which rapidly grew into a biography of the Buddha; and by the birth stories, which coalesced with the current folklore, and were intelligible to all the world, doubtless played a great part. Further, although Gautama appears not to have meddled with the caste system, he refused to recognize any distinction, save that of perfection in the way of salvation, among his followers; and by such teaching, no less than by the inculcation of love and benevolence to all sentient beings, he practically levelled every social, political, and racial barrier. A third important condition was the organization of the Buddhists into monastic communities for the stricter professors, while the laity were permitted a wide indulgence in practice and were allowed to hope for accommodation in some of the temporary abodes of bliss. With a few hundred thousand years of immediate paradise in sight, the average man could be content to shut his eyes to what might follow.

Note 11 (p. 41)

In ancient times it was the fashion, even among the Greeks themselves, to derive all Greek wisdom from Eastern sources; not long ago it was as generally denied that Greek philosophy had any connection with Oriental speculation; it seems probable, however, that the truth lies between these extremes.

The Ionian intellectual movement does not stand alone. It is only one of several sporadic indications of the working of some powerful mental ferment over the whole of the area comprised between the Aegean and Northern Hindostan during the eighth, seventh, and sixth centuries before our era. In these three hundred years, prophetism attained its apogee among the Semites of Palestine; Zoroasterism grew and became the creed of a conquering race, the Iranic Aryans; Buddhism rose and spread with marvelous rapidity among the Aryans of Hindostan; while scientific naturalism took its rise among the Aryans of Ionia. It would be difficult to find another three centuries which have given birth to four events of equal importance. All the principal existing religions of mankind have grown out of the first three: while the fourth is the little spring, now swollen into the great stream of positive science. So far as physical possibilities go, the prophet Jeremiah and the oldest Ionian philosopher might have met and conversed. If they had done so, they would probably have disagreed a good deal; and it is interesting to reflect that their discussions might have embraced questions which, at the present day, are still hotly controverted.

The old Ionian philosophy, then, seems to be only one of many results of a stirring of the moral and intellectual life of the Aryan and the Semitic populations of Western Asia. The conditions of this general awakening were doubtless manifold, but there is one which modern research had brought into great prominence. This is the existence of extremely ancient and highly advanced societies in the valleys of the Euphrates and of the Nile.

It is now known that, more than a thousand—perhaps more than two thousand—years before the sixth century BC, civilization had attained a relatively high pitch among the Babylonians and the Egyptians. Not only had painting, sculpture, architecture, and the industrial arts reached a remarkable development; but in Chaldæa, at any rate, a vast amount of knowledge had been accumulated and methodized, in the departments of grammar, mathematics, astronomy, and natural history. Where such traces of the scientific spirit are visible, naturalistic speculation is rarely far off, though, so far as I know, no remains of an Accadian, or Egyptian, philosophy, properly so called, have yet been recovered.

Geographically, Chaldæa occupied a central position among the oldest seats of civilization. Commerce, largely aided by the intervention of those colossal pedlars, the Phoenicians, had brought Chaldæa into connection with all of them, for a thousand years before the epoch at present under consideration. And in the ninth, eighth and seventh centuries, the Assyrian, the depositary of Chaldæan civilization, as the Macedonian and the Roman, at a later date, were the depositaries of Greek culture, had added irresistible force to the other agencies for the wide distribution of Chaldæan literature, art, and science.

I confess that I find it difficult to imagine that the Greek immigrants—who stood in somewhat the same relation to the Babylonians and the Egyptians as the later Germanic barbarians to the Romans of the Empire—should not have been immensely influenced by the new life with which they became acquainted. But there is abundant direct evidence of the magnitude of this influence in certain spheres. I suppose it is not doubted that the Greek went to school with the Oriental for his primary instruction in reading, writing, and arithmetic; and that Semitic theology supplied him with some of his mythological lore. Nor does there now seem to be any question about the large indebtedness of Greek art to that of Chaldæa, and that of Egypt.

But the manner of that indebtedness is very instructive. The obligation is clear, but its limits are no less definite. Nothing better exemplifies the indomitable originality of the Greeks than the relations of their art to that of the Orientals. Far from being subdued into mere imitators by the technical excellence of their teachers, they lost no time in bettering the instruction they received, using their models as mere stepping stones on the way to those unsurpassed and unsurpassable achievements which are all their own. The shibboleth of Art is the human figure. The ancient Chaldæans and Egyptians, like the modern Japanese, did wonders in the representation of birds and quadrupeds; they even attained to something more than respectability in human portraiture. But their utmost efforts never brought them within range of the best Greek embodiments of the grace of womanhood, or of the severer beauty of manhood.

It is worthwhile to consider the probable effect upon the acute and critical Greek mind of the conflict of ideas, social, political, and theological, which arose out of the conditions of life in the Asiatic colonies. The Ionian polities had passed through the whole gamut of social and political changes, from patriarchal and occasionally oppressive kingship to rowdy and still more burdensome mobship— no doubt with infinitely eloquent and copious argumentation, on both sides, at every stage of their progress towards that arbitrament of force which settles most political questions. The marvelous speculative faculty, latent in the Ionian, had come in contact with Mesopotamian, Egyptian, Phœnician theologies and cosmogonies; with the illuminati of Orphism and the fanatics and dreamers of the

Mysteries; possibly with Buddhism and Zoroasterism; possibly even with Judaism. And it has been observed that the mutual contradictions of antagonistic supernaturalisms are apt to play a large part among the generative agencies of naturalism.

Thus, various external influences may have contributed to the rise of philosophy among the Ionian Greeks of the sixth century. But the assimilative capacity of the Greek mind—its power of Hellenizing whatever it touched—has here worked so effectually, that, so far as I can learn, no indubitable traces of such extraneous contributions are now allowed to exist by the most authoritative historians of Philosophy. Nevertheless, I think it must be admitted that the coincidences between the Heracleito-stoical doctrines and those of the older Hindu philosophy are extremely remarkable. In both, the cosmos pursues an eternal succession of cyclical changes. The great year, answering to the Kalpa, covers an entire cycle from the origin of the universe as a fluid to its dissolution in fire—"*Humor initium, ignis exitus mundi,*" as Seneca has it. In both systems, there is immanent in the cosmos a source of energy, Brahma, or the Logos, which works according to fixed laws. The individual soul is an efflux of this world-spirit, and returns to it. Perfection is attainable only by individual effort, through ascetic discipline, and is rather a state of painlessness than of happiness; if indeed it can be said to be a state of anything, save the negation of perturbing emotion. The hatchment motto "*In Cœlo Quies*" would serve both Hindu and Stoic; and absolute quiet is not easily distinguishable from annihilation.

Zoroasterism, which, geographically, occupies a position intermediate between Hellenism and Hinduism, agrees with the latter in recognizing the essential evil of the cosmos; but differs from both in its intensely anthropomorphic personification of the two antagonistic principles, to the one of which it ascribes all the good; and, to the other, all the evil. In fact, it assumes the existence of two worlds, one good and one bad; the latter created by the evil power for the purpose of damaging the former. The existing cosmos is a mere mixture of the two, and the "last judgment" is a root-and-branch extirpation of the work of Ahriman.

Note 12 (p. 41)

There is no snare in which the feet of a modern student of ancient lore are more easily entangled, than that which is spread by the similarity of the language of antiquity to modern modes of expression. I do not presume to interpret the obscurest of Greek philosophers; all I wish is to point out, that his words, in the sense accepted by competent interpreters, fit modern ideas singularly well.

So far as the general theory of evolution goes there is no difficulty. The aphorism about the river; the figure of the child playing on the shore; the kingship and fatherhood of strife, seem decisive. The ὁδός ἄνω κάτω μίη expresses, with singular aptness, the cyclical aspect of the one process of organic evolution in individual plants and animals: yet it may be a question whether the Heracleitean strife included any distinct conception of the struggle for existence. Again, it is tempting to compare the part played by the Heracleitean "fire" with that ascribed by the moderns to heat, or rather to that cause of motion, of which heat is one expression; and a little ingenuity might find a foreshadowing of the doctrine of the conservation of energy, in the saying that all the things are changed into fire and fire into all things, as gold into goods and goods into gold.

Note 13 (p. 42)

Popes lines in the *Essay on Man* (Ep. i. 267-8),

> All are but parts of one stupendous whole,
> Whose body Nature is, and God the soul,

simply paraphrase Seneca's *"quem in hoc mundo locum deus obtinet, hunc in homine animus: quod est illic materia, id nobis corpus est."*—(Ep. lxv. 24); which again is a Latin version of the old Stoical doctrine, εἰς ἅπαν τοῦ κόσμου μέρος διήκει ὁ νοῦς, καθάπερ ἀφ' ἡμῶν ἡ ψυχή.

So far as the testimony for the universality of what ordinary people call "evil" goes, there is nothing better than the writings of the Stoics themselves. They might serve as a storehouse for the epigrams of the ultra-pessimists. Heracleitus *(circa* 500 BC) says just as hard things about ordinary humanity as his disciples centuries later; and there really seems no need to seek for the causes of this dark view of life in the circumstances of the time of Alexander's successors or of the early Emperors of Rome. To the man with an ethical ideal, the world, including himself, will always seem full of evil.

Note. 14 (p. 43)

I use the well-known phrase, but decline responsibility for the libel upon Epicurus, whose doctrines were far less compatible with existence in a stye than those of the Cynics. If it were steadily borne in mind that the conception of the "flesh" as the source of evil, and the great saying "*Initium est salutis notitia peccati,*" are the property of Epicurus, fewer illusions about Epicureanism would pass muster for accepted truth.

Note 15 (p. 44)

The Stoics said that man was a ζῷον λογικὸν πολιτικὸν φιλάλληον, or a rational, a political, and an altruistic or philanthropic animal. In their view, his higher nature tended to develop in these three directions, as a plant tends to grow up into its typical form. Since, without the introduction of any consideration of pleasure or pain, whatever thwarted the realization of its type by the plant might be said to be bad, and whatever helped it good; so virtue, in the Stoical sense, as the conduct which tended to the attainment of the rational, political, and philanthropic ideal, was good in itself, and irrespectively of its emotional concomitants.

Man is an "*animal sociale communi bono genitum.*" The safety of society depends upon practical recognition of the fact. "*Salva autem esse societas nisi custodia et amore partium non possit,*" says Seneca. (*De. Ira,* ii. 31.)

Note 16 (p. 44)

The importance of the physical doctrine of the Stoics lies in its clear recognition of the universality of the law of causation, with its corollary, the order of nature: the exact form of that order is an altogether secondary consideration.

Many ingenious persons now appear to consider that the incompatibility of pantheism, of materialism, and of any doubt about the immortality of the soul, with religion and morality, is to be held as an axiomatic truth. I confess that I have a certain difficulty in accepting this dogma. For the Stoics were notoriously materialists and pantheists of the most extreme character; and while no strict Stoic believed in the eternal duration of the individual soul, some even denied its persistence after death. Yet it is equally certain that of all gentile philosophies, Stoicism exhibits the highest ethical development, is animated by the most religious spirit, and has exerted the profoundest influence upon the moral and religious development not merely of the best men among the Romans, but among the moderns down to our own day.

Seneca was claimed as a Christian and placed among the saints by the fathers of the early Christian Church; and the genuineness of a correspondence between him and the apostle Paul has been hotly maintained in our own time, by orthodox writers. That the letters, as we possess them, are worthless forgeries is obvious; and writers as wide apart as Baur and Lightfoot agree that the whole story is devoid of foundation.

The dissertation of the late Bishop of Durham *(Epistle to the Phillippians)* is particularly worthy of study, apart from this question, on account of the evidence which it supplies of the numerous similarities of thought between Seneca and the writer of the Pauline epistles. When it is remembered that the writer of the Acts puts a quotation from Aratus, or Cleanthes, into the mouth of the apostle; and that Tarsus was a great seat of philosophical and especially stoical learning (Chrysippus himself was a native of the adjacent town of Sôli), there is no difficulty in understanding the origin of these resemblances. See, on this subject, Sir Alexander Grant's dissertation in his edition of *The Ethics of Aristotle* (where there is an interesting reference to the stoical character of Bishop Butler's ethics), the concluding pages of Dr. Weygoldt's instructive little work *Die Philosophie der Stoa,* and Aubertin's *Sénèque et Saint Paul.*

It is surprising that a writer of Dr. Lightfoot's stamp should speak of Stoicism as a philosophy of "despair." Surely, rather, it was a philosophy of men who, having cast off all illusions, and the child-ishness of despair among them, were minded to endure in patience whatever conditions the cosmic process might create, so long as those conditions were compatible with the progress towards virtue, which alone, for them, conferred a worthy object on existence. There is no note of despair in the stoical declaration that the perfected "wise man" is the equal of Zeus in everything but the duration of his existence. And, in my judgment, there is as little pride about it, often as it serves for the text of discourses on stoical arrogance. Grant the stoical postulate that there is no good except virtue; grant that the perfected wise man is altogether virtuous, in consequence of being guided in all things by the reason, which is an effluence of Zeus, and there seems no escape from the stoical conclusion.

Note 17 (p. 45)

Our "Apathy" carries such a different set of connotations from its Greek original that I have ventured on using the latter as a technical term.

Note 18 (p. 46)

Many of the stoical philosophers recommended their disciples to take an active share in public affairs; and in the Roman world, for several centuries, the best public men were strongly inclined to Stoicism. Nevertheless, the logical tendency of Stoicism seems to me to be fulfilled only in such men as Diogenes and Epictetus.

Note 19 (p. 47)

"Criticisms on the Origin of Species," 1864. *Collected Essays,* vol. ii. p. 91. [1894.]

Note 20 (p. 48)

Of course, strictly speaking, social life, and the ethical process in virtue of which it advances towards perfection, are part and parcel of the general process of evolution, just as the gregarious habit of innu-merable plants and animals, which has been of immense advantage to them, is so. A hive of bees is an organic polity, a society in which the part played by each member is determined by organic necessities. Queens, workers, and drones are, so to speak, castes, divided from one another by marked physical barriers. Among birds and mammals, societies are formed, of which the bond in many cases seems to be purely psychological; that is to say, it appears to depend upon the liking of the individuals for one another's company. The tendency of individuals to over self-assertion is kept down by fighting. Even in these rudimentary forms of society, love and fear come into play, and enforce a greater or less renunciation of self-will. To this extent the general cosmic process begins to be checked by a rudimentary ethical process, which is, strictly speaking, part of the former, just as the "governor" in a steam-engine is part of the mechanism of the engine.

Note 21 (p. 49)

See "Government: Anarchy or Regimentation," *Collected Essays*, vol. i. pp. 413–418. It is this form of political philosophy to which I conceive the epithet of "reasoned savagery" to be strictly applicable. [1894.]

Note 22 (p. 49)

"*L'homme n'est qu'un roseau, le plus faible de la nature, mais c'est un roseau pensant. Il ne faut pas que l'univers entier s'arme pour l'écraser. Une vapeur, une goutte d'eau, suffit pour le tuer. Mais quand l'univers l'écraserait, l'homme serait encore plus noble que ce qui le tue, parce qu'il sait qu'il meurt; et l'avantage que l'univers a sur lui, l'univers n'en sait rien.*"

—*Pensées de Pascal.*

Note 23 (p. 50)

The use of the word "Nature" here may be criticized. Yet the manifestation of the natural tendencies of men is so profoundly modified by training that it is hardly too strong. Consider the suppression of the sexual instinct between near relations.

Note 24 (p. 51)

A great proportion of poetry is addressed by the young to the young; only the great masters of the art are capable of divining, or think it worth while to enter into, the feelings of retrospective age. The two great poets whom we have so lately lost, Tennyson and Browning, have done this, each in his own inimitable way; the one in the *Ulysses*, from which I have borrowed; the other in that wonderful fragment "Childe Roland to the dark Tower came."

CHAPTER THREE

SCIENCE AND MORALS

[1886]

IN SPITE OF LONG AND, PERHAPS, NOT UNJUSTIFIABLE HESITATION, I begin to think that there must be something in telepathy. For evidence, which I may not disregard, is furnished by the last number of the *Fortnightly Review* that among the hitherto undiscovered endowments of the human species, there may be a power even more wonderful than the mystic faculty by which the esoterically Buddhistic sage "upon the farthest mountain in Cathay" reads the inmost thoughts of a dweller within the homely circuit of the London postal district. Great indeed is the insight of such a seer; but how much greater is his who combines the feat of reading, not merely the thoughts of which the thinker is aware, but those of which he knows nothing; who sees him unconsciously drawing the conclusions which he repudiates, and supporting the doctrines which he detests. To reflect upon the confusion which the working of such a power as this may introduce into one's ideas of personality and responsibility is perilous—madness lies that way. But truth is truth, and I am almost fain to believe in this magical visibility of the non-existent when the only alternative is the supposition that the writer of the article on "Materialism and Morality" in vol. xl. (1886) of the *Fortnightly Review*, in spite of his manifest ability and honesty, has pledged himself, so far as I am concerned, to what, if I may trust my own knowledge of my own thoughts, must be called a multitude of errors of the first magnitude.

I so much admire Mr. Lilly's outspokenness, I am so completely satisfied with the uprightness of his intentions, that it is repugnant to me to quarrel with anything he may say; and I sympathize so warmly with his manly scorn of the vileness of much that passes under the name of literature in these times, that I would willingly be silent under his by no means unkindly exposition of his theory of my own tenets, if I thought that such personal abnegation would serve the interest of the cause we both have at heart. But I cannot think so. My creed may be an ill-favored thing, but it is mine own, as Touchstone says of his ladylove; and I have so high an opinion of the solid virtues of the object of my affections that I cannot calmly see her personated by a wench who is much uglier and has no virtue worth speaking of. I hope I should be ready to stand by a falling cause if I had ever adopted it; but suffering for a falling cause, which one has done one's best to bring to the ground, is a kind of martyrdom for which I have no taste. In my opinion, the philosophical theory which Mr. Lilly attributes to me—but which I have over and over again disclaimed—is untenable and destined to extinction; and I not unreasonably demur to being counted among its defenders.

After the manner of a mediæval disputant, Mr. Lilly posts up three theses, which, as he conceives, embody the chief heresies propagated by the late Professor Clifford, Mr. Herbert Spencer, and myself. He says that we agree "(1) in putting aside, as unverifiable, everything which the senses cannot verify; (2) everything beyond the bounds of physical science; (3) everything which cannot be brought into a laboratory and dealt with chemically" (p. 578).

My lamented young friend Clifford, sweetest of natures though keenest of disputants, is out of reach of our little controversies, but his works speak for him, and those who run may read a refutation of Mr. Lilly's assertions in them. Mr. Herbert Spencer, hitherto, has shown no lack either of ability or of inclination to speak for himself; and it would be a superfluity, not to say an impertinence, on my part, to take up the cudgels for him. But, for myself, if my knowledge of my own consciousness may be assumed to be adequate (and I make not the least pretension to acquaintance with what goes on in my "*Unbewusstsein*"), I may be permitted to observe that the first proposition appears to me to be not true; that the second is in the same case; and that, if there be gradations in untrueness, the third is so monstrously untrue that it hovers on the verge of absurdity, even if it does not actually flounder in that logical limbo. Thus, to all three theses, I reply in appropriate fashion, *Nego*—I say No; and I proceed to state the grounds of that negation, which the proprieties do not permit me to make quite so emphatic as I could desire.

Let me begin with the first assertion, that I "put aside, as unverifiable, everything which the senses cannot verify." Can such a statement as this be seriously made in respect of any human being? But I am not appointed apologist for mankind in general; and confining my observations to myself, I beg leave to point out that, at this present moment, I entertain an unshakable conviction that Mr. Lilly is the victim of a patent and enormous misunderstanding, and that I have not the slightest intention of putting that conviction aside because I cannot "verify" it either by touch, or taste, or smell, or hearing, or sight, which (in the absence of any trace of telepathic faculty) make up the totality of my senses.

Again, I may venture to admire the clear and vigorous English in which Mr. Lilly embodies his views; but the source of that admiration does not lie in anything which my five senses enable me to discover in the pages of his article, and of which an orang-outang might be just as acutely sensible. No, it lies in an appreciation of literary form and logical structure by æsthetic and intellectual faculties which are not senses, and which are not unfrequently sadly wanting where the senses are in full vigor. My poor relation may beat me in the matter of sensation; but I am quite confident that, when style and syllogisms are to be dealt with, he is nowhere.

If there is anything in the world which I do firmly believe in, it is the universal validity of the law of causation; but that universality cannot be proved by any amount of experience, let alone that which comes to us through the senses. And when an effort of volition changes the current of my thoughts, or when an idea calls up another associated idea, I have not the slightest doubt that the process to which the first of the phenomena, in each case, is due stands in the relation of cause to the second. Yet the attempt to verify this belief by sensation would be sheer lunacy. Now I am quite sure that Mr. Lilly does not doubt my sanity; and the only alternative seems to be the admission that his first proposition is erroneous.

The second thesis charges me with putting aside "as unverifiable" "everything beyond the bounds of physical science." Again I say, No. Nobody, I imagine, will credit me with a desire to limit the empire of physical science, but I really feel bound to confess that a great many very familiar and, at the same time, extremely important phenomena he quite beyond its legitimate limits. I cannot conceive, for example, how the phenomena of consciousness, as such and apart from the physical process by which they are called into existence, are to be brought within the bounds of physical science. Take the simplest possible example, the feeling of redness. Physical science tells us that it commonly arises as a consequence of molecular changes propagated from the eye to a certain part of the substance of the brain, when vibrations of the luminiferous ether of a certain character fall upon the retina. Let us suppose the process of physical analysis pushed so far that one could view the last link of this chain of molecules, watch their movements as if they were billiard balls, weigh them, measure them, and know all that is physically knowable about them. Well, even in that case, we should be just as far from being able to include the resulting phenomenon of consciousness, the feeling of redness, within the bounds of physical science, as we are at present. It would remain as unlike the phenomena we know under the names of matter and motion as it is now. If there is any plain truth upon which I have made it my business to insist over and over again it is this—and whether it is a truth or not, my insistence upon it leaves not a shadow of justification for Mr. Lilly's assertion.

But I ask in this case also, how is it conceivable that any man, in possession of all his natural faculties, should hold such an opinion? I do not suppose that I am exceptionally endowed because I have all my life enjoyed a keen perception of the beauty offered us by nature and by art. Now physical science may and probably will, someday, enable our posterity to set forth the exact physical concomitants and conditions of the strange rapture of beauty. But if ever that day arrives, the rapture will remain, just as it is now, outside and beyond the physical world; and, even in the mental world, something superadded to mere sensation. I do not wish to crow unduly over my humble cousin the orang, but in the æsthetic province, as in that of the intellect, I am afraid he is nowhere. I doubt not he would detect a fruit amidst a wilderness of leaves where I could see nothing; but I am tolerably confident that he has never been awestruck, as I have been, by the dim religious gloom, as of a temple devoted to the earthgods, of the tropical forests which he inhabits. Yet I doubt not that our poor long-armed and short-legged friend, as he sits meditatively munching his durian fruit, has something behind that sad Socratic face of his which is utterly "beyond the bounds of physical science." Physical science may know all about his clutching the fruit and munching it and digesting it, and how the physical titillation of his palate is transmitted to some microscopic cells of the gray matter of his brain. But the feelings of sweetness and of satisfaction which, for a moment, hang out their signal lights in his melancholy eyes, are as utterly outside the bounds of physics as is the "fine frenzy" of a human rhapsodist.

Does Mr. Lilly really believe that, putting me aside, there is any man with the feeling of music in him who disbelieves in the reality of the delight which he derives from it, because that delight lies outside the bounds of physical science, not less than outside the region of the mere sense of hearing? But, it may be, that he includes music, painting, and sculpture under the head of physical science, and in that case I can only regret I am unable to follow him in his ennoblement of my favorite pursuits.

The third thesis runs that I put aside "as unverifiable" "everything which cannot be brought into a laboratory and dealt with chemically"; and, once more, I say No. This wondrous allegation is no novelty; it has not unfrequently reached me from that region where gentle (or ungentle) dulness so often holds unchecked sway—the pulpit. But I marvel to find that a writer of Mr. Lilly's intelligence and good faith is willing to father such a wastrel. If I am to deal with the thing seriously, I find myself met by one of the two horns of a dilemma. Either some meaning, as unknown to usage as to the dictionaries, attaches to "laboratory" and "chemical," or the proposition is (what am I to say in my sore need for a gentle and yet appropriate word?)—well—unhistorical.

Does Mr. Lilly suppose that I put aside "as unverifiable" all the truths of mathematics, of philology, of history? And if I do not, will he have the great goodness to say how the binomial theorem is to be dealt with "chemically," even in the best-appointed "laboratory"; or where the balances and crucibles are kept by which the various theories of the nature of the Basque language may be tested; or what reagents will extract the truth from any given History of Rome, and leave the errors behind as a residual calx?

I really cannot answer these questions, and unless Mr. Lilly can, I think he would do well hereafter to think more than twice before attributing such preposterous notions to his fellow-men, who, after all, as a learned counsel said, are vertebrated animals.

The whole thing perplexes me much; and I am sure there must be an explanation which will leave Mr. Lilly's reputation for common sense and fair dealing untouched. Can it be—I put this forward quite tentatively—that Mr. Lilly is the victim of a confusion, common enough among thoughtless people, and into which he has fallen unawares? Obviously, it is one thing to say that the logical methods of physical science are of universal applicability, and quite another to affirm that all subjects of thought lie within the province of physical science. I have often declared my conviction that there is only one method by which intellectual truth can be reached, whether the subject-matter of investigation belongs to the world of physics or to the world of consciousness; and one of the arguments in favor of the use of physical science as an instrument of education which I have oftenest used is that, in my opinion, it exercises young minds in the appreciation of inductive evidence better than any other study. But while I repeat my conviction that the physical sciences probably furnish the best and most easily appreciable illustrations of the one and indivisible mode of ascertaining truth by the use of reason, I beg leave to add that I have never thought of suggesting that other branches of knowledge may not afford the same discipline; and assuredly I have never given the slightest ground for the attribution to me of the ridiculous contention that there is nothing true outside the bounds of physical science. Doubtless people who wanted to say something damaging, without too nice a regard to its truth or falsehood, have often enough misrepresented my plain meaning. But Mr. Lilly is not one of these folks at whom one looks and passes by, and I can but sorrowfully wonder at finding him in such company.

So much for the three theses which Mr. Lilly has nailed on to the page of this Review. I think I have shown that the first is inaccurate, that the second is inaccurate, and that the third is inaccurate; and that these three inaccurates constitute one prodigious, though I doubt not unintentional, misrepresentation. If Mr. Lilly and I were dialectic gladiators, fighting in the arena of the *Fortnightly*, under the eye of an editorial lanista, for the delectation of the public, my best tactics would now be to leave the field of battle. For the question whether I do, or do not, hold certain opinions is a matter of fact, with regard to which my evidence is likely to be regarded as conclusive—at least until such time as the telepathy of the unconscious is more generally recognized.

However, some other assertions are made by Mr. Lilly which more or less involve matters of opinion whereof the rights and wrongs are less easily settled, but in respect of which he seems to me to err quite as seriously as about the topics we have been hitherto discussing. And the importance of these subjects leads me to venture upon saying something about them, even though I am thereby compelled to leave the safe ground of personal knowledge.

Before launching the three torpedoes which have so sadly exploded on board his own ship, Mr. Lilly says that with whatever "rhetorical ornaments I may gild my teaching," it is "Materialism." Let me observe, in passing, that rhetorical ornament is not in my way, and that gilding refined gold would, to my mind, be less objectionable than varnishing the fair face of truth with that pestilent cosmetic, rhetoric. If I believed that I had any claim to the title of "Materialist," as that term is understood in the language of philosophy and not in that of abuse, I should not attempt to hide it by any sort of gilding. I have not found reason to care much for hard names in the course of the last thirty years, and I am too old to develop a new sensitiveness. But, to repeat what I have more than once taken pains to say in the most unadorned of plain language, I repudiate, as philosophical error, the doctrine of Materialism as I understand it, just as I repudiate the doctrine of Spiritualism as Mr. Lilly presents it, and my reason for thus doing is, in both cases, the same; namely, that, whatever their differences. Materialists and Spiritualists agree in making very positive assertions about matters of which I am certain I know nothing, and about which I believe they are, in truth, just as ignorant. And further, that, even when their assertions are confined to topics which lie within the range of my faculties, they often appear to me to be in the wrong. And there is yet another reason for objecting to be identified with either of these sects; and that is that each is extremely fond of attributing to the other, by way of reproach, conclusions which are the property of neither, though they infallibly flow from the logical development of the first principles of both. Surely a prudent man is not to be reproached because he keeps clear of the squabbles of these philosophical Bianchi and Neri, by refusing to have anything to do with either?

I understand the main tenet of Materialism to be that there is nothing in the universe but matter and force; and that all the phenomena of nature are explicable by deduction from the properties assignable to these two primitive factors. That great champion of Materialism whom Mr. Lilly appears to consider to be an authority in physical science, Dr. Büchner, embodies this article of faith on his title page. *Kraft und Stoff*—force and matter—are paraded as the Alpha and Omega of existence. This I apprehend is the fundamental article of the faith materialistic; and whosoever does not hold it is condemned by the more zealous of the persuasion (as I have some reason to know) to the Inferno appointed for fools or hypocrites. But all this I heartily disbelieve; and at the risk of being charged with wearisome repetition of an old story, I will briefly give my reasons for persisting in my infidelity. In the first place, as I have already hinted, it seems to me pretty plain that there is a third thing in the universe, to wit, consciousness, which, in the hardness of my heart or head, I cannot see to be matter, or force, or any conceivable modification of either, however intimately the manifestations of the phenomena of consciousness may be connected with the phenomena known as matter and force. In the second place, the arguments used by Descartes and Berkeley to show that our certain knowledge does not extend beyond our states of consciousness, appear to me to be as irrefragable now as they did when I first became acquainted with them some half-century ago. All the materialistic writers I know of who have tried to bite that file have simply broken their teeth. But, if this is true, our one certainty is the existence of the mental world, and that of *Kraft und Stoff* falls into the rank of, at best, a highly probable hypothesis.

Thirdly, when I was a mere boy, with a perverse tendency to think when I ought to have been playing, my mind was greatly exercised by this formidable problem, What would become of things if they lost their qualities? As the qualities had no objective existence, and the thing without qualities was nothing, the solid world seemed whittled away—to my great horror. As I grew older, and learned to use the terms matter and force, the boyish problem was revived, *mutato nomine*. On the one hand, the notion of matter without force seemed to resolve the world into a set of geometrical ghosts, too dead even to jabber. On the other hand, Boscovich's hypothesis, by which matter was resolved into centers of force, was very attractive. But when one tried to think it out, what in the world became of force considered as an objective entity? Force, even the most materialistic of philosophers will agree with the most idealistic, is nothing but a name for the cause of motion. And if, with Boscovich, I resolved things into centers of force, then matter vanished altogether and left immaterial entities in its place. One might as well frankly accept Idealism and have done with it.

I must make a confession, even if it be humiliating. I have never been able to form the slightest conception of those "forces" which the Materialists talk about, as if they had samples of them many years in bottle. They tell me that matter consists of atoms, which are separated by mere space devoid of contents; and that, through this void, radiate the attractive and repulsive forces whereby the atoms affect one another. If anybody can clearly conceive the nature of these things which not only exist in nothingness, but pull and push there with great vigor, I envy him for the possession of an intellect of larger grasp, not only than mine, but than that of Leibnitz or of Newton.[1] To me the "*chimæra, bombinans in vacuo quia comedit secundas intentiones*" of the schoolmen is a familiar and domestic creature compared with such "forces." Besides, by the hypothesis, the forces are not matter; and thus all that is of any particular consequence in the world turns out to be not matter on the Materialist's own showing. Let it not be supposed that I am casting a doubt upon the propriety of the employment of the terms "atom" and "force," as they stand among the working hypotheses of physical science. As formulæ which can be applied, with perfect precision and great convenience, in the interpretation of nature, their value is incalculable; but, as real entities, having an objective existence, an indivisible particle which nevertheless occupies space is surely inconceivable; and with respect to the operation of that atom, where it is not, by the aid of a "force" resident in nothingness, I am as little able to imagine it as I fancy anyone else is.

Unless and until anybody will resolve all these doubts and difficulties for me, I think I have a right to hold aloof from Materialism. As to Spiritualism, it lands me in even greater difficulties when I want to get change for its notes-of-hand in the solid coin of reality. For the assumed substantial entity, spirit, which is supposed to underlie the phenomena of consciousness, as matter underlies those of physical nature, leaves not even a geometrical ghost when these phenomena are abstracted. And, even if we suppose the existence of such an entity apart from qualities—that is to say, a bare existence—for mind, how does anybody know that it differs from that other entity, apart from qualities, which is the supposed substratum of matter? Spiritualism is, after all, little better than Materialism turned upside down. And if I try to think of the "spirit" which a man, by this hypothesis, carries about under his hat, as something devoid of relation to space, and as something indivisible, even in thought, while it is, at the same time, supposed to be in that place and to be possessed of half a dozen different faculties, I confess I get quite lost.

As I have said elsewhere, if I were forced to choose between Materialism and Idealism, I should elect for the latter; and I certainly would have nothing to do with the effete mythology of Spiritualism. But I am not aware that I am under any compulsion to choose either the one or the other. I have always entertained a strong suspicion that the sage who maintained that man is the measure of the universe was sadly in the wrong; and age and experience have not weakened that conviction. In following these lines of speculation I am reminded of the quarter-deck walks of my youth. In taking that form of exercise you may perambulate through all points of the compass with perfect safety, so long as you keep within certain limits: forget those limits, in your ardor, and mere smothering and spluttering, if not worse, await you. I stick by the deck and throw a lifebuoy now and then to the struggling folk who have gone overboard; and all I get for my humanity is the abuse of all whenever they leave off abusing one another.

Tolerably early in life I discovered that one of the unpardonable sins, in the eyes of most people, is for a man to presume to go about unlabeled. The world regards such a person as the police do an unmuzzled dog, not under proper control. I could find no label that would suit me, so, in my desire to range myself and be respectable, I invented one; and, as the chief thing I was sure of was that I did not know a great many things that the—ists and the—ites about me professed to be familiar with, I called myself an Agnostic. Surely no denomination could be more modest or more appropriate; and I cannot imagine why I should be every now and then haled out of my refuge and declared sometimes to be a Materialist, sometimes an Atheist, sometimes a Positivist; and sometimes, alas and alack, a cowardly or reactionary Obscurantist.

I trust that I have, at last, made my case clear, and that henceforth I shall be allowed to rest in peace—at least, after a further explanation or two, which Mr. Lilly proves to me may be necessary. It has been seen that my excellent critic has original ideas respecting the meaning of the words "laboratory" and "chemical"; and, as it appears to me, his definition of "Materialist" is quite as much peculiar to himself. For, unless I misunderstand him, and I have taken pains not to do so, he puts me down as a Materialist (over and above the grounds which I have shown to have no foundation); firstly, because I have said that consciousness is a function of the brain; and, secondly, because I hold by determinism. With respect to the first point, I am not aware that there is anyone who doubts that, in the proper physiological sense of the word function, consciousness, in certain forms at any rate, is a cerebral function. In physiology we call function that effect, or series of effects, which results from the activity of an organ. Thus, it is the function of muscle to give rise to motion; and the muscle gives rise to motion when the nerve which supplies it is stimulated. If one of the nerve-bundles in a man's arm is laid bare and a stimulus is applied to certain of the nervous filaments, the result will be production of motion in that arm. If others are stimulated, the result will be the production of the state of consciousness called pain. Now, if I trace these last nerve-filaments, I find them to be ultimately connected with part of the substance of the brain, just as the others turn out to be connected with muscular substance. If the production of motion in the one case is properly said to be the function of the muscular substance, why is the production of a state of consciousness in the other case not to be called a function of the cerebral substance? Once upon a time, it is true, it was supposed that a certain "animal spirit" resided in muscle and was the real active agent. But we have done with that wholly superfluous fiction so far as the muscular organs are concerned. Why are we to retain a corresponding fiction for the nervous organs?

If it is replied that no physiologist, however spiritual his leanings, dreams of supposing that simple sensations require a "spirit" for their production, then I must point out that we are all agreed that consciousness is a function of matter, and that particular tenet must be given up as a mark of Materialism. Any further argument will turn upon the question, not whether consciousness is a function of the brain, but whether all forms of consciousness are so. Again, I hold it would be quite correct to say that material changes are the causes of psychical phenomena (and, as a consequence, that the organs in which these changes take place have the production of such phenomena for their function), even if the spiritualistic hypothesis had any foundation. For nobody hesitates to say that an event A is the cause of an event Z, even if there are as many intermediate terms, known and unknown, in the chain of causation as there are letters between

A and Z. The man who pulls the trigger of a loaded pistol placed close to another's head certainly is the cause of that other's death, though, in strictness, he "causes" nothing but the movement of the finger upon the trigger. And, in like manner, the molecular change which is brought about in a certain portion of the cerebral substance by the stimulation of a remote part of the body would be properly said to be the cause of the consequent feeling, whatever unknown terms were interposed between the physical agent and the actual psychical product. Therefore, unless Materialism has the monopoly of the right use of language, I see nothing materialistic in the phraseology which I have employed.

The only remaining justification which Mr. Lilly offers for dubbing me a Materialist, *malgré moi*, arises out of a passage which he quotes, in which I say that the progress of science means the extension of the province of what we call matter and force, and the concomitant gradual banishment from all regions of human thought of what we call spirit and spontaneity. I hold that opinion now, if anything, more firmly than I did when I gave utterance to it a score of years ago, for it has been justified by subsequent events. But what that opinion has to do with Materialism I fail to discover. In my judgment, it is consistent with the most thorough-going Idealism, and the grounds of that judgment are really very plain and simple.

The growth of science, not merely of physical science, but of all science, means the demonstration of order and natural causation among phenomena which had not previously been brought under those conceptions. Nobody who is acquainted with the progress of scientific thinking in every department of human knowledge, in the course of the last two centuries, will be disposed to deny that immense provinces have been added to the realm of science; or to doubt that the next two centuries will be witnesses of a vastly greater annexation. More particularly in the region of the physiology of the nervous system is it justifiable to conclude from the progress that has been made in analysing the relations between material and psychical phenomena, that vast further advances will be made; and that, sooner or later, all the so-called spontaneous operations of the mind will have, not only their relations to one another, but their relations to physical phenomena, connected in natural series of causes and effects, strictly defined. In other words, while, at present, we know only the nearer moiety of the chain of causes and effects, by which the phenomena we call material give rise to those which we call mental; hereafter, we shall get to the further end of the series.

In my innocence, I have been in the habit of supposing that this is merely a statement of facts, and that the good Bishop Berkeley, if he were alive, would find such facts fit into his system without the least difficulty. That Mr. Lilly should play into the hands of his foes, by declaring that unmistakable facts make for them, is an exemplification of ways that are dark, quite unintelligible to me. Surely Mr. Lilly does not hold that the disbelief in spontaneity—which term, if it has any meaning at all, means uncaused action—is a mark of the beast Materialism? If so, he must be prepared to tackle many of the Cartesians (if not Descartes himself), Spinoza and Leibnitz among the philosophers, Augustine, Thomas Aquinas, Calvin and his followers among theologians, as Materialists—and that surely is a sufficient *reductio ad absurdum* of such a classification.

The truth is, that in his zeal to paint "Materialism," in large letters, on everything he dislikes, Mr. Lilly forgets a very important fact, which, however, must be patent to everyone who has paid attention to the history of human thought; and that fact is, that everyone of the speculative difficulties which beset Kant's three problems, the existence of a Deity, the freedom of the will, and immortality, existed ages before anything that can be called physical science, and would continue to exist if modern physical science were swept away. All that physical science has done has been to make, as it were, visible and tangible some difficulties that formerly were more hard of apprehension. Moreover, these difficulties exist just as much on the hypothesis of Idealism as on that of Materialism.

The student of nature, who starts from the axiom of the universality of the law of causation, cannot refuse to admit an eternal existence; if he admits the conservation of energy, he cannot deny the possibility of an eternal energy; if he admits the existence of immaterial phenomena in the form of consciousness, he must admit the possibility, at any rate, of an eternal series of such phenomena;

and, if his studies have not been barren of the best fruit of the investigation of nature, he will have enough sense to see that when Spinoza says, *"Per Deum intelligo ens absolute infinitum, hoc est substantiam constantem infinitis attributis,"* the God so conceived is one that only a very great fool would deny, even in his heart. Physical science is as little Atheistic as it is Materialistic.

So with respect to immortality. As physical science states this problem, it seems to stand thus: "Is there any means of knowing whether the series of states of consciousness, which has been casually associated for threescore years and ten with the arrangement and movements of innumerable millions of successively different material molecules, can be continued, in like association, with some substance which has not the properties of matter and force?" As Kant said, on a like occasion, if anybody can answer that question, he is just the man I want to see. If he says that consciousness cannot exist, except in relation of cause and effect with certain organic molecules, I must ask how he knows that; and if he says it can, I must put the same question. And I am afraid that, like jesting Pilate, I shall not think it worth while (having but little time before me) to wait for an answer.

Lastly, with respect to the old riddle of the freedom of the will. In the only sense in which the word freedom is intelligible to me—that is to say, the absence of any restraint upon doing what one likes within certain limits—physical science certainly gives no more ground for doubting it than the common sense of mankind does. And if physical science, in strengthening our belief in the universality of causation and abolishing chance as an absurdity, leads to the conclusions of determinism, it does no more than follow the track of consistent and logical thinkers in philosophy and in theology, before it existed or was thought of. Whoever accepts the universality of the law of causation as a dogma of philosophy, denies the existence of uncaused phenomena. And the essence of that which is improperly called the freewill doctrine is that occasionally, at any rate, human volition is self-caused, that is to say, not caused at all; for to cause oneself one must have anteceded oneself—which is, to say the least of it, difficult to imagine.

Whoever accepts the existence of an omniscient Deity as a dogma of theology, affirms that the order of things is fixed from eternity to eternity; for the fore-knowledge of an occurrence means that the occurrence will certainly happen; and the certainty of an event happening is what is meant by its being fixed or fated.[2]

Whoever asserts the existence of an omnipotent Deity, that he made and sustains all things, and is the *causa causarum*, cannot, without a contradiction in terms, assert that there is any cause independent of him; and it is a mere subterfuge to assert that the cause of all things can "permit" one of these things to be an independent cause.

Whoever asserts the combination of omniscience and omnipotence as attributes of the Deity, does implicitly assert predestination. For he who knowingly makes a thing and places it in circumstances the operation of which on that thing he is perfectly acquainted with, does predestine that thing to whatever fate may befall it.

Thus, to come, at last, to the really important part of all this discussion, if the belief in a God is essential to morality, physical science offers no obstacle thereto; if the belief in immortality is essential to morality, physical science has no more to say against the probability of that doctrine than the most ordinary experience has, and it effectually closes the mouths of those who pretend to refute it by objections deduced from merely physical data. Finally, if the belief in the uncausedness of volition is essential to morality, the student of physical science has no more to say against that absurdity than the logical philosopher or theologian. Physical science, I repeat, did not invent determinism, and the deterministic doctrine would stand on just as firm a foundation as it does if there were no physical science. Let anyone who doubts this read Jonathan Edwards, whose demonstrations are derived wholly from philosophy and theology.

Thus, when Mr. Lilly, like another Solomon Eagle, goes about proclaiming "Woe to this wicked city," and denouncing physical science as the evil genius of modern days—mother of materialism, and fatalism, and all sorts of other condemnable isms—I venture to beg him to lay the blame on the right shoulders; or, at least, to put in the dock, along with Science, those sinful sisters of hers, Philosophy and Theology, who, being so much older, should have known better than the poor Cinderella of the schools and universities over which they have so long dominated. No doubt modern society is diseased enough; but then it does not differ from older civilizations in that respect. Societies of men are fermenting masses, and, as beer has what the Germans call *"Oberhefe"* and *"Unterhefe,"* so every society that has existed has had its scum at the top and its dregs at the bottom; but I doubt if any of the "ages of faith" had less scum or less dregs, or even showed a proportionally greater quantity of sound wholesome stuff in the vat. I think it would puzzle Mr. Lilly, or anyone else, to adduce convincing evidence that, at any period of the world's history, there was a more widespread sense of social duty, or a greater sense of justice, or of the obligation of mutual help, than in this England of ours. Ah! But, says Mr. Lilly, these are all products of our Christian inheritance; when Christian dogmas vanish virtue will disappear too, and the ancestral ape and tiger will have full play. But there are a good many people who think it obvious that Christianity also inherited a good deal from Paganism and from Judaism; and that, if the Stoics and the Jews revoked their bequest, the moral property of Christianity would realize very little. And, if morality has survived the stripping off of several sets of clothes which have been found to fit badly, why should it not be able to get on very well in the light and handy garments which Science is ready to provide?

But this by the way. If the diseases of society consist in the weakness of its faith in the existence of the God of the theologians, in a future state, and in uncaused volitions, the indication, as the doctors say, is to suppress Theology and Philosophy, whose bickerings about things of which they know nothing have been the prime cause and continual sustenance of that evil scepticism which is the Nemesis of meddling with the unknowable.

Cinderella is modestly conscious of her ignorance of these high matters. She lights the fire, sweeps the house, and provides the dinner; and is rewarded by being told that she is a base creature, devoted to low and material interests. But in her garret she has fairy visions out of the ken of the pair of shrews who are quarrelling down stairs. She sees the order which pervades the seeming disorder of the world; the great drama of evolution, with its full share of pity and terror, but also with abundant goodness and beauty, unrolls itself before her eyes; and she learns, in her heart of hearts, the lesson, that the foundation of morality is to have done, once and for all, with lying; to give up pretending to believe that for which there is no evidence, and repeating unintelligible propositions about things beyond the possibilities of knowledge.

She knows that the safety of morality lies neither in the adoption of this or that philosophical speculation, or this or that theological creed, but in a real and living belief in that fixed order of nature which sends social disorganization upon the track of immorality, as surely as it sends physical disease after physical trespasses. And of that firm and lively faith it is her high mission to be the priestess.

CHAPTER FOUR

CAPITAL—THE MOTHER OF LABOR

An economical problem discussed from a physiological point of view

[1890]

THE FIRST ACT OF A NEWBORN CHILD IS TO DRAW A DEEP BREATH. IN fact, it will never draw a deeper, inasmuch as the passages and chambers of the lungs, once distended with air, do not empty themselves again; it is only a fraction of their contents which passes in and out with the flow and the ebb of the respiratory tide. Mechanically, this act of drawing breath, or inspiration, is of the same nature as that by which the handles of a bellows are separated, in order to fill the bellows with air; and, in like manner, it involves that expenditure of energy which we call exertion, or work, or labor. It is, therefore, no mere metaphor to say that man is destined to a life of toil: the work of respiration which began with his first breath ends only with his last; nor does one born in the purple get off with a lighter task than the child who first sees light under a hedge.

How is it that the newborn infant is enabled to perform this first instalment of the sentence of life-long labor which no man may escape? Whatever else a child may be, in respect of this particular question, it is a complicated piece of mechanism, built up out of materials supplied by its mother; and in the course of such building-up, provided with a set of motors—the muscles. Each of these muscles contains a stock of substance capable of yielding energy under certain conditions, one of which is a change of state in the nerve fibers connected with it. The powder in a loaded gun is such another stock of substance capable of yielding energy in consequence of a change of state in the mechanism of the lock, which intervenes between the finger of the man who pulls the trigger and the cartridge. If that change is brought about, the potential energy of the powder passes suddenly into actual energy, and does the work of propelling the bullet. The powder, therefore, may be appropriately called *work-stuff*, not only because it is stuff which is easily made to yield work in the physical sense, but because a good deal of work in the economical sense has contributed to its production. Labor was necessary to collect, transport, and purify the raw sulphur and saltpetre; to cut wood and convert it into powdered charcoal; to mix these ingredients in the right proportions; to give the mixture the proper grain, and so on. The powder once formed part of the stock, or capital, of a powder-maker: and it is not only certain natural bodies which are collected and stored in the gun-powder, but the labor bestowed on the operations mentioned may be figuratively said to be incorporated in it.

In principle, the work-stuff stored in the muscles of the newborn child is comparable to that stored in the gun-barrel. The infant is launched into altogether new surroundings; and these operate through the mechanism of the nervous machinery, with the result that the potential energy of some of the work-stuff in the muscles which bring about inspiration is suddenly converted into actual energy; and this, operating through the mechanism of the respiratory apparatus, gives rise to an act of inspiration. As the bullet is propelled by the "going off" of the powder, as it might be said that the ribs are raised and the midriff depressed by the "going off" of certain portions of muscular work-stuff. This work-stuff is part of a stock or capital of that commodity stored up in the child's organism before birth, at the expense of the mother; and the mother has made good her expenditure by drawing upon the capital of food-stuffs which furnished her daily maintenance.

Under these circumstances, it does not appear to me to be open to doubt that the primary act of outward labor in the series which necessarily accompany the life of man is dependent upon the pre-existence of a stock of material which is not only of use to him, but which is disposed in such a manner as to be utilizable with facility. And I further imagine that the propriety of the application of the term "capital" to this stock of useful substance cannot be justly called in question; inasmuch as it is easy to prove that the essential constituents of the work-stuff accumulated is the child's muscles have merely been transferred from the store of food-stuffs, which everybody admits to be capital, by means of the maternal organism to that of the child, in which they are again deposited to await use. Every subsequent act of labor, in like manner, involves an equivalent consumption of the child's store of work-stuff—its vital capital; and one of the main objects of the process of breathing is to get rid of some of the effects of that consumption. It follows, then, that, even if no other than the respiratory work were going on in the organism, the capital of work-stuff, which the child brought with it into the world, must sooner or later be used up, and the movements of breathing must come to an end; just as the see-saw of the piston of a steam-engine stops when the coal in the fireplace has burnt away.

Milk, however, is a stock of materials which essentially consists of savings from the food-stuffs supplied to the mother. And these savings are in such a physical and chemical condition that the organism of the child can easily convert them into work-stuff. That is to say, by borrowing directly from the vital capital of the mother, indirectly from the store in the natural bodies accessible to her, it can make good the loss of its own. The operation of borrowing, however, involves further work; that is, the labor of sucking, which is a mechanical operation of much the same nature as breathing. The child thus pays for the capital it borrows in labor; but as the value in work-stuff of the milk obtained is very far greater than the value of that labor, estimated by the consumption of work-stuff it involves, the operation yields a large profit to the infant. The overplus of food-stuff suffices to increase the child's capital of work-stuff; and to supply not only the materials for the enlargement of the "buildings and machinery" which is expressed by the child's growth, but also the energy required to put all these materials together, and to carry them to their proper places. Thus, throughout the years of infancy, and so long thereafter as the youth or man is not thrown upon his own resources, he lives by consuming the vital capital provided by others. To use a terminology which is more common than appropriate, whatever work he performs (and he does a good deal, if only in mere locomotion) is unproductive.

Let us now suppose the child come to man's estate in the condition of a wandering savage, dependent for his food upon what he can pick up or catch, after the fashion of the Australian aborigines. It is plain that the place of mother, as the supplier of vital capital, is now taken by the fruits, seeds, and roots of plants and by various kinds of animals. It is they alone which contain stocks of those substances which can be converted within the man's organism into work-stuff; and of the other matters, except air and water, required to supply the constant consumption of his capital and to keep his organic machinery going. In no way does the savage contribute to the production of these substances. Whatever labor he bestows upon such vegetable and animal bodies, on the contrary, is devoted to their destruction; and it is a mere matter of accident whether a little labor yields him a great deal—as in the case, for example, of a stranded whale; or whether much labor yields next to nothing—as in times of long-continued drought. The savage, like the child, borrows the capital he needs, and, at any rate, intentionally, does nothing towards repayment; it would plainly be an improper use of the word "produce" to say that his labor in hunting for the roots, or the fruits, or the eggs, or the grubs and snakes, which he finds and eats, "produces" or contributes to "produce" them. The same thing is true of more advanced tribes, who are still merely hunters, such as the Esquimaux. They may expend more labor and skill; but it is spent in destruction.

When we pass from these to men who lead a purely pastoral life, like the South American Gauchos, or some Asiatic nomads, there is an important change. Let us suppose the owner of a flock of sheep to live on the milk, cheese, and flesh which they yield. It is obvious that the flock stands to him in the economic relation of the mother to the child, inasmuch as it supplies him with food-stuffs competent to make good the daily and hourly losses of his capital of work-stuff. If we imagine our sheep-owner to have access to extensive pastures and to be troubled neither by predacious animals nor by rival shepherds, the performance of his pastoral functions will hardly involve the expenditure of any more labor than is needful to provide him with the exercise required to maintain health. And this is true, even if we take into account the trouble originally devoted to the domestication of the sheep. It surely would be a most singular pretension for the shepherd to talk of the flock as the "produce" of his labor in any but a very limited sense. In truth, his labor would have been a mere accessory of production of very little consequence. Under the circumstances supposed, a ram and some ewes, left to themselves for a few years, would probably generate as large a flock; and the superadded labor of the shepherd would have little more effect upon their production than upon that of the blackberries on the bushes about the pastures. For the most part the increment would be thoroughly unearned; and, if it is a rule of absolute political ethics that owners have no claim upon "betterment" brought about independently of their own labor, then the shepherd would have no claim to at least nine-tenths of the increase of the flock.

But if the shepherd has no real claim to the title of "producer," who has? Are the rams and ewes the true "producers"? Certainly their title is better if, borrowing from the old terminology of chemistry, they only claim to be regarded as the "proximate principles" of production. And yet, if strict justice is to be dispensed, even they are to be regarded rather as collectors and distributors than as "producers." For all that they really do is to collect, slightly modify, and render easily accessible, the vital capital which already exists in the green herbs on which they feed, but in such a form as to be practically out of the reach of man.

Thus, from an economic point of view, the sheep are more comparable to confectioners than to producers. The usefulness of biscuit lies in the raw flour of which it is made; but raw flour does not answer as an article of human diet, and biscuit does. So the usefulness of mutton lies mainly in certain chemical compounds which it contains: the sheep gets them out of grass; we cannot live on grass, but we can on mutton.

Now, herbaceous and all other green plants stand alone among terrestrial natural bodies, in so far as, under the influence of light, they possess the power to build up, out of the carbonic acid gas in the atmosphere, water and certain nitrogenous and mineral salts, those substances which in the animal organism are utilized as work-stuff. They are the chief and, for practical purposes, the sole producers of that vital capital which we have seen to be the necessary antecedent of every act of labor. Every green plant is a laboratory in which, so long as the sun shines upon it, materials furnished by the mineral world, gases, water, saline compounds, are worked up into those food-stuffs without which animal life cannot be carried on. And since, up to the present time, synthetic chemistry has not advanced so far as to achieve this feat, the green plant may be said to be the only living worker whose labor directly results in the production of that vital capital which is the necessary antecedent of human labor.[1] Nor is this statement a paradox involving perpetual motion, because the energy by which the plant does its work is supplied by the sun— the primordial capitalist so far as we are concerned. But it cannot be too strongly impressed upon the mind that sunshine, air, water, the best soil that is to be found on the surface of the earth, might co-exist; yet without plants, there is no known agency competent to generate the so-called "protein compounds," by which alone animal life can be permanently supported. And not only are plants thus essential; but, in respect of particular kinds of animals, they must be plants of a particular nature. If there were no terrestrial green plants but, say, cypresses and mosses, pastoral and agricultural life would be alike impossible; indeed, it is difficult to imagine the possibility of the existence of any large animal, as the labor required to get at a sufficiency of the store of food-stuffs, contained in such plants as these, could hardly extract from them an equivalent for the waste involved in that expenditure of work.

We are compact of dust and air; from that we set out, and to that complexion must we come at last. The plant either directly, or by some animal intermediary, lends us the capital which enables us to carry on the business of life, as we flit through the upper world, from the one term of our journey to the other. Popularly, no doubt, it is permissible to speak of the soil as a "producer," just as we may talk of the daily movement of the sun. But, as I have elsewhere remarked, propositions which are to bear any deductive strain that may be put upon them must run the risk of seeming pedantic, rather than that of being inaccurate. And the statement that land, in the sense of cultivable soil, is a producer, or even one of the essentials of economic production, is anything but accurate. The process of water-culture, in which a plant is not "planted" in any soil, but is merely supported in water containing in solution the mineral ingredients essential to that plant, is now thoroughly understood; and, if it were worth while, a crop yielding abundant food-stuffs could be raised on an acre of fresh water, no less than on an acre of dry land. In the Arctic regions, again, land has nothing to do with "production" in the social economy of the Esquimaux, who live on seals and other marine animals; and might, like Proteus, shepherd the flocks of Poseidon if they had a mind for pastoral life. But the seals and the bears are dependent on other inhabitants of the sea, until, somewhere in the series, we come to the minute green plants which float in the ocean, and are the real "producers" by which the whole of its vast animal population is supported.[2]

Thus, when we find set forth as an "absolute" truth the statement that the essential factors in economic production are land, capital and labor—when this is offered as an axiom whence all sorts of other important truths may be deduced—it is needful to remember that the assertion is true only with a qualification. Undoubtedly "vital capital" is essential; for, as we have seen, no human work can be done unless it exists, not even that internal work of the body which is necessary to passive life. But, with respect to labor (that is, human labor) I hope to have left no doubt on the reader's mind that, in regard to production, the importance of human labor may be so small as to be almost a vanishing quantity. Moreover, it is certain that there is no approximation to a fixed ratio between the expenditure of labor and the production of that vital capital which is the foundation of all wealth. For, suppose that we introduce into our suppositions pastoral paradise beasts of prey and rival shepherds, the amount of labor thrown upon the sheep-owner may increase almost indefinitely, and its importance as a condition of production may be enormously augmented, while the quantity of produce remains stationary. Compare for a moment the unimportance of the shepherd's labor, under the circumstances first defined, with its indispensability in countries in which the water for the sheep has to be drawn from deep wells, or in which the flock has to be defended from wolves or from human depredators. As to land, it has been shown that, except as affording mere room and standing ground, the importance of land, great as it may be, is secondary. The one thing needful for economic production is the green plant, as the sole producer of vital capital from natural inorganic bodies. Men might exist without labor (in the ordinary sense) and without land; without plants they must inevitably perish.

That which is true of the purely pastoral condition is *a fortiori* true of the purely agricultural[3] condition, in which the existence of the cultivator is directly dependent on the production of vital capital by the plants which he cultivates. Here, again, the condition precedent of the work of each year is vital capital. Suppose that a man lives exclusively upon the plants which he cultivates. It is obvious that he must have food-stuffs to live upon, while he prepares the soil for sowing and throughout the period which elapses between this and harvest. These food-stuffs must be yielded by the stock remaining over from former crops. The result is the same as before—the pre-existence of vital capital is the necessary antecedent of labor. Moreover, the amount of labor which contributes, as an accessory condition, to the production of the crop varies as widely in the case of plant-raising as in that of cattle-raising. With favorable soil, climate and other conditions, it may be very small, with unfavorable, very great, for the same revenue or yield of food-stuffs.

Thus, I do not think it is possible to dispute the following proposition: the existence of any man, or of any number of men, whether organized into a polity or not, depends on the production of food-stuffs (that is, vital capital) readily accessible to man, either directly or indirectly, by plants. But it follows that the number of men who can exist, say for one year, on any given area of land, taken by itself, depends upon the quantity of food-stuffs produced by such plants growing on the area in one year. If a is that quantity, and b the minimum of food-stuffs required for each man, $\frac{a}{b} = n$, the maximum number of men who can exist on the area. Now the amount of production (a) is limited by the extent of area occupied; by the quantity of sunshine which falls upon the area; by the range and distribution of temperature; by the force of the winds; by the supply of water; by the composition and the physical characters of the soil; by animal and vegetable competitors and destroyers. The labor of man neither does, nor can, produce vital capital; all that it can do is to modify, favorably or unfavorably, the conditions of its production. The most important of these—namely, sunshine, range of daily and nightly temperature, wind—are practically out of men's reach.[4] On the other hand, the supply of water, the physical and chemical qualities of the soil, and the influences of competitors and destroyers, can often, though by no means always, be largely affected by labor and skill. And there is no harm in calling the effect of such labor "production," if it is clearly understood that "production" in this sense is a very different thing from the "production" of food-stuffs by a plant.

We have been dealing hitherto with suppositions the materials of which are furnished by everyday experience, not with mere a priori assumptions. Our hypothetical solitary shepherd with his flock, or the solitary farmer with his grain field, are mere bits of such experience, cut out, as it were, for easy study. Still borrowing from daily experience, let us suppose that either sheep-owner or farmer, for any reason that may be imagined, desires the help of one or more other men; and that, in exchange for their labor, he offers so many sheep, or quarts of milk, or pounds of cheese, or so many measures of grain, for a year's service. I fail to discover any a priori "rights of labor" in virtue of which these men may insist on being employed, if they are not wanted. But, on the other hand, I think it is clear that there is only one condition upon which the persons to whom the offer of these "wages" is made can accept it; and that is that the things offered in exchange for a year's work shall contain at least as much vital capital as a man uses up in doing the year's work. For no rational man could knowingly and willingly accept conditions which necessarily involve starvation. Therefore there is an irreducible minimum of wages; it is such an amount of vital capital as suffices to replace the inevitable consumption of the person hired. Now, surely, it is beyond a doubt that these wages, whether at or above the irreducible minimum, are paid out of the capital disposable after the wants of the owner of the flock or of the crop of grain are satisfied; and, from what has been said already, it follows that there is a limit to the number of men, whether hired, or brought in in any other way, who can be maintained by the sheepowner or landowner out of his own resources. Since no amount of labor can produce an ounce of food-stuff beyond the maximum producible by a limited number of plants, under the most favorable circumstances in regard to those conditions which are not affected by labor, it follows that, if the number of men to be fed increases indefinitely, a time must come when some will have to starve. That is the essence of the so-called Malthusian doctrine; and it is a truth which, to my mind, is as plain as the general proposition that a quantity which constantly increases will, sometime or other, exceed any greater quantity the amount of which is fixed.

The foregoing considerations leave no doubt about the fundamental condition of the existence of any polity, or organized society of men, either in a purely pastoral or purely agricultural state, or in any mixture of both states. It must possess a store of vital capital to start with, and the means of repairing the consumption of that capital which takes place as a consequence of the work of the members of the society. And, if the polity occupies a completely isolated area of the earth's surface, the numerical strength of that polity can never exceed the quotient of the maximum quantity of food-stuffs producible by the green plants on that area, in each year, divided by the quantity necessary for the maintenance of each person during the year. But, there is a third mode of existence possible to a polity; it may, conceivably, be neither purely pastoral nor purely agricultural, but purely manufacturing. Let us suppose three islands, like Gran Canaria, Teneriffe and Lanzerote, in the Canaries, to be quite cut off from the rest of the world. Let Gran Canaria be inhabited by grain-raisers, Teneriffe by cattle-breeders; while the population of Lanzerote (which we may suppose to be utterly barren) consists of carpenters, woollen manu-facturers, and shoemakers. Then the facts of daily experience teach us that the people of Lanzerote could never have existed unless they came to the island provided with a stock of food-stuffs; and that they could not continue to exist, unless that stock, as it was consumed, was made up by contributions from the vital capital of either Gran Canaria, or Teneriffe, or both. Moreover, the carpenters of Lanzerote could do nothing, unless they were provided with wood from the other islands; nor could the wool spinners and weavers or the shoemakers work without wool and skins from the same sources. The wood and the wool and the skins are, in fact, the capital without which their work as manufacturers in their respective trades is impossible—so that the vital and other capital supplied by Gran Canaria and Teneriffe is most indubitably the necessary antecedent of the industrial labor of Lanzerote. It is perfectly true that by the time the wood, the wool, and the skins reached Lanzerote a good deal of labor in cutting, shearing, skinning, transport, and so on, would have been spent upon them. But this does not alter the fact that the only "production" which is essential to the existence of the population of Teneriffe and Gran Canaria is that effected by the green plants in both islands; and that all the labor spent upon the raw produce useful in manufacture, directly or indirectly yielded by them—by the inhabitants of these islands and by those of Lanzerote into the bargain—will not provide one solitary Lanzerotian with a dinner, unless the Teneriffians and Canariotes happen to want his goods and to be willing to give some of their vital capital in exchange for them.

Under the circumstances defined, if Teneriffe and Gran Canaria disappeared, or if their inhabitants ceased to care for carpentry, clothing, or shoes, the people of Lanzerote must starve. But if they wish to buy, then the Lanzerotians, by "cultivating" the buyers, indi-rectly favor the cultivation of the produce of those buyers.

Thus, if the question is asked whether the labor employed in manufacture in Lanzerote is "productive" or "unproductive" there can be only one reply. If anybody will exchange vital capital, or that which can be exchanged for vital capital, for Lanzerote goods, it is productive; if not, it is unproductive.

In the case of the manufacturer, the dependence of labor upon capital is still more intimate than in that of the herdsman or agriculturist. When the latter are once started they can go on, without troubling themselves about the existence of any other people. But the manufacturer depends on pre-existing capital, not only at the beginning, but at the end of his operations. However great the expenditure of his labor and of his skill, the result, for the purpose of maintaining his existence, is just the same as if he had done nothing, unless there is a customer able and willing to exchange food-stuffs for that which his labor and skill have achieved.

There is another point concerning which it is very necessary to have clear ideas. Suppose a carpenter in Lanzerote to be engaged in making chests of drawers. Let us suppose that a, the timber, and b, the grain and meat needful for the man's sustenance until he can finish a chest of drawers, have to be paid for by that chest. Then the capital with which he starts is represented by $a + b$. He could not start at all unless he had it; day by day, he must destroy more or less of the substance and of the general adaptability of a in order to work it up into the special forms needed to constitute the chest of drawers; and, day by day, he must use up at least so much of b as will replace his loss of vital capital by the work of that day. Suppose it takes the carpenter and his workmen ten days to saw up the timber, to plane the boards, and to give them the shape and size proper for the various parts of the chest of drawers. And suppose that he then offers his heap of boards to the advancer of $a + b$ as an equivalent for the wood + ten days" supply of vital capital? The latter will surely say: "No. I did not ask for a heap of boards. I asked for a chest of drawers. Up to this time, so far as I am concerned, you have done nothing and are as much in my debt as ever." And if the carpenter maintained that he had "virtually" created two-thirds of a chest of drawers, inasmuch as it would take only five days more to put together the pieces of wood, and that the heap of boards ought to be accepted as the equivalent of two-thirds of his debt, I am afraid the creditor would regard him as little better than an impudent swindler. It obviously makes no sort of difference whether the Canariote or Teneriffian buyer advanced the wood and the food-stuffs, on which the carpenter had to maintain himself; or whether the carpenter had a stock of both, the consumption of which must be recouped by the exchange of a chest of drawers for a fresh supply. In the latter case, it is even less doubtful that, if the carpenter offered his boards to the man who wanted a chest of drawers, the latter would laugh in his face. And if he took the chest of drawers for himself, then so much of his vital capital would be sunk in it past recovery. Again, the payment of goods in a lump, for the chest of drawers, comes to the same thing as the payment of daily wages for the fifteen days that the carpenter was occupied in making it. If, at the end of each day, the carpenter chose to say to himself, "I have "virtually" created, by my day's labor, a fifteenth of what I shall get for the chest of drawers—therefore my wages are the produce of my day's labor"—there is no great harm in such metaphorical speech, so long as the poor man does not delude himself into the supposition that it represents the exact truth. "Virtually" is apt to cover more intellectual sins than "charity" does moral delicts. After what has been said, it surely must be plain enough that each day's work has involved the consumption of the carpenter's vital capital, and the fashioning of his timber, at the expense of more or less consumption of those forms of capital. Whether the $a + b$ to be exchanged for the chest has been advanced as a *loan*, or is paid daily or weekly as *wages*, or, at some later time, as the *price* of a finished commodity—the essential element of the transaction, and the only essential element, is, that it must, at least, effect the replacement of the vital capital consumed. Neither boards nor chest of drawers are eatable; and, so far from the carpenter having produced the essential part of his wages by each day's labor, he has merely wasted that labor, unless somebody who happens to want a chest of drawers offers to exchange vital capital, or something that can procure it, equivalent to the amount consumed during the process of manufacture.[5]

That it should be necessary, at this time of day, to set forth such elementary truths as these may well seem strange; but no one who consults that interesting museum of political delusions, *Progress and Poverty*, some of the treasures of which I have already brought to light, will doubt the fact, if he bestows proper attention upon the first book of that widely read work. At page 9 it is thus written:

The proposition I shall endeavor to prove is: that wages, instead of being drawn from capital, are, in reality, drawn from the product of the labor for which they are paid.

Again at page 11:

In every case in which labor is exchanged for commodities, production really precedes enjoyment . . . wages are the earnings—that is to say, the makings—of labor—not the advances of capital.

And the proposition which the author endeavors to disprove is the hitherto generally accepted doctrine

that labor is maintained and paid out of existing capital, before the product which constitutes the ultimate object is secured (p. 10).

The doctrine respecting the relation of capital and wages, which is thus opposed in *Progress and Poverty*, is that illustrated in the foregoing pages; the truth of which, I conceive, must be plain to anyone who has apprehended the very simple arguments by which I have endeavored to demonstrate it. One conclusion or the other must be hopelessly wrong; and, even at the cost of going once more over some of the ground traversed in this essay and that on *Natural and Political Rights*,[6] I propose to show that the error lies with *Progress and Poverty*; in which work, so far as political science is concerned, the poverty is, to my eye, much more apparent than the progress.

To begin at the beginning. The author propounds a definition of wealth: "Nothing which nature supplies to man without his labor is wealth" (p. 17). Wealth consists of "natural substances or products which have been adapted by human labor to human use or gratification, their value depending upon the amount of labor which, upon the average, would be required to produce things of like kind" (p. 16). The following examples of wealth are given:

> Buildings, cattle, tools, machinery, agricultural and mineral products, manufactured goods, ships, waggons, furniture, and the like (p. 16).

I take it that native metals, coal and brick clay, are "mineral products"; and I quite believe that they are properly termed "wealth." But when a seam of coal crops out at the surface, and lumps of coal are to be had for the picking up; or when native copper lies about in nuggets, or when brick clay forms a superficial stratum, it appears to me that these things are supplied to, nay almost thrust upon, man without his labor. According to the definition, therefore, they are not "wealth." According to the enumeration, however, they are "wealth": a tolerably fair specimen of a contradiction in terms. Or does *Progress and Poverty* really suggest that a coal seam which crops out at the surface is not wealth; but that if somebody breaks off a piece and carries it away, the bestowal of this amount of labor upon that particular lump makes it wealth; while the rest remains "not wealth"? The notion that the value of a thing bears any necessary relation to the amount of labor (average or otherwise) bestowed upon it, is a fallacy which needs no further refutation than it has already received. The average amount of labor bestowed upon warming-pans confers no value upon them in the eyes of a Gold-Coast negro; nor would an Esquimaux give a slice of blubber for the most elaborate of ice-machines.

So much for the doctrine of *Progress and Poverty* touching the nature of wealth. Let us now consider its teachings respecting capital as wealth or a part of wealth. Adam Smith's definition "that part of a man's stock which he expects to yield him a revenue is called his capital" is quoted with approval (p. 19); elsewhere capital is said to be that part of wealth "which is devoted to the aid of production" (p. 17); and yet again it is said to be

> *wealth in course of exchange,*[7] understanding exchange to include, not merely the passing from hand to hand, but also such transmutations as occur when the reproductive or transforming forces of nature are utilized for the increase of wealth (p. 19).

But if too much pondering over the possible senses and scope of these definitions should weary the reader, he will be relieved by the following acknowledgment:

Nor is the definition of capital I have suggested of any importance (p. 20).

The author informs us, in fact, that he is "not writing a textbook," thereby intimating his opinion that it is less important to be clear and accurate when you are trying to bring about a political revolution than when a merely academic interest attaches to the subject treated. But he is not busy about anything so serious as a textbook: no, he "is only attempting to discover the laws which control a great social problem"—a mode of expression which indicates perhaps the high-water mark of intellectual muddlement. I have heard, in my time, of "laws" which control other "laws"; but this is the first occasion on which "laws" which "control a problem" have come under my notice. Even the disquisitions "of those flabby writers who have burdened the press and darkened counsel by numerous volumes which are dubbed political economy" (p. 17) could hardly furnish their critics with a finer specimen of that which a hero of the *Dunciad*, by the one flash of genius recorded of him, called "clotted nonsense."

Doubtless it is a sign of grace that the author of these definitions should attach no importance to any of them; but since, unfortunately, his whole argument turns upon the tacit assumption that they are important, I may not pass them over so lightly. The third I give up. Why anything should be capital when it is "in course of exchange," and not be capital under other circumstances, passes my understanding. We are told that "that part of a farmer's crop held for sale or for seed, or to feed his help, in part payment of wages, would be accounted capital; that held for the care of his family would not be" (p. 18). But I fail to discover any ground of reason or authority for the doctrine that it is only when a crop is about to be sold or sown, or given as wages, that it may be called capital. On the contrary, whether we consider custom or reason, so much of it as is stored away in ricks and barns during harvest, and remains there to be used in any of these ways months or years afterwards, is customarily and rightly termed capital. Surely, the meaning of the clumsy phrase that capital is "wealth in the course of exchange" must be that it is "wealth capable of being exchanged" against labor or anything else. That, in fact, is the equivalent of the second definition, that capital is "that part of wealth which is devoted to the aid of production." Obviously, if you possess that for which men will give labor, you can aid production by means of that labor. And, again, it agrees with the first definition (borrowed from Adam Smith) that capital is "that part of a man's stock which he expects to yield him a revenue." For a revenue is both etymologically and in sense a "return." A man gives his labor in sowing grain, or in tending cattle, because he expects a "return"—a "revenue"—in the shape of the increase of the grain or of the herd; and also, in the latter case, in the shape of their labor and manure which "aid the production" of such increase. The grain and cattle of which he is possessed immediately after harvest is his capital; and his revenue for the twelvemonth, until the next harvest, is the surplus of grain and cattle over and above the amount with which he started. This is disposable for any purpose for which he may desire to use it, leaving him just as well off as he was at the beginning of the year. Whether the man keeps the surplus grain for sowing more land, and the surplus cattle for occupying more pasture; whether he exchanges them for other commodities, such as the use of the land (as rent); or labor (as wages); or whether he feeds himself and his family, in no way alters their nature as revenue, or affects the fact that this revenue is merely disposable capital.

That (even apart from etymology) cattle are typical examples of capital cannot be denied (*Progress and Poverty*, p. 25); and if we seek for that particular quality of cattle which makes them "capital," neither has the author of *Progress and Poverty* supplied, nor is anyone else very likely to supply, a better account of the matter than Adam Smith has done. Cattle are "capital" because they are "stock which yields revenue." That is to say, they afford to their owner a supply of that which he desires to possess. And, in this particular case, the "revenue" is not only desirable, but of supreme importance, inasmuch as it is capable of maintaining human life. The herd yields a revenue of food-stuffs as milk and meat; a revenue of skins; a revenue of manure; a revenue of labor; a revenue of exchangeable commodities in the shape of these things, as well as in that of live cattle. In each and all of these capacities cattle are capital; and, conversely, things which possess any or all of these capacities are capital.

Therefore what we find at page 25 of *Progress and Poverty* must be regarded as a welcome lapse into clearness of apprehension:

> A fertile field, a rich vein of ore, a falling stream which supplies power, may give the possessor advantages equivalent to the possession of capital; but to class such things as capital would be to put an end to the distinction between land and capital.

Just so. But the fatal truth is that these things are capital; and that there really is no fundamental distinction between land and capital. Is it denied that a fertile field, a rich vein of ore, or a falling stream, may form part of a man's stock, and that, if they do, they are capable of yielding revenue? Will not somebody pay a share of the produce in kind, or in money, for the privilege of cultivating the first; royalties for that of working the second; and a like equivalent for that of erecting a mill on the third? In what sense, then, are these things less "capital" than the buildings and tools which on page 27 of *Progress and Poverty* are admitted to be capital? Is it not plain that if these things confer "advantages equivalent to the possession of capital," and if the "advantage" of capital is nothing but the yielding of revenue, then the denial that they are capital is merely a roundabout way of self-contradiction?

All this confused talk about capital, however, is lucidity itself compared with the exposition of the remarkable thesis, "Wages not drawn from capital, but produced by labor," which occupies the third chapter of *Progress and Poverty*.

> If, for instance, I devote my labor to gathering birds'
> eggs or picking wild berries, the eggs or berries I thus
> get are my wages. Surely no one will contend that, in
> such a case, wages are drawn from capital. There is no
> capital in the case (p. 20).

Nevertheless, those who have followed what has been said in the
first part of this essay surely neither will, nor can, have any hesitation about substantially adopting the challenged contention,
though they may possibly have qualms as to the propriety of the use
of the term "wages."[8] They will have no difficulty in apprehending
the fact that birds' eggs and berries are stores of food-stuffs, or vital
capital; that the man who devotes his labor to getting them does
so at the expense of his personal vital capital; and that, if the eggs
and the berries are "wages" for his work, they are so because they
enable him to restore to his organism the vital capital which he has
consumed in doing the work of collection. So that there is really a
great deal of "capital in the case."

Our author proceeds:

> An absolutely naked man, thrown on an island where
> no human being has before trod, may gather birds' eggs
> or pick berries (p. 20).

No doubt. But those who have followed my argument thus far will be
aware that a man's vital capital does not reside in his clothes; and,
therefore, they will probably fail, as completely as I do, to discover the
relevancy of the statement.

Again:

> Or, if I take a piece of leather and work it up into a pair
> of shoes, the shoes are my wages—the reward of my
> exertion. Surely they are not drawn from capital—either
> my capital or anybody else's capital—but are brought
> into existence by the labor of which they became the
> wages; and, in obtaining this pair of shoes as the wages

of my labor, capital is not even momentarily lessened one iota. For if we call in the idea of capital, my capital at the beginning consists of the piece of leather, the thread, &c. (p. 20).

It takes away one's breath to have such a concatenation of fallacies administered in the space of half a paragraph. It does not seem to have occurred to our economical reformer to imagine whence his "capital at the beginning," the "leather, thread, &c." came. I venture to suppose that leather to have been originally cattle-skin; and since calves and oxen are not flayed alive, the existence of the leather implies the lessening of that form of capital by a very considerable iota. It is, therefore, as sure as anything can be that, in the long run, the shoes are drawn from that which is capital *par excellence;* to wit, cattle. It is further beyond doubt that the operation of tanning must involve loss of capital in the shape of bark, to say nothing of other losses; and that the use of the awls and knives of the shoemaker involves loss of capital in the shape of the store of iron; further, the shoemaker has been enabled to do his work not only by the vital capital expended during the time occupied in making the pair of shoes, but by that expended from the time of his birth, up to the time that he earned wages that would keep him alive.

Progress and Poverty continues:

As my labor goes on, value is steadily added until, when my labor results in the finished shoes, I have my capital plus the difference in value between the material and the shoes. In obtaining this additional value—my wages—how is capital, at anytime, drawn upon? (p. 20).

In return we may inquire, how can anyone propound such a question? Capital is drawn upon all the time. Not only when the shoes are commenced, but while they are being made, and until they are either used by the shoemaker himself or are purchased by somebody else; that is, exchanged for a portion of another man's capital. In fact (supposing that the shoemaker does not want shoes himself), it is the existence of vital capital in the possession of another person and the willingness of that person to part with more or less of it in exchange for the shoes—it is these two conditions, alone, which prevent the shoemaker from having consumed his capital unproductively, just as much as if he had spent his time in chopping up the leather into minute fragments.

Thus, the examination of the very case selected by the advocate of the doctrine that labor bestowed upon manufacture, without, any intervention of capital, can produce wages, proves to be a delusion of the first magnitude; even though it be supported by the dictum of Adam Smith which is quoted in its favor (p. 20)—

> The produce of labor constitutes the natural recompense or wages of labor. In that original state of things which precedes both the appropriation of land and the accumulation of stock, the whole produce of labor belongs to the laborer. He has neither landlord nor master to share with him (*Wealth of Nations*, ch. xvii.).

But the whole of this passage exhibits the influence of the French Physiocrats by whom Adam Smith was inspired, at their worst; that is to say, when they most completely forsook the ground of experience for a priori speculation. The confident reference to "that original state of things" is quite in the manner of the *Essai sur l'Inégalité*. Now, the state of men before the "appropriation of land" and the "accumulation of stock" must surely have been that of purely savage hunters. As, by the supposition, nobody would have possessed land, certainly no man could have had a landlord; and, if there was no accumulation of stock in a transferable form, as surely there could be no master, in the sense of hirer. But hirer and hire (that is, wages) are correlative terms, like mother and child. As "child" implies "mother," so does "hire" or "wages" imply a "hirer" or "wage-giver." Therefore, when a man in "the original state of things" gathered fruit or killed game for his own sustenance, the fruit or the game could be called his "wages" only in a figurative sense; as one sees if the term "hire," which has a more limited connotation, is substituted for "wage." If not, it must be assumed that the savage hired himself to get his own dinner; whereby we are led to the tolerably absurd conclusion that, as in the "state of nature" he was his own employer, the "master" and the laborer, in that model age, appropriated the produce in equal shares! And if this should be not enough, it has already been seen that, in the hunting state, man is not even an accessory of production of vital capital; he merely consumes what nature produces.

According to the author of *Progress and Poverty* political economists have been deluded by a "fallacy which has entangled some of the most acute minds in a web of their own spinning."

> It is in the use of the term capital in two senses. In the primary proposition that capital is necessary to the exertion of productive labor, the term "capital" is understood as including all food, clothing, shelter, &c.; whereas in the deductions finally drawn from it, the term is used in its common and legitimate meaning of wealth devoted, not to the immediate gratification of desire, but to the procurement of more wealth—of wealth in the hands of employers as distinguished from laborers (p. 23).

I am by no means concerned to defend the political economists who are thus charged with blundering; but I shall be surprised to learn that any have carried the art of self-entanglement to the degree of perfection exhibited by this passage. Who has ever imagined that wealth which, in the hands of an employer, is capital, ceases to be capital if it is in the hands of a laborer? Suppose a workman to be paid thirty shillings on Saturday evening for six days' labor, that thirty shillings comes out of the employer's capital, and receives the name of "wages" simply because it is exchanged for labor. In the workman's pocket, as he goes home, it is a part of his capital, in exactly the same sense as, half an hour before, it was part of the employer's capital; he is a capitalist just as much as if he were a Rothschild. Suppose him to be a single man, whose cooking and household matters are attended to by the people of the house in which he has a room; then the rent which he pays them out of this capital is, in part, wages for their labor, and he is, so far, an employer. If he saves one shilling out of his thirty, he has, to that extent, added to his capital when the next Saturday comes round. And if he puts his saved shillings week by week into the Savings Bank, the difference between him and the most bloated of bankers is simply one of degree.

At page 24, we are confidently told that "laborers by receiving wages" cannot lessen "even temporarily" the "capital of the employer," while at page 26 it is admitted that in certain cases the capitalist "pays out capital in wages." One would think that the "paying out" of capital is hardly possible without at least a "temporary" diminution of the capital from which payment is made. But *Progress and Poverty* changes all that by a little verbal legerdemain:

> For where wages are paid before the object of the labor is obtained, or is finished—as in agriculture, where ploughing and sowing must precede by several months the harvesting of the crop; as in the erection of buildings, the construction of ships, railroads, canals, &c. it is clear that the owners of the capital paid in wages cannot expect an immediate return, but, as the phrase is, must "outlay it" or "lie out of it" for a time which sometimes amounts to many years. And hence, if first principles are not kept in mind, it is easy to jump to the conclusion that Wages are advanced by capital (p. 26).

Those who have paid attention to the argument of former parts of this paper may not be able to understand how, if sound "first principles are kept in mind," any other conclusion can be reached, whether by jumping, or by any other mode of logical progression. But the first principle which our author "keeps in mind" possesses just that amount of ambiguity which enables him to play hocus-pocus with it. It is this; that "the creation of value does not depend upon the finishing of the product" (p. 26).

There is no doubt that, under certain limitations, this proposition is correct. It is not true that "labor always adds to capital by its exertion before it takes from capital its wages" (p. 26), but it is true that it may, and often does, produce that effect.

To take one of the examples given, the construction of a ship. The shaping of the timbers undoubtedly gives them a value (for a shipbuilder) which they did not possess before. When they are put together to constitute the framework of the ship, there is a still further addition of value (for a shipbuilder); and when the outside planking is added, there is another addition (for a shipbuilder). Suppose everything else about the hull is finished, except the one little item of caulking the seams, there is no doubt that it has still more value for a shipbuilder. But for whom else has it any value, except perhaps for a firewood merchant? What price will anyone who wants a ship—that is to say, something that will carry a cargo from one port to another—give for the unfinished vessel which would take water in at every seam and go down in half an hour, if she were launched? Suppose the shipbuilder's capital to fail before the vessel is caulked, and that he cannot find another shipbuilder who cares to buy and finish it, what sort of proportion does the value created by the labor, for which he has paid out of his capital, stand to that of his advances? Surely no one will give him one-tenth of the capital disbursed in wages, perhaps not so much even as the prime cost of the raw materials. Therefore, though the assertion that "the creation of value does not depend on the finishing of the product" may be strictly true under certain circumstances, it need not be and is not always true. And, if it is meant to imply or suggest that the creation of value in a manufactured article does not depend upon the finishing of that article, a more serious error could hardly be propounded.

Is there not a prodigious difference in the value of an uncaulked and in that of a finished ship; between the value of a house in which only the tiles of the roof are wanting and a finished house; between that of a clock which only lacks the escapement and a finished clock?

As ships, house, and clock, the unfinished articles have no value whatever—that is to say, no person who wanted to purchase one of these things, for immediate use, would give a farthing for either.

The only value they can have, apart from that of the materials they contain, is that which they possess for someone who can finish them, or for someone who can make use of parts of them for the construction of other things. A man might buy an unfinished house for the sake of the bricks; or he might buy an incomplete clock to use the works for some other piece of machinery.

Thus, though every stage of the labor bestowed on raw material, for the purpose of giving rise to a certain product, confers some additional value on that material in the estimation of those who are engaged in manufacturing that product, the ratio of that accumulated value, at any stage of the process, to the value of the finished product is extremely inconstant, and often small; while, to other persons, the value of the unfinished product may be nothing, or even a *minus* quantity. A house-timber merchant, for example, might consider that wood which had been worked into the ribs of a ship was spoiled—that is, had less value than it had as a log.

According to *Progress and Poverty*, there was, really, no advance of capital while the great St. Gothard tunnel was cut. Suppose that, as the Swiss and the Italian halves of the tunnel approached to within half a kilometer, that half-kilometer had turned out to be composed of practically impenetrable rock—would anybody have given a centime for the unfinished tunnel? And if not, how comes it that "the creation of value does not depend on the finishing of the product"?

I think it may be not too much to say that, of all the political delusions which are current in this queer world, the very stupidest are those which assume that labor and capital are necessarily antagonistic; that all capital is produced by labor and therefore, by natural right, is the property of the laborer; that the possessor of capital is a robber who preys on the workman and appropriates to himself that which he has had no share in producing.

On the contrary, capital and labor are, necessarily, close allies; capital is never a product of human labor alone; it exists apart from human labor; it is the necessary antecedent of labor; and it furnishes the materials on which labor is employed. The only indispensable form of capital—vital capital—cannot be produced by human labor.

All that man can do is to favor its formation by the real producers. There is no intrinsic relation between the amount of labor bestowed on an article and its value in exchange. The claim of labor to the total result of operations which are rendered possible only by capital is simply an a priori iniquity.

CHAPTER FIVE

SOCIAL DISEASES AND WORSE REMEDIES

Letters to the *Times* on Mr. Booth's scheme
With a preface and introductory essay

[1891]

PREFACE

THE LETTERS WHICH ARE HERE COLLECTED TOGETHER WERE published in the *Times* in the course of the months of December 1890 and January 1891.

The circumstances which led me to write the first letter are sufficiently set forth in its opening sentences; and the materials on which I based my criticisms of Mr. Booth's scheme, in this and in the second letter, were wholly derived from Mr. Booth's book. I had some reason to know, however, that when anybody allows his sense of duty so far to prevail over his sense of the blessedness of peace as to write a letter to the *Times*, on any subject of public interest, his reflections, before he has done with the business, will be very like those of Johnny Gilpin, "who little thought, when he set out, of running such a rig." Such undoubtedly are mine when I contemplate these twelve documents, and call to mind the distinct addition to the revenue of the Post Office which must have accrued from the mass of letters and pamphlets which have been delivered at my door; to say nothing of the unexpected light upon my character, motives, and doctrines, which has been thrown by some of the *Times'* correspondents, and by no end of comments elsewhere.

If self-knowledge is the highest aim of man, I ought by this time to have little to learn. And yet, if I am awake, some of my teachers— unable, perhaps, to control the divine fire of the poetic imagination which is so closely akin to, if not a part of, the mythopœic faculty— have surely dreamed dreams. So far as my humbler and essentially prosaic faculties of observation and comparison go, plain facts are against them. But, as I may be mistaken, I have thought it well to prefix to the letters (by way of "Prolegomena") an essay which appeared in the "Nineteenth Century" for January 1888 in which the principles that, to my mind, lie at the bottom of the "social question" are stated. So far as Individualism and Regimental Socialism are concerned, this paper simply emphasizes and expands the opinions expressed in an address to the members of the Midland Institute, delivered seventeen years earlier, and still more fully developed in several essays published in the "Nineteenth Century" in 1889, which I hope, before long, to republish.[1]

The fundamental proposition which runs through the writings, which thus extend over a period of twenty years, is that the common a priori doctrines and methods of reasoning about political and social questions are essentially vicious; and that argumentation on this basis leads, with equal logical force, to two contradictory and extremely mischievous systems, the one that of Anarchic Individualism, the other that of despotic or Regimental Socialism. Whether I am right or wrong, I am at least consistent in opposing both to the best of my ability. Mr. Booth's system appears to me, and, as I have shown, is regarded by Socialists themselves, to be mere autocratic Socialism, masked by its theological exterior. That the "fantastic" religious skin will wear away, and the Socialistic reality it covers will show its real nature, is the expressed hope of one candid Socialist, and may be fairly conceived to be the unexpressed belief of the despotic leader of the new Trades Union, who has shown his zeal, if not his discretion, in championing Mr. Booth's projects. [See Letter VIII.]

Yet another word to commentators upon my letters. There are some who rather chuckle, and some who sneer, at what they seem to consider the dexterity of an "old controversial hand," exhibited by the contrast which I have drawn between the methods of conversion depicted in the New Testament and those pursued by fanatics of the Salvationist type, whether they be such as are now exploited by Mr. Booth, or such as those who, from the time of the Anabaptists, to go no further back, have worked upon similar lines.

Whether such observations were intended to be flattering or sarcastic, I must respectfully decline to accept the compliment, or to apply the sarcasm to myself. I object to obliquity of procedure and ambiguity of speech in all shapes. And I confess that I find it difficult to understand the state of mind which leads anyone to suppose, that deep respect for single-minded devotion to high aims is incompatible with the unhesitating conviction that those aims include the propagation of doctrines which are devoid of foundation—perhaps even mischievous.

The most degrading feature of the narrower forms of Christianity (of which that professed by Mr. Booth is a notable example) is their insistence that the noblest virtues, if displayed by those who reject their pitiable formulæ, are, as their pet phrase goes, "splendid sins." But there is, perhaps, one step lower; and that is that men, who profess freedom of thought, should fail to see and appreciate that large soul of goodness which often animates even the fanatical adherents of such tenets. I am sorry for any man who can read the epistles to the Galatians and the Corinthians without yielding a large meed of admiration to the fervent humanity of Paul of Tarsus; who can study the lives of Francis of Assisi, or of Catherine of Siena, without wishing that, for the furtherance of his own ideals, he might be even as they; or who can contemplate unmoved the steadfast veracity and true heroism which loom through the fogs of mystical utterance in George Fox. In all these great men and women there lay the root of the matter; a burning desire to amend the condition of their fellow-men, and to put aside all other things for that end. If, in spite of all the dogmatic helps or hindrances in which they were entangled, these people are not to be held in high honor, who are?

I have never expressed a doubt—for I have none—that, when Mr. Booth left the Methodist connection, and started that organization of the Salvation Army upon which, comparatively recently, such ambitious schemes of social reform have been grafted, he may have deserved some share of such honor. I do not say that, so far as his personal desires and intentions go, he may not still deserve it. But the correlate of despotic authority is unlimited responsibility. If Mr. Booth is to take credit for any good that the Army system has effected, he must be prepared to bear blame for its inherent evils. As it seems to me, that has happened to him which sooner or later happens to all despots: he has become the slave of his own creation— the prosperity and glory of the soul-saving machine have become the end, instead of a means, of soul-saving; and to maintain these at the proper pitch, the "General" is led to do things which the Mr. Booth of twenty years ago would probably have scorned.

And those who desire, as I most emphatically desire, to be just to Mr. Booth, however badly they may think of the working of the organization he has founded, will bear in mind that some astute backers of his probably care little enough for Salvationist religion; and, perhaps, are not very keen about many of Mr. Booth's projects. I have referred to the rubbing of the hands of the Socialists over Mr. Booth's success;[2] but, unless I err greatly, there are politicians of a certain school to whom it affords still greater satisfaction. Consider what electioneering agents the captains of the Salvation Army, scattered through all our towns, and directed from a political "bureau" in London, would make! Think how political adversaries could be harassed by our local attorney—"tribune of the people," I mean; and how a troublesome man, on the other side, could be "hunted down" upon any convenient charge, whether true or false, brought by our Vigilance-familiar![3]

I entirely acquit Mr. Booth of any complicity in far-reaching schemes of this kind; but I did not write idly when, in my first letter, I gave no vague warning of what might grow out of the organized force, drilled in the habit of unhesitating obedience, which he has created.

INTRODUCTORY ESSAY

The struggle for existence in human society

[1888]

THE VAST AND VARIED PROCESSION OF EVENTS, WHICH WE CALL
Nature, affords a sublime spectacle and an inexhaustible wealth of
attractive problems to the speculative observer. If we confine our
attention to that aspect which engages the attention of the intellect,
nature appears a beautiful and harmonious whole, the incarnation
of a faultless logical process, from certain premises in the past to an
inevitable conclusion in the future. But if it be regarded from a less
elevated, though more human, point of view; if our moral sympathies
are allowed to influence our judgment, and we permit ourselves
to criticize our great mother as we criticize one another; then our
verdict, at least so far as sentient nature is concerned, can hardly be
so favorable.

In sober truth, to those who have made a study of the phenomena
of life as they are exhibited by the higher forms of the animal world,
the optimistic dogma, that this is the best of all possible worlds, will
seem little better than a libel upon possibility. It is really only another
instance to be added to the many extant, of the audacity of à priori
speculators who, having created God in their own image, find no
difficulty in assuming that the Almighty must have been actuated
by the same motives as themselves. They are quite sure that, had any
other course been practicable, He would no more have made infinite

suffering a necessary ingredient of His handiwork than a respectable philosopher would have done the like.

But even the modified optimism of the time-honored thesis of physico-theology, that the sentient world is, on the whole, regulated by principles of benevolence, does but ill stand the test of impartial confrontation with the facts of the case. No doubt it is quite true that sentient nature affords hosts of examples of subtle contrivances directed towards the production of pleasure or the avoidance of pain; and it may be proper to say that these are evidences of benevolence. But if so, why is it not equally proper to say of the equally numerous arrangements, the no less necessary result of which is the production of pain, that they are evidences of malevolence?

If a vast amount of that which, in a piece of human workmanship, we should call skill, is visible in those parts of the organization of a deer to which it owes its ability to escape from beasts of prey, there is at least equal skill displayed in that bodily mechanism of the wolf which enables him to track, and sooner or later to bring down, the deer. Viewed under the dry light of science, deer and wolf are alike admirable; and, if both were non-sentient automata, there would be nothing to qualify our admiration of the action of the one on the other. But the fact that the deer suffers, while the wolf inflicts suffering, engages our moral sympathies. We should call men like the deer innocent and good, men such as the wolf malignant and bad; we should call those who defended the deer and aided him to escape brave and compassionate, and those who helped the wolf in his bloody work base and cruel. Surely, if we transfer these judgments to nature outside the world of man at all, we must do so impartially. In that case, the goodness of the right hand which helps the deer, and the wickedness of the left hand which eggs on the wolf, will neutralize one another: and the course of nature will appear to be neither moral nor immoral, but non-moral.

This conclusion is thrust upon us by analogous facts in every part of the sentient world; yet, inasmuch as it not only jars upon prevalent prejudices, but arouses the natural dislike to that which is painful, much ingenuity has been exercised in devising an escape from it.

From the theological side, we are told that this is a state of proba-
tion, and that the seeming injustices and immoralities of nature
will be compensated by and by. But how this compensation is to be
effected, in the case of the great majority of sentient things, is not
clear. I apprehend that no one is seriously prepared to maintain that
the ghosts of all the myriads of generations of herbivorous animals
which lived during the millions of years of the earth's duration,
before the appearance of man, and which have all that time been
tormented and devoured by carnivores, are to be compensated by a
perennial existence in clover; while the ghosts of carnivores are to
go to some kennel where there is neither a pan of water nor a bone
with any meat on it. Besides, from the point of view of morality, the
last stage of things would be worse than the first. For the carnivores,
however brutal and sanguinary, have only done that which, if there
is any evidence of contrivance in the world, they were expressly
constructed to do. Moreover, carnivores and herbivores alike have
been subject to all the miseries incidental to old age, disease, and
over-multiplication, and both might well put in a claim for "compensation" on this score.

On the evolutionist side, on the other hand, we are told to take
comfort from the reflection that the terrible struggle for existence
tends to final good, and that the suffering of the ancestor is paid for
by the increased perfection of the progeny. There would be something in this argument if, in Chinese fashion, the present generation
could pay its debts to its ancestors; otherwise it is not clear what
compensation the *Eohippus* gets for his sorrows in the fact that,
some millions of years afterwards, one of his descendants wins the
Derby. And, again, it is an error to imagine that evolution signifies
a constant tendency to increased perfection. That process undoubtedly involves a constant re-modelling of the organism in adaptation
to new conditions; but it depends on the nature of those conditions
whether the direction of the modifications effected shall be upward
or downward. Retrogressive is as practicable as progressive metamorphosis. If what the physical philosophers tell us, that our globe
has been in a state of fusion, and, like the sun, is gradually cooling
down, is true; then the time must come when evolution will mean

adaptation to an universal winter, and all forms of life will die out, except such low and simple organisms as the Diatom of the arctic and antarctic ice and the Protococcus of the red snow. If our globe is proceeding from a condition in which it was too hot to support any but the lowest living thing to a condition in which it will be too cold to permit of the existence of any others, the course of life upon its surface must describe a trajectory like that of a ball fired from a mortar; and the sinking half of that course is as much a part of the general process of evolution as the rising.

From the point of view of the moralist the animal world is on about the same level as a gladiator's show. The creatures are fairly well treated, and set to fight—whereby the strongest, the swiftest, and the cunningest live to fight another day. The spectator has no need to turn his thumbs down, as no quarter is given. He must admit that the skill and training displayed are wonderful. But he must shut his eyes if he would not see that more or less enduring suffering is the meed of both vanquished and victor. And since the great game is going on in every corner of the world, thousands of times a minute; since, were our ears sharp enough, we need not descend to the gates of hell to hear—

  . . . *sospiri, pianti, ed alti guai.*

   * * * * *

  Voci alte e fioche, e suon di man con elle

—it seems to follow that, if this world is governed by benevolence, it must be a different sort of benevolence from that of John Howard.

But the old Babylonians wisely symbolized Nature by their great goddess Istar, who combined the attributes of Aphrodite with those of Ares. Her terrible aspect is not to be ignored or covered up with shams; but it is not the only one. If the optimism of Leibnitz is a foolish though pleasant dream, the pessimism of Schopenhauer is a nightmare, the more foolish because of its hideousness. Error which is not pleasant is surely the worst form of wrong.

This may not be the best of all possible worlds, but to say that it is the worst is mere petulant nonsense. A worn-out voluptuary may find nothing good under the sun, or a vain and inexperienced youth, who cannot get the moon he cries for, may vent his irritation in pessimistic moanings; but there can be no doubt in the mind of any reasonable person that mankind could, would, and in fact do, get on fairly well with vastly less happiness and far more misery than find their way into the lives of nine people out of ten. If each and all of us had been visited by an attack of neuralgia, or of extreme mental depression, for one hour in every twenty-four—a supposition which many tolerably vigorous people know, to their cost, is not extravagant—the burden of life would have been immensely increased without much practical hindrance to its general course. Men with any manhood in them find life quite worth living under worse conditions than these.

There is another sufficiently obvious fact, which renders the hypothesis that the course of sentient nature is dictated by malevolence quite untenable. A vast multitude of pleasures, and these among the purest and the best, are superfluities, bits of good which are to all appearance unnecessary as inducements to live, and are, so to speak, thrown into the bargain of life. To those who experience them, few delights can be more entrancing than such as are afforded by natural beauty, or by the arts, and especially by music; but they are products of, rather than factors in, evolution, and it is probable that they are known, in any considerable degree, to but a very small proportion of mankind.

The conclusion of the whole matter seems to be that, if Ormuzd has not had his way in this world, neither has Ahriman. Pessimism is as little consonant with the facts of sentient existence as optimism. If we desire to represent the course of nature in terms of human thought, and assume that it was intended to be that which it is, we must say that its governing principle is intellectual and not moral; that it is a materialized logical process, accompanied by pleasures and pains, the incidence of which, in the majority of cases, has not the slightest reference to moral desert. That the rain falls alike upon the just and the unjust, and that those upon whom the Tower of Siloam fell were no worse than their neighbors, seem to be Oriental modes of expressing the same conclusion.

In the strict sense of the word "nature," it denotes the sum of the phenomenal world, of that which has been, and is, and will be; and society, like art, is therefore a part of nature. But it is convenient to distinguish those parts of nature in which man plays the part of immediate cause, as something apart; and, therefore, society, like art, is usefully to be considered as distinct from nature. It is the more desirable, and even necessary, to make this distinction, since society differs from nature in having a definite moral object; whence it comes about that the course shaped by the ethical man—the member of society or citizen—necessarily runs counter to that which the non-ethical man—the primitive savage, or man as a mere member of the animal kingdom—tends to adopt. The latter fights out the struggle for existence to the bitter end, like any other animal; the former devotes his best energies to the object of setting limits to the struggle.[1]

In the cycle of phenomena presented by the life of man, the animal, no more moral end is discernible than in that presented by the lives of the wolf and of the deer. However imperfect the relics of prehistoric men may be, the evidence which they afford clearly tends to the conclusion that, for thousands and thousands of years, before the origin of the oldest known civilizations, men were savages of a very low type. They strove with their enemies and their competitors; they preyed upon things weaker or less cunning than themselves; they were born, multiplied without stint, and died, for thousands of generations, alongside the mammoth, the urus, the lion, and the hyæna, whose lives were spent in the same way; and they were no more to be praised or blamed, on moral grounds, than their less erect and more hairy compatriots.

As among these, so among primitive men, the weakest and stupidest went to the wall, while the toughest and shrewdest, those who were best fitted to cope with their circumstances, but not the best in any other sense, survived. Life was a continual free fight, and beyond the limited and temporary relations of the family, the Hobbesian war of each against all was the normal state of existence. The human species, like others, plashed and floundered amid the general stream of evolution, keeping its head above water as it best might, and thinking neither of whence nor whither.

The history of civilization—that is, of society—on the other hand, is the record of the attempts which the human race has made to escape from this position. The first men who substituted the state of mutual peace for that of mutual war, whatever the motive which impelled them to take that step, created society. But, in establishing peace, they obviously put a limit upon the struggle for existence. Between the members of that society, at any rate, it was not to be pursued à outrance. And of all the successive shapes which society has taken, that most nearly approaches perfection in which the war of individual against individual is most strictly limited. The primitive savage, tutored by Istar, appropriated whatever took his fancy, and killed whomsoever opposed him, if he could. On the contrary, the ideal of the ethical man is to limit his freedom of action to a sphere in which he does not interfere with the freedom of others; he seeks the common weal as much as his own; and, indeed, as an essential part of his own welfare. Peace is both end and means with him; and he founds his life on a more or less complete self-restraint, which is the negation of the unlimited struggle for existence. He tries to escape from his place in the animal kingdom, founded on the free development of the principle of non-moral evolution, and to establish a kingdom of Man, governed upon the principle of moral evolution. For society not only has a moral end, but in its perfection, social life, is embodied morality.

But the effort of ethical man to work towards a moral end by no means abolished, perhaps has hardly modified, the deep-seated organic impulses which impel the natural man to follow his non-moral course. One of the most essential conditions, if not the chief cause, of the struggle for existence, is the tendency to multiply without limit, which man shares with all living things. It is notable that "increase and multiply" is a commandment traditionally much older than the ten; and that it is, perhaps, the only one which has been spontaneously and *ex animo* obeyed by the great majority of the human race. But, in civilized society, the inevitable result of such obedience is the re-establishment, in all its intensity, of that struggle for existence—the war of each against all—the mitigation or abolition of which was the chief end of social organization.

It is conceivable that, at some period in the history of the fabled Atlantis, the production of food should have been exactly sufficient to meet the wants of the population, that the makers of the commodities of the artificer should have amounted to just the number supportable by the surplus food of the agriculturists. And, as there is no harm in adding another monstrous supposition to the foregoing, let it be imagined that every man, woman, and child was perfectly virtuous, and aimed at the good of all as the highest personal good. In that happy land, the natural man would have been finally put down by the ethical man. There would have been no competition, but the industry of each would have been serviceable to all; nobody being vain and nobody avaricious, there would have been no rivalries; the struggle for existence would have been abolished, and the millennium would have finally set in. But it is obvious that this state of things could have been permanent only with a stationary population. Add ten fresh mouths; and as, by the supposition, there was only exactly enough before, somebody must go on short rations. The Atlantis society might have been a heaven upon earth, the whole nation might have consisted of just men, needing no repentance, and yet somebody must starve. Reckless Istar, non-moral Nature, would have riven the ethical fabric. I was once talking with a very eminent physician[2] about the *vis medicatrix naturæ*. "Stuff!" said he; "nine times out of ten nature does not want to cure the man: she wants to put him in his coffin." And Istar-Nature appears to have equally little sympathy with the ends of society. "Stuff! She wants nothing but a fair field and free play for her darling the strongest."

Our Atlantis may be an impossible figment, but the antagonistic tendencies which the fable adumbrates have existed in every society which was ever established, and, to all appearance, must strive for the victory in all that will be. Historians point to the greed and ambition of rulers, to the reckless turbulence of the ruled, to the debasing effects of wealth and luxury, and to the devastating wars which have formed a great part of the occupation of mankind, as the causes of the decay of states and the foundering of old civilizations, and thereby point their story with a moral. No doubt immoral motives of all sorts have figured largely among the minor causes of these events. But beneath all this superficial turmoil lay the deep-seated impulse given by unlimited multiplication. In the swarms of colonies thrown out by Phœnicia and by old Greece; in the *ver sacrum* of the Latin races; in the floods of Gauls and of Teutons which burst over the frontiers of the old civilization of Europe; in the swaying to and fro of the vast Mongolian hordes in late times, the population problem comes to the front in a very visible shape. Nor is it less plainly manifest in the everlasting agrarian questions of ancient Rome than in the Arreoi societies of the Polynesian Islands.

In the ancient world, and in a large part of that in which we live the practice of infanticide was, or is, a regular and legal custom; famine, pestilence, and war were and are normal factors in the struggle for existence, and they have served, in a gross and brutal fashion, to mitigate the intensity of the effects of its chief cause.

But, in the more advanced civilizations, the progress of private and public morality has steadily tended to remove all these checks. We declare infanticide murder, and punish it as such; we decree, not quite so successfully, that no one shall die of hunger; we regard death from preventible causes of other kinds as a sort of constructive murder, and eliminate pestilence to the best of our ability; we declaim against the curse of war, and the wickedness of the military spirit, and we are never weary of dilating on the blessedness of peace and the innocent beneficence of Industry. In their moments of expansion, even statesmen and men of business go thus far. The finer spirits look to an ideal *civitas Dei;* a state when every man, having reached the point of absolute self-negation, and having nothing but moral perfection to strive after, peace will truly reign, not merely among nations, but among men, and the struggle for existence will be at an end.

Whether human nature is competent, under any circumstances, to reach, or even seriously advance towards, this ideal condition, is a question which need not be discussed. It will be admitted that mankind has not yet reached this stage by a very long way, and my business is with the present. And that which I wish to point out is that, so long as the natural man increases and multiplies without restraint, so long will peace and industry not only permit, but they will necessitate, a struggle for existence as sharp as any that ever went on under the *régime* of war. If Istar is to reign on the one hand, she will demand her human sacrifices on the other.

Let us look at home. For seventy years peace and industry have had their way among us with less interruption and under more favorable conditions than in any other country on the face of the earth. The wealth of Crœsus was nothing to that which we have accumulated, and our prosperity has filled the world with envy. But Nemesis did not forget Crœsus: has she forgotten us?

I think not. There are now 36,000,000 of people in our islands, and every year considerably more than 300,000 are added to our numbers.[3] That is to say, about every hundred seconds, or so, a new claimant to a share in the common stock of maintenance presents him or herself among us. At the present time, the produce of the soil does not suffice to feed half its population. The other moiety has to be supplied with food which must be bought from the people of food-producing countries. That is to say, we have to offer them the things which they want in exchange for the things we want. And the things they want and which we can produce better than they can are mainly manufactures—industrial products.

The insolent reproach of the first Napoleon had a very solid foundation. We not only are, but, under penalty of starvation, we are bound to be, a nation of shopkeepers. But other nations also lie under the same necessity of keeping shop, and some of them deal in the same goods as ourselves. Our customers naturally seek to get the most and the best in exchange for their produce. If our goods are inferior to those of our competitors, there is no ground, compatible with the sanity of the buyers, which can be alleged, why they should not prefer the latter. And, if that result should ever take place on a large and general scale, five or six millions of us would soon have nothing to eat. We know what the cotton famine was; and we can therefore form some notion of what a dearth of customers would be.

Judged by an ethical standard, nothing can be less satisfactory than the position in which we find ourselves. In a real, though incomplete, degree we have attained the condition of peace which is the main object of social organization; and, for argument's sake, it may be assumed that we desire nothing but that which is in itself innocent and praiseworthy—namely, the enjoyment of the fruits of honest industry. And lo! In spite of ourselves, we are in reality engaged in an internecine struggle for existence with our presumably no less peaceful and well-meaning neighbors. We seek peace and we do not ensue it. The moral nature in us asks for no more than is compatible with the general good; the non-moral nature proclaims and acts upon that fine old Scottish family motto, "Thou shalt starve ere I want." Let us be under no illusions, then. So long as unlimited multiplication goes on, no social organization which has ever been devised, or is likely to be devised, no fiddle-faddling with the distribution of wealth, will deliver society from the tendency to be destroyed by the reproduction within itself, in its intensest form, of that struggle for existence the limitation of which is the object of society. And however shocking to the moral sense this eternal competition of man against man and of nation against nation may be; however revolting may be the accumulation of misery at the negative pole of society, in contrast with that of monstrous wealth at the positive pole;[4] this state of things must abide, and grow continually worse, so long as Istar holds her way unchecked. It is the true riddle of the Sphinx; and every nation which does not solve it will sooner or later be devoured by the monster itself has generated.

The practical and pressing question for us, just now, seems to me to be how to gain time. "Time brings counsel," as the Teutonic proverb has it; and wiser folk among our posterity may see their way out of that which at present looks like an *impasse.*

It would be folly to entertain any ill-feeling towards those neighbors and rivals who, like ourselves, are slaves of Istar; but, if somebody is to be starved, the modern world has no Oracle of Delphi to which the nations can appeal for an indication of the victim. It is open to us to try our fortune; and, if we avoid impending fate, there will be a certain ground for believing that we are the right people to escape. *Securus judicat orbis.*

To this end, it is well to look into the necessary conditions of our salvation by works. They are two, one plain to all the world and hardly needing insistence; the other seemingly not so plain, since too often it has been theoretically and practically left out of sight. The obvious condition is that our produce shall be better than that of others.

There is only one reason why our goods should be preferred to those of our rivals—our customers must find them better at the price. That means that we must use more knowledge, skill, and industry in producing them, without a proportionate increase in the cost of production; and, as the price of labor constitutes a large element in that cost, the rate of wages must be restricted within certain limits. It is perfectly true that cheap production and cheap labor are by no means synonymous; but it is also true that wages cannot increase beyond a certain proportion without destroying cheapness. Cheapness, then, with, as part and parcel of cheapness, a moderate price of labor, is essential to our success as competitors in the markets of the world.

The second condition is really quite as plainly indispensable as the first, if one thinks seriously about the matter. It is social stability. Society is stable, when the wants of its members obtain as much satisfaction as, life being what it is, commonsense and experience show may be reasonably expected. Mankind, in general, care very little for forms of government or ideal considerations of any sort; and nothing really stirs the great multitude to break with custom and incur the manifest perils of revolt except the belief that misery in this world, or damnation in the next, or both, are threatened by the continuance of the state of things in which they have been brought up. But when they do attain that conviction, society becomes as unstable as a package of dynamite, and a very small matter will produce the explosion which sends it back to the chaos of savagery.

It needs no argument to prove that when the price of labor sinks below a certain point, the worker infallibly falls into that condition which the French emphatically call *la misère*—a word for which I do not think there is any exact English equivalent. It is a condition in which the food, warmth, and clothing which are necessary for the mere maintenance of the functions of the body in their normal state cannot be obtained; in which men, women, and children are forced to crowd into dens wherein decency is abolished and the most ordinary conditions of healthful existence are impossible of attainment; in which the pleasures within reach are reduced to bestiality and drunkenness; in which the pains accumulate at compound interest, in the shape of starvation, disease, stunted development, and moral degradation; in which the prospect of even steady and honest industry is a life of unsuccessful battling with hunger, rounded by a pauper's grave.

That a certain proportion of the members of every great aggregation of mankind should constantly tend to establish and populate such a Slough of Despond as this is inevitable, so long as some people are by nature idle and vicious, while others are disabled by sickness or accident, or thrown upon the world by the death of their breadwinners. So long as that proportion is restricted within tolerable limits, it can be dealt with; and, so far as it arises only from such causes, its existence may and must be patiently borne. But, when the organization of society, instead of mitigating this tendency, tends to continue and intensify it; when a given social order plainly makes for evil and not for good, men naturally enough begin to think it high time to try a fresh experiment. The animal man, finding that the ethical man has landed him in such a slough, resumes his ancient sovereignty, and preaches anarchy; which is, substantially, a proposal to reduce the social cosmos to chaos, and begin the brute struggle for existence once again.

Anyone who is acquainted with the state of the population of all great industrial centers, whether in this or other countries, is aware that, amidst a large and increasing body of that population, *la misère* reigns supreme. I have no pretensions to the character of a philanthropist, and I have a special horror of all sorts of sentimental rhetoric; I am merely trying to deal with facts, to some extent within my own knowledge, and further evidenced by abundant testimony, as a naturalist; and I take it to be a mere plain truth that, throughout industrial Europe, there is not a single large manufacturing city which is free from a vast mass of people whose condition is exactly that described; and from a still greater mass who, living just on the edge of the social swamp, are liable to be precipitated into it by any lack of demand for their produce. And, with every addition to the population, the multitude already sunk in the pit and the number of the host sliding towards it continually increase.

Argumentation can hardly be needful to make it clear that no society in which the elements of decomposition are thus swiftly and surely accumulating can hope to win in the race of industries. Intelligence, knowledge, and skill are undoubtedly conditions of success; but of what avail are they likely to be unless they are backed up by honesty, energy, goodwill, and all the physical and moral faculties that go to the making of manhood, and unless they are stimulated by hope of such reward as men may fairly look to? And what dweller in the slough of want, dwarfed in body and soul, demoralized, hopeless, can reasonably be expected to possess these qualities?

Any full and permanent development of the productive powers of an industrial population, then, must be compatible with and, indeed, based upon a social organization which will secure a fair amount of physical and moral welfare to that population; which will make for good and not for evil. Natural science and religious enthusiasm rarely go hand in hand, but on this matter their concord is complete; and the least sympathetic of naturalists can but admire the insight and the devotion of such social reformers as the late Lord Shaftesbury, whose recently published *Life and Letters* gives a vivid picture of the condition of the working classes fifty years ago, and of the pit which our industry, ignoring these plain truths, was then digging under its own feet.

There is, perhaps, no more hopeful sign of progress among us, in the last half-century, than the steadily increasing devotion which has been and is directed to measures for promoting physical and moral welfare among the poorer classes. Sanitary reformers, like most other reformers whom I have had the advantage of knowing, seem to need a good dose of fanaticism, as a sort of moral coca, to keep them up to the mark, and, doubtless, they have made many mistakes; but that the endeavor to improve the condition under which our industrial population live, to amend the drainage of densely peopled streets, to provide baths, washhouses, and gymnasia, to facilitate habits of thrift, to furnish some provision for instruction and amusement in public libraries and the like, is not only desirable from a philanthropic point of view, but an essential condition of safe industrial development, appears to me to be indisputable. It is by such means alone, so far as I can see, that we can hope to check the constant gravitation of industrial society towards *la misère*, until the general progress of intelligence and morality leads men to grapple with the sources of that tendency. If it is said that the carrying out of such arrangements as those indicated must enhance the cost of production, and thus handicap the producer in the race of competition, I venture, in the first place, to doubt the fact; but if it be so, it results that industrial society has to face a dilemma, either alternative of which threatens destruction.

On the one hand, a population the labor of which is sufficiently remunerated may be physically and morally healthy and socially stable, but may fail in industrial competition by reason of the dearness of its produce. On the other hand, a population the labor of which is insufficiently remunerated must become physically and morally unhealthy, and socially unstable; and though it may succeed for a while in industrial competition, by reason of the cheapness of its produce, it must in the end fall, through hideous misery and degradation, to utter ruin.

Well, if these are the only possible alternatives, let us for ourselves and our children choose the former, and, if need be, starve like men. But I do not believe that a stable society made up of healthy, vigorous, instructed, and self-ruling people would ever incur serious risk of that fate. They are not likely to be troubled with many competitors of the same character, just yet; and they may be safely trusted to find ways of holding their own.

Assuming that the physical and moral well-being and the stable social order, which are the indispensable conditions of permanent industrial development, are secured, there remains for consideration the means of attaining that knowledge and skill without which, even then, the battle of competition cannot be successfully fought. Let us consider how we stand. A vast system of elementary education has now been in operation among us for sixteen years, and has reached all but a very small fraction of the population. I do not think that there is any room for doubt that, on the whole, it has worked well, and that its indirect no less than its direct benefits have been immense. But, as might be expected, it exhibits the defects of all our educational systems—fashioned as they were to meet the wants of a bygone condition of society. There is a widespread and, I think, well-justified complaint that it has too much to do with books and too little to do with things. I am as little disposed as anyone can well be to narrow early education and to make the primary school a mere annexe of the shop. And it is not so much in the interests of industry, as in that of breadth of culture, that I echo the common complaint against the bookish and theoretical character of our primary instruction.

If there were no such things as industrial pursuits, a system of education which does nothing for the faculties of observation, which trains neither the eye nor the hand, and is compatible with utter ignorance of the commonest natural truths, might still be reasonably regarded as strangely imperfect. And when we consider that the instruction and training which are lacking are exactly those which are of most importance for the great mass of our population, the fault becomes almost a crime, the more that there is no practical difficulty in making good these defects. There really is no reason why drawing should not be universally taught, and it is an admirable training for both eye and hand. Artists are born, not made; but everybody may be taught to draw elevations, plans, and sections; and pots and pans are as good, indeed better, models for this purpose than the Apollo Belvedere. The plant is not expensive; and there is this excellent quality about drawing of the kind indicated, that it can be tested almost as easily and severely as arithmetic. Such drawings are either right or wrong, and if they are wrong the pupil can be made to see that they are wrong. From the industrial point of view, drawing has the further merit that there is hardly any trade in which the power of drawing is not of daily and hourly utility. In the next place, no good reason, except the want of capable teachers, can be assigned why elementary notions of science should not be an element in general instruction. In this case, again, no expensive or elaborate apparatus is necessary. The commonest thing—a candle, a boy's squirt, a piece of chalk—in the hands of a teacher who knows his business, may be made the starting-points whence children may be led into the regions of science as far as their capacity permits, with efficient exercise of their observational and reasoning faculties on the road. If object lessons often prove trivial failures, it is not the fault of object lessons, but that of the teacher, who has not found out how much the power of teaching a little depends on knowing a great deal, and that thoroughly; and that he has not made that discovery is not the fault of the teachers, but of the detestable system of training them which is widely prevalent.[5]

As I have said, I do not regard the proposal to add these to the present subjects of universal instruction as made merely in the interests of industry. Elementary science and drawing are just as needful at Eton (where I am happy to say both are now parts of the regular course) as in the lowest primary school. But their importance in the education of the artisan is enhanced, not merely by the fact that the knowledge and skill thus gained—little as they may amount to—will still be of practical utility to him; but, further, because they constitute an introduction to that special training which is commonly called "technical education."

I conceive that our wants in this last direction may be grouped under three heads: (1) Instruction in the principles of those branches of science and of art which are peculiarly applicable to industrial pursuits, which may be called preliminary scientific education. (2) Instruction in the special branches of such applied science and art, as technical education proper. (3) Instruction of teachers in both these branches. (4) Capacity-catching machinery.

A great deal has already been done in each of these directions, but much remains to be done. If elementary education is amended in the way that has been suggested, I think that the school-boards will have quite as much on their hands as they are capable of doing well. The influences under which the members of these bodies are elected do not tend to secure fitness for dealing with scientific or technical education; and it is the less necessary to burden them with an uncongenial task, as there are other organizations, not only much better fitted to do the work, but already actually doing it.

In the matter of preliminary scientific education, the chief of these is the Science and Art Department, which has done more during the last quarter of a century for the teaching of elementary science among the masses of the people than any organization which exists either in this or in any other country. It has become veritably a people's university, so far as physical science is concerned. At the foundation of our old universities they were freely open to the poorest, but the poorest must come to them. In the last quarter of a century, the Science and Art Department, by means of its classes spread all over the country and open to all, has conveyed instruction to the poorest. The University Extension movement shows that our older learned corporations have discovered the propriety of following suit.

Technical education, in the strict sense, has become a necessity for two reasons. The old apprenticeship system has broken down, partly by reason of the changed conditions of industrial life, and partly because trades have ceased to be "crafts," the traditional secrets whereof the master handed down to his apprentices. Invention is constantly changing the face of our industries, so that "use and wont," "rule of thumb," and the like, are gradually losing their importance, while that knowledge of principles which alone can deal successfully with changed conditions is becoming more and more valuable. Socially, the "master" of four or five apprentices is disappearing in favor of the "employer" of forty, or four hundred, or four thousand, "hands," and the odds and ends of technical knowledge, formerly picked up in a shop, are not, and cannot be, supplied in the factory. The instruction formerly given by the master must therefore be more than replaced by the systematic teaching of the technical school.

Institutions of this kind on varying scales of magnitude and completeness, from the splendid edifice set up by the City and Guilds Institute to the smallest local technical school, to say nothing of classes, such as those in technology instituted by the Society of Arts (subsequently taken over by the City Guilds), have been established in various parts of the country, and the movement in favor of their increase and multiplication is rapidly growing in breadth and intensity. But there is much difference of opinion as to the best way in which the technical instruction, so generally desired, should be given. Two courses appear to be practicable: the one is the establishment of special technical schools with a systematic and lengthened course of instruction demanding the employment of the whole time of the pupils. The other is the setting afoot of technical classes, especially evening classes, comprising a short series of lessons on some special topic, which may be attended by persons already earning wages in some branch of trade or commerce.

There is no doubt that technical schools, on the plan indicated under the first head, are extremely costly; and, so far as the teaching of artizans is concerned, it is very commonly objected to them that, as the learners do not work under trade conditions, they are apt to fall into amateurish habits, which prove of more hindrance than service in the actual business of life. When such schools are attached to factories under the direction of an employer who desires to train up a supply of intelligent workmen, of course this objection does not apply; nor can the usefulness of such schools for the training of future employers and for the higher grade of the employed be doubtful; but they are clearly out of the reach of the great mass of the people, who have to earn their bread as soon as possible. We must therefore look to the classes, and especially to evening classes, as the great instrument for the technical education of the artizan. The utility of such classes has now been placed beyond all doubt; the only question which remains is to find the ways and means of extending them.

We are here, as in all other questions of social organization, met by two diametrically opposed views. On the one hand, the methods pursued in foreign countries are held up as our example. The state is exhorted to take the matter in hand, and establish a great system of technical education. On the other hand, many economists of the individualist school exhaust the resources of language in condemning and repudiating, not merely the interference of the general government in such matters, but the application of a farthing of the funds raised by local taxation to these purposes. I entertain a strong conviction that, in this country, at any rate, the State had much better leave purely technical and trade instruction alone. But, although my personal leanings are decidedly towards the individualists, I have arrived at that conclusion on merely practical grounds. In fact, my individualism is rather of a sentimental sort, and I sometimes think I should be stronger in the faith if it were less vehemently advocated.[6] I am unable to see that civil society is anything but a corporation established for a moral object—namely, the good of its members—and therefore that it may take such measures as seem fitting for the attainment of that which the general voice decides to be the general good. That the suffrage of the majority is by no means a scientific test of social good and evil is unfortunately too true; but, in practice, it is the only test we can apply, and the refusal to abide by it means anarchy. The purest despotism that ever existed is as much based upon that will of the majority (which is usually submission to the will of a small minority) as the freest republic. Law is the expression of the opinion of the majority; and it is law, and not mere opinion, because the many are strong enough to enforce it.

I am as strongly convinced as the most pronounced individualist can be, that it is desirable that every man should be free to act in every way which does not limit the corresponding freedom of his fellow-man. But I fail to connect that great induction of political science with the practical corollary which is frequently drawn from it: that the State—that is, the people in their corporate capacity—has no business to meddle with anything but the administration of justice and external defense. It appears to me that the amount of freedom which incorporate society may fitly leave to its members is not a fixed quantity, to be determined a priori by deduction from the fiction called "natural rights"; but that it must be determined by, and vary with, circumstances. I conceive it to be demonstrable that the higher and the more complex the organization of the social body, the more closely is the life of each member bound up with that of the whole; and the larger becomes the category of acts which cease to be merely self-regarding, and which interfere with the freedom of others more or less seriously.

If a squatter, living ten miles away from any neighbor, chooses to burn his house down to got rid of vermin, there may be no necessity (in the absence of insurance offices) that the law should interfere with his freedom of action; his act can hurt nobody but himself. But, if the dweller in a street chooses to do the same thing, the State very properly makes such a proceeding a crime, and punishes it as such. He does meddle with his neighbor's freedom, and that seriously. So it might, perhaps, be a tenable doctrine, that it would be needless, and even tyrannous, to make education compulsory in a sparse agricultural population, living in abundance on the produce of its own soil; but, in a densely populated manufacturing country, struggling for existence with competitors, every ignorant person tends to become a burden upon, and, so far, an infringer of the liberty of, his fellows, and an obstacle to their success. Under such circumstances an education rate is, in fact, a war tax, levied for purposes of defense.

That State action always has been more or less misdirected, and always will be so, is, I believe, perfectly true. But I am not aware that it is more true of the action of men in their corporate capacity than it is of the doings of individuals. The wisest and most dispassionate man in existence, merely wishing to go from one stile in a field to the opposite, will not walk quite straight—he is always going a little wrong, and always correcting himself; and I can only congratulate the individualist who is able to say that his general course of life has been of a less undulatory character. To abolish State action, because its direction is never more than approximately correct, appears to me to be much the same thing as abolishing the man at the wheel altogether, because, do what he will, the ship yaws more or less. "Why should I be robbed of my property to pay for teaching another man's children?" is an individualist question, which is not unfrequently put as if it settled the whole business. Perhaps it does, but I find difficulties in seeing why it should. The parish in which I live makes me pay my share for the paving and lighting of a great many streets that I never pass through; and I might plead that I am robbed to smooth the way and lighten the darkness of other people. But I am afraid the parochial authorities would not let me off on this plea; and I must confess I do not see why they should.

I cannot speak of my own knowledge, but I have every reason to believe that I came into this world a small reddish person, certainly without a gold spoon in my mouth, and in fact with no discernible abstract or concrete "rights" or property of any description. If a foot was not set upon me, at once, as a squalling nuisance, it was either the natural affection of those about me, which I certainly had done nothing to deserve, or the fear of the law which, ages before my birth, was painfully built up by the society into which I intruded, that prevented that catastrophe. If I was nourished, cared for, taught, saved from the vagabondage of a wastrel, I certainly am not aware that I did anything to deserve those advantages. And, if I possess anything now, it strikes me that, though I may have fairly earned my day's wages for my day's work, and may justly call them my property—yet, without that organization of society, created out of the toil and blood of long generations before my time, I should probably have had nothing but a flint axe and an indifferent hut to call my own; and even those would be mine only so long as no stronger savage came my way.

· So that if society, having, quite gratuitously, done all these things for me, asks me in turn to do something towards its preservation— even if that something is to contribute to the teaching of other men's children—I really, in spite of all my individualist leanings, feel rather ashamed to say no. And if I were not ashamed, I cannot say that I think that society would be dealing unjustly with me in converting the moral obligation into a legal one. There is a manifest unfairness in letting all the burden be borne by the willing horse.

It does not appear to me, then, that there is any valid objection to taxation for purposes of education; but, in the case of technical schools and classes, I think it is practically expedient that such a taxation should be local. Our industrial population accumulates in particular towns and districts; these districts are those which immediately profit by technical education; and it is only in them that we can find the men practically engaged in industries, among whom some may reasonably be expected to be competent judges of that which is wanted, and of the best means of meeting the want.

In my belief, all methods of technical training are at present tentative, and, to be successful, each must be adapted to the special peculiarities of its locality. This is a case in which we want twenty years, not of "strong government," but of cheerful and hopeful blundering; and we may be thankful if we get things straight in that time.

The principle of the Bill introduced, but dropped, by the Government last session, appears to me to be wise, and some of the objections to it I think are due to a misunderstanding. The Bill proposed in substance to allow localities to tax themselves for purposes of technical education—on the condition that any scheme for such purpose should be submitted to the Science and Art Department, and declared by that department to be in accordance with the intention of the Legislature.

A cry was raised that the Bill proposed to throw technical education into the hands of the Science and Art Department. But, in reality, no power of initiation, nor even of meddling with details, was given to that Department—the sole function of which was to decide whether any plan proposed did or did not come within the limits of "technical education." The necessity for such control, somewhere, is obvious. No legislature, certainly not ours, is likely to grant the power of self-taxation without setting limits to that power in some way; and it would neither have been practicable to devise a legal definition of technical education, nor commendable to leave the question to the Auditor-General, to be fought out in the law-courts. The only alternative was to leave the decision to an appropriate State authority. If it is asked, what is the need of such control if the people of the localities are the best judges, the obvious reply is that there are localities and localities, and that while Manchester, or Liverpool, or Birmingham, or Glasgow might, perhaps, be safely left to do as they thought fit, smaller towns, in which there is less certainty of full discussion by competent people of different ways of thinking, might easily fall a prey to crotcheteers.

Supposing our intermediate science teaching and our technical schools and classes are established, there is yet a third need to be supplied, and that is the want of good teachers. And it is necessary not only to get them, but to keep them when you have got them.

It is impossible to insist too strongly upon the fact that efficient teachers of science and of technology are not to be made by the processes in vogue at ordinary training colleges. The memory loaded with mere bookwork is not the thing wanted—is, in fact, rather worse than useless—in the teacher of scientific subjects. It is absolutely essential that his mind should be full of knowledge and not of mere learning, and that what he knows should have been learned in the laboratory rather than in the library. There are happily already, both in London and in the provinces, various places in which such training is to be had, and the main thing at present is to make it in the first place accessible, and in the next indispensable, to those who undertake the business of teaching. But when the well-trained men are supplied, it must he recollected that the profession of teacher is not a very lucrative or otherwise tempting one, and that it may be advisable to offer special inducements to good men to remain in it. These, however, are questions of detail into which it is unnecessary to enter further.

Last, but not least, comes the question of providing the machinery for enabling those who are by nature specially qualified to undertake the higher branches of industrial work, to reach the position in which they may render that service to the community. If all our educational expenditure did nothing but pick one man of scientific or inventive genius, each year, from amidst the hewers of wood and drawers of water, and give him the chance of making the best of his inborn faculties, it would be a very good investment. If there is one such child among the hundreds of thousands of our annual increase, it would be worth any money to drag him either from the slough of misery, or from the hotbed of wealth, and teach him to devote himself to the service of his people. Here, again, we have made a beginning with our scholarships and the like, and need only follow in the tracks already worn.

The program of industrial development briefly set forth in the preceding pages is not what Kant calls a "*Hirngespinnst*," a cobweb spun in the brain of a Utopian philosopher. More or less of it has taken bodily shape in many parts of the country, and there are towns of no great size or wealth in the manufacturing districts (Keighley, for example) in which almost the whole of it has, for some time, been carried out, so far as the means at the disposal of the energetic and public-spirited men who have taken the matter in hand permitted. The thing can be done; I have endeavored to show good grounds for the belief that it must be done, and that speedily, if we wish to hold our own in the war of industry. I doubt not that it will be done, whenever its absolute necessity becomes as apparent to all those who are absorbed in the actual business of industrial life as it is to some of the lookers on.

[Perhaps it is necessary for me to add that technical education is not here proposed as a panacea for social diseases, but simply as a medicament which will help the patient to pass through an imminent crisis.]

An ophthalmic surgeon may recommend an operation for cataract in a man who is going blind, without being supposed to undertake that it will cure him of gout. And I may pursue the metaphor so far as to remark, that the surgeon is justified in pointing out that a diet of pork chops and burgundy will probably kill his patient, though he may be quite unable to suggest a mode of living which will free him from his constitutional disorder.

Mr. Booth asks me, Why do you not propose some plan of your own? Really, that is no answer to my argument that his treatment will make the patient very much worse. [Note added in *Social Diseases and Worse Remedies, January,* 1891.]

LETTERS TO THE *TIMES*
ON THE
DARKEST ENGLAND SCHEME

I

The Times, *December 1st, 1890*

Sir—A short time ago a generous and philanthropic friend wrote to me, placing at my disposal a large sum of money for the furtherance of the vast scheme which the "General" of the Salvation Army has propounded, if I thought it worthy of support. The responsibility of advising my benevolent correspondent has weighed heavily upon me, but I felt that it would be cowardly, as well as ungracious, to refuse to accept it. I have therefore studied Mr. Booth's book with some care, for the purpose of separating the essential from the accessory features of his project, and I have based my judgment—I am sorry to say an unfavorable one—upon the data thus obtained. Before communicating my conclusions to my friend, however, I am desirous to know what there may be to be said in arrest of that judgment; and the matter is of such vast public importance that I trust you will aid me by publishing this letter, notwithstanding its length.

There are one or two points upon which I imagine all thinking men have arrived at the same convictions as those from which Mr. Booth starts. It is certain that there is an immense amount of remediable misery among us; that, in addition to the poverty, disease, and degradation which are the consequences of causes beyond human control, there is a vast, probably a very much larger, quantity of misery which is the result of individual ignorance, or misconduct, and of faulty social arrangements. Further, I think it is not to be doubted that, unless this remediable misery is effectually dealt with, the hordes of vice and pauperism will destroy modern civilization as effectually as uncivilized tribes of another kind destroyed the great social organization which preceded ours. Moreover, I think all will agree that no reforms and improvements will go to the root of the evil unless they attack it in its ultimate source—namely, the motives of the individual man. Honest, industrious, and self-restraining men will make a very bad social organization prosper; while vicious, idle, and reckless citizens will bring to ruin the best that ever was, or ever will be, invented.

The leading propositions which are peculiar to Mr. Booth I take to be these:

1. That the only adequate means to such reformation of the individual man is the adoption of that form of somewhat corybantic Christianity of which the soldiers of the Salvation Army are the militant missionaries. This implies the belief that the excitement of the religious emotions (largely by processes described by their employers as "rousing" and "convivial") is a desirable and trustworthy method of permanently amending the conduct of mankind.

I demur to these propositions. I am of opinion that the testimony of history, no less than the cool observation of that which lies within the personal experience of many of us, is wholly adverse to it.

2. That the appropriate instrument for the propagation and maintenance of this peculiar sacramental enthusiasm is the Salvation Army—a body of devotees, drilled and disciplined as a military organization, and provided with a numerous hierarchy of officers, everyone of whom is pledged to blind and unhesitating obedience to the "General," who frankly tells us that the first condition of the service is "implicit, unquestioning obedience." "A telegram from me will send any of them to the uttermost parts of the earth"; everyone "has taken service on the express condition that he or she will obey, without questioning, or gainsaying, the orders from headquarters" (Darkest England, *p. 243*).

This proposition seems to me to be indisputable. History confirms it. Francis of Assisi and Ignatius Loyola made their great experiments on the same principle. Nothing is more certain than that a body of religious enthusiasts (perhaps we may even say fanatics) pledged to blind obedience to their chief, is one of the most efficient instruments for effecting any purpose that the wit of man has yet succeeded in devising. And I can but admire the insight into human nature which has led Mr. Booth to leave his unquestioning and unhesitating instruments unbound by vows. A volunteer slave is worth ten sworn bondsmen.

3. That the success of the Salvation Army, with its present force of 9416 officers "wholly engaged in the work," its capital of three quarters of a million, its income of the same amount, its 1375 corps at home, and 1499 in the colonies and foreign countries (Appendix, pp. 2 and 3), is a proof that Divine assistance has been vouchsafed to its efforts.

Here I am not able, to agree with the sanguine Commander-in-chief of the new model, whose labors in creating it have probably interfered with his acquisition of information respecting the fate of previous enterprises of like kind.

It does not appear to me that his success is in any degree more remarkable than that of Francis of Assisi or that of Ignatius Loyola, than that of George Fox, or even than that of the Mormons, in our own time. When I observe the discrepancies of the doctrinal foundations from which each of these great movements set out, I find it difficult to suppose that supernatural aid has been given to all of them; still more, that Mr. Booth's smaller measure of success is evidence that it has been granted to him.

But what became of the Franciscan experiment[1]? If there was one rule rather than another on which the founder laid stress, it was that his army of friars should be absolute mendicants, keeping themselves sternly apart from all worldly entanglements. Yet, even before the death of Francis, in 1226, a strong party, headed by Elias of Cortona, the deputy of his own appointment, began to hanker after these very things; and, within thirty years of that time, the Franciscans had become one of the most powerful, wealthy, and worldly corporations in Christendom, with their fingers in every sink of political and social corruption, if so be profit for the order could be fished out of it; their principal interest being to fight their rivals, the Dominicans, and to persecute such of their own brethren as were honest enough to try to carry out their founder's plainest injunctions. We also know what has become of Loyola's experiment. For two centuries the Jesuits have been the hope of the enemies of the Papacy; whenever it becomes too prosperous, they are sure to bring about a catastrophe by their corrupt use of the political and social influence which their organization and their wealth secure.

With these examples of that which may happen to institutions founded by noble men, with high aims, in the hands of successors of a different stamp, armed with despotic authority, before me, common prudence surely requires that, before advising the handing over of a large sum of money to the general of a new order of mendicants, I should ask what guarantee there is that, thirty years hence, the "General" who then autocratically controls the action, say, of one hundred thousand officers pledged to blind obedience, distributed through the whole length and breadth of the poorer classes, and each with his finger on the trigger of a mine charged with discontent and religious fanaticism; with the absolute control, say, of eight or ten millions sterling of capital and as many of income; with barracks in every town, with estates scattered over the country, and with settlements in the colonies—will exercise his enormous powers, not merely honestly, but wisely? What shadow

*of security is there that the person who wields this uncontrolled
authority over many thousands of men shall use it solely for
those philanthropic and religious objects which, I do not doubt,
are alone in the mind of Mr. Booth? Who is to say that the
Salvation Army, in the year 1920, shall not be a replica of what
the Franciscan order had become in the year 1260?*

*The personal character and the intentions of the founders
of such organizations as we are considering count for very
little in the formation of a forecast of their future; and if they
did, it is no disrespect to Mr. Booth to say that he is not the
peer of Francis of Assisi. But if Francis' judgment of men
was so imperfect as to permit him to appoint an ambitious
intriguer of the stamp of Brother Elias his deputy, we have
no right to be sanguine about the perspicacity of Mr. Booth
in a like matter.*

*Adding to all these considerations the fact that Mr. Llewelyn
Davies, the warmth of whose philanthropy is beyond question,
and in whose competency and fairness I, for one, place implicit
reliance, flatly denies the boasted success of the Salvation Army
in its professed mission, I have arrived at the conclusion that,
as at present advised, I cannot be the instrument of carrying
out my friend's proposal.*

*Mr. Booth has pithily characterized certain benevolent
schemes as doing sixpennyworth of good and a shilling's worth
of harm. I grieve to say that, in my opinion, the definition
exactly fits his own project. Few social evils are of greater magnitude than uninstructed and unchastened religious fanaticism;
no personal habit more surely degrades the conscience and the
intellect than blind and unhesitating obedience to unlimited
authority. Undoubtedly, harlotry and intemperance are sore
evils, and starvation is hard to bear, or even to know of; but
the prostitution of the mind, the soddening of the conscience, the
dwarfing of manhood are worse calamities. It is a greater evil
to have the intellect of a nation put down by organized fanaticism; to see its political and industrial affairs at the mercy of a
despot whose chief thought is to make that fanaticism prevail;*

to watch the degradation of men, who should feel themselves individually responsible for their own and their country's fates, to mere brute instruments, ready to the hand of a master for any use to which he may put them.

But that is the end to which, in my opinion, all such organizations as that to which kindly people, who do not look to the consequences of their acts, are now giving their thousands, inevitably tend. Unless clear proof that I am wrong is furnished, another thousand shall not be added by my instrumentality.

I am, Sir, your obedient servant,

T. H. Huxley

NOTE

An authoritative contemporary historian, Matthew Paris, writes thus of the Minorite, or Franciscan, Friars in England in 1235, just nine years after the death of Francis of Assisi:

At this time some of the Minorite brethren, as well as some of the Order of Preachers, unmindful of their profession and the restrictions of their order, impudently entered the territories of some noble monasteries, under pretence of fulfilling their duties of preaching, as if intending to depart after preaching the next day. Under pretence of sickness, or on some other pretext, however, they remained, and, constructing an altar of wood, they placed on it a consecrated stone altar, which they had brought with them, and clandestinely and in a low voice performed mass, and even received the confessions of many of the parishioners, to the prejudice of the priests. . . . And if by chance they were not satisfied with this, they broke forth in insults and threats, reviling every other order except their own, and asserting that all the rest were doomed to damnation, and that they would not spare the soles of their feet till they had exhausted the wealth of their opposers, however great it might be. The religious men, therefore, gave way to them

*in many points, yielding to avoid scandal, and offending
those in power. For they were the councillors and messengers
of the nobles, and even secretaries of the Pope, and therefore obtained much secular favor. Some, however, finding
themselves opposed at the Court of Rome, were restrained by
obvious reasons, and went away in confusion; for the Supreme
Pontiff, with a scowling look, said to them, "What means
this, my brethren? To what lengths are you going? Have you
not professed voluntary poverty, and that you would traverse
towns and castles and distant places, as the case required,
barefooted and unostentatiously in order to preach the word of
God in all humility? And do you now presume to usurp these
estates to yourselves against the will of the lords of these fees?
Your religion appears to be in a great measure dying away,
and your doctrines to be confuted."*

Under date of 1243, Matthew writes:

*For three or four hundred years or more the monastic order did
not hasten to destruction so quickly as their order [Minorites
and Preachers] of whom now the brothers, twenty-tour years
having scarcely elapsed, had first built in England dwellings
which rivalled regal palaces in height. These are they who daily
expose to view their inestimable treasures, in enlarging their
sumptuous edifices, and erecting lofty walls, thereby impudently transgressing the limits of their original poverty and
violating the basis of their religion, according to the prophecy of
German Hildegarde. When noblemen and rich men are at the
point of death, whom they know to be possessed of great riches,
they, in their love of gain, diligently urge them to the injury and
loss of the ordinary pastors, and extort confessions and hidden
wills, landing themselves and their own order only, and placing themselves before all others. So no faithful man now believes
he can be saved, except he is directed by the counsels of the
Preachers and Minorites. Matthew Paris'* English History.
Translated by the Rev. J. A. Giles, 1889, Vol. I.

II

The Times, *December 9ᵗʰ, 1890*

Sir—The purpose of my previous letter about Mr. Booth's scheme was to arouse the contributors to the military chest of the Salvation Army to a clear sense of what they are doing. I thought it desirable that they should be distinctly aware that they are setting up and endowing a sect, in many ways analogous to the "Ranters" and "Revivalists" of undesirable notoriety in former times; but with this immensely important difference, that it possesses a strong, far-reaching, centralized organization, the disposal of the physical, moral, and financial strength of which rests with an irresponsible chief, who, according to his own account, is assured of the blind obedience of nearly ten thousand subordinates. I wish them to ask themselves. Ought prudent men and good citizens to aid in the establishment of an organization which, under sundry, by no means improbable, contingencies, may easily become a worse and more dangerous nuisance than the mendicant friars of the middle ages? If this is an academic question, I really do not know what questions deserve to be called practical. As you divined, I purposely omitted any consideration of the details of the Salvationist scheme, and of the principles which animate those who work it, because I desired that the public appreciation of the evils, necessarily inherent in all such plans of despotic social and religious regimentation should not be obscured by the raising of points of less comparative, however great absolute, importance.

But it is now time to undertake a more particular criticism of Darkest England. *At the outset of my examination of that work, I was startled to find that Mr. Booth had put forward his scheme with an almost incredibly imperfect knowledge of what had been done and is doing in the same direction. A simple reader might well imagine that the author of* Darkest England *posed as the Columbus, or at any rate the Cortez, of that region. "Go to Mudie's," he tells us, and you will be surprised to see how few books there are upon the social problem. That may or may not be correct; but if Mr. Booth had gone to a certain reading-room not far from Mudie's, I undertake to say that the well-informed and obliging staff of the national library in Bloomsbury would have provided him with more books on this topic, in almost all European languages, than he would read in three months. Has socialism no literature? And what is socialism but an incarnation of the social question? Moreover, I am persuaded that even* Mudie's *resources could have furnished Mr.* Booth with the Life of Lord Shaftesbury *and Carlyle's works. Mr. Booth seems to have undertaken to instruct the world without having heard of* Past and Present *or of* Latter-Day Pamphlets; *though, somewhat late in the day, a judicious friend calls his attention to them. To those of my contemporaries on whom, as on myself, Carlyle's writings on this topic made an ineffaceable impression forty years ago, who know that, for all that time, hundreds of able and devoted men, both clerical and lay, have worked heart and soul for the permanent amendment of the condition of the poor, Mr. Booth's* Go to Mudie's *affords an apt measure of the depth of his preliminary studies. However, I am bound to admit that these earlier laborers in the field labored in such a different fashion, that the originality of the plan started by Mr. Booth remains largely unaffected. For them no drums have beat, no trombones brayed; no sanctified buffoonery, after the model of the oration of the Friar in Wallenstein's camp dear to the readers of Schiller, has tickled the ears of the groundlings on their behalf. Sadly behind the great age of rowdy self-advertisement in which their lot has fallen, they seem not to have advanced one whit beyond John the Baptist and the Apostles, 1800 years ago, in their notions of the way in which the* metanoia, *the change of mind of the ill-doer, is to be brought about. Yet the new model was there, ready for the imitation of those ancient savers of souls. The ranting and roaring mystagogues of some of the most venerable of Greek and Syrian cults also had their processions and banners, their fifes and cymbals and holy chants, their hierarchy of officers to whom the art of making collections was not wholly unknown; and who, as freely as their modern imitators, promised an Elysian future to contributory converts. The success of these antique Salvation armies was enormous. Simon Magus was quite as notorious a personage, and probably had as strong a following as Mr. Booth. Yet the Apostles, with their old-fashioned ways, would not accept such a success as a satisfactory sign of the Divine sanction, nor depart from their own methods of leading the way to the higher life.*

I deem it unessential to verify Mr. Booth's statistics. The exact strength of the population of the realm of misery, be it one, two, or three millions, has nothing to do with the efficacy of any means proposed for the highly desirable end of reducing it to a minimum. *The sole question for consideration at present is whether the scheme, keeping specially in view the spirit in which it is to be worked, is likely to do more good than harm.*

Mr. Booth tells us, with commendable frankness, that "it is primarily and mainly for the sake of saving the soul that I seek the salvation of the body" (p. 26), which language, being interpreted, means that the propagation of the special Salvationist creed comes first, and the promotion of the physical, intellectual, and purely moral welfare of mankind second in his estimation. Men are to be made sober and industrious, mainly, that, as washed, shorn, and docile sheep, they may be driven into the narrow theological fold which Mr. Booth patronizes. If they refuse to enter, for all their moral cleanliness, they will have to take their place among the goats as sinners, only less dirty than the rest.

I have been in the habit of thinking (and I believe the opinion is largely shared by reasonable men) that self-respect and thrift are the rungs of the ladder by which men may most surely climb out of the slough of despond of want; and I have regarded them as perhaps the most eminent of the practical virtues. That is not Mr. Booth's opinion. For him they are mere varnished sins—nothing better than "Pride re-baptized" (p. 27). Shutting his eyes to the necessary consequences of the struggle for life, the existence of which he accepts as fully as any Darwinian,[2] Mr. Booth tells men, whose evil case is one of those consequences, that envy is a corner-stone of our competitive system. With thrift and self-respect denounced as sin, with the suffering of starving men referred to the sins of the capitalist, the gospel according to Mr. Booth may save souls, but it will hardly save society.

In estimating the social and political influence which the Salvation Army is likely to exert, it is important to reflect that the officers (pledged to blind obedience to their "General") are not to confine themselves to the functions of mere deacons and catechists (though, under a "General" like Cyril, Alexandria knew to her cost what even they could effect); they are to be "tribunes of the people," who are to act as their gratuitous legal advisers; and, when law is not sufficiently effective, the whole force of the army is to obtain what the said tribunes may conceive to be justice, by the practice of ruthless intimidation. Society, says Mr. Booth, needs "mothering"; and he sets forth, with much complacency, a variety of "cases," by which we may estimate the sort of "mothering" to be expected at his parental hands. Those who study the materials thus set before them will, I think, be driven to the conclusion that the "mother" has already proved herself a most unscrupulous meddler, even if she has not fallen within reach of the arm of the law.

Consider this "case." A, asserting herself to have been seduced twice, "applied to our people. We hunted up the man, followed him to the country, threatened him with public exposure, and forced from him the payment to his victim of £60 down, an allowance of £1 a week, and an insurance policy on his life for £450 in her favor" (p. 138).

Jedburgh justice this. "We" constitute ourselves prosecutor, judge, jury, sheriff's officer, all in one; "we" practice intimidation as deftly as if we were a branch of another League; and, under threat of exposure, "we" extort a tolerably heavy hush-money in payment of our silence.

Well, really, my poor moral sense is unable to distinguish these remarkable proceedings of the new popular tribunate from what, in French, is called chantage *and, in plain English, blackmailing. And when we consider that anybody, for any reason of jealousy, or personal spite, or party hatred, might*

*be thus "hunted," "followed," "threatened," and financially
squeezed or ruined, without a particle of legal investigation,
at the will of a man whom the familiar charged with the
inquisitorial business dare not hesitate to obey, surely it is not
unreasonable to ask how far does the Salvation Army, in its
"tribune of the people" aspect, differ from a Sicilian Mafia? I
am no apologist of men guilty of the acts charged against the
person who yet, I think, might be as fairly called a "victim," in
this case, as his partner in wrong-doing. It is possible that,
in so peculiar a case, Solomon himself might have been puzzled
to apportion the relative moral delinquency of the parties.
However that may be, the man was morally and legally bound
to support his child, and anyone would have been justified in
helping the woman to her legal rights, and the man to the legal
consequences (in which exposure is included) of his fault.*

*The action of the "General" of the Salvation Army in extort-
ing the heavy fine he chose to impose as the price of his silence,
however excellent his motives, appears to me to be as immoral
as, I hope, it is illegal.*

*So much for the Salvation Army as a teacher of question-
able ethics and of eccentric economics, as the legal adviser who
recommends and practices the extraction of money by intimidation, as the fairy godmother who proposes to "mother" society,
in a fashion which is not to my taste, however much it may
commend itself to some of Mr. Booth's supporters.*

I am, Sir, your obedient servant,
T. H. Huxley

III

The Times, *December 11ᵗʰ, 1890*
*Sir—When I first addressed you on the subject of the projected
operations of the Salvation Army, all that I knew about that body
was derived from the study of Mr. Booth's book, from common
repute, and from occasional attention to the sayings and doings*

of his noisy squadrons, with which my walks about London, in past years, have made me familiar. I was quite unaware of the existence of evidence respecting the present administration of the Salvation forces, which would have enabled me to act upon the sagacious maxim of the American humorist, "Don't prophesy unless you know." The letter you were good enough to publish has brought upon me a swarm of letters and pamphlets. Some favor me with abuse; some thoughtful correspondents warmly agree with me, and then proceed to point out how much worthier certain schemes of their own are of my friend's support; some send valuable encouragement, for which I offer my hearty thanks, and ask them to excuse anymore special acknowledgment. But that which I find most to the purpose, just now, is the revelation made by some of the documents which have reached me, of a fact of which I was wholly ignorant—namely, that persons who have faithfully and zealously served in the Salvation Army, who express unchanged attachment to its original principles and practice, and who have been in close official relations with the "General," have publicly declared that the process of degradation of the organization into a mere engine of fanatical intolerance and personal ambition, which I declared was inevitable, has already set in and is making rapid progress.

It is out of the question, Sir, that I should occupy the columns of the Times *with a detailed exposition and criticism of these* pièces justificatives *of my forecast. I say criticism, because the assertions of persons who have quitted any society must, in fairness, be taken with the caution that is required in the case of all* ex parte *statements of hostile witnesses. But it is, at any rate, a notable fact that there are parts of my first letter, indicating the inherent and necessary evil consequences of any such organization, which might serve for abstracts of portions of this evidence, long since printed and published under the public responsibility of the witnesses.*

Let us ask the attention of your readers, in the first place, to An Ex-Captain's Experience of the Salvation Army, *by J. J. R. Redstone, the genuineness of which is guaranteed* by the preface (dated April 5th, 1888) which the Rev. Dr. Cunningham Geikie has supplied. Mr. Redstone's story is well worth reading on its own account. Told in simple, direct language such as John Bunyan might have used, it permits no doubt of the single-minded sincerity of the man, who gave up everything to become an officer of the Salvation Army, but, exhibiting a sad want of that capacity for unhesitating and blind obedience on which Mr. Booth lays so much stress, was thrown aside, penniless—no, I am wrong, with 2s. 4d. for his last week's salary—to shift, with his equally devoted wife, as he best might. I wish I could induce intending contributors to Mr. Booth's army chest to read Mr. Redstone's story. I would particularly ask them to contrast the pure simplicity of his plain tale with the artificial pietism and slobbering unction of the letters which Mr. Ballington Booth addresses to his "dear boy" (a married man apparently older than himself), so long as the said "dear boy" is facing brickbats and starvation, as per order.

I confess that my opinion of the chiefs of the Salvation Army has been so distinctly modified by the perusal of this pamphlet that I am glad to be relieved from the necessity of expressing it. It will be much better that I should cite a few sentences from the preface written by Dr. Cunningham Geikie, who expresses warm admiration for the early and uncorrupted work of the Salvation Army, and cannot possibly be accused of prejudice against it on religious grounds:

1. The Salvation Army "is emphatically a family concern. Mr. Booth, senior, is General; one son is chief of the staff, and the remaining sons and daughters engross the other chief positions. It is Booth all over; indeed, like the sun in your eyes, you can see nothing else wherever you. turn." And, as Dr. Geikie shrewdly remarks, "to be the head of a widely spread sect carries with it many advantages—not all exclusively spiritual."

2. Whoever becomes a Salvation officer is henceforth a slave, helplessly exposed to the caprice of his superiors.

Mr. Redstone bore an excellent character both before he entered the army and when he left it. To join it, though a *married man, he gave up a situation which he had held for five years, and he served Mr. Booth two years, working hard in most difficult posts. His one fault, Major Lawley tells us, was, that he was "too straight"—that is, too honest, truthful, and manly—or, in other words, too real a Christian. Yet without trial, without formulated charges, on the strength of secret complaints which were never, apparently, tested, he was dismissed with less courtesy than most people would show a beggar—with 2s. 4d. for his last week's salary. If there be any mistake in this matter, I shall be glad to learn it.*

3. Dr. Geikie confirms, on the ground of information given confidentially by other officers, Mr. Redstone's assertion that they are watched and reported by spies from headquarters.

4. Mr. Booth refuses to guarantee his officers any fixed amount of salary. While he and his family of high officials live in comfort, if not in luxury, the pledged slaves whose devotion is the foundation of any true success the Army has met with often have "hardly food enough to sustain life. One good fellow frankly told me that when he had nothing he just went and begged."

At this point, it is proper that I should interpose an apology for having hastily spoken of such men as Francis of Assisi, even for purposes of warning, in connection with Mr. Booth. Whatever may be thought of the wisdom of the plans of the founders of the great monastic orders of the middle ages, they took their full share of suffering and privation, and never shirked in their own persons the sacrifices they imposed on their followers.

I have already expressed the opinion, that whatever the ostensible purpose of the scheme under discussion, one of its consequences will be the setting up and endowment of a new Ranter-Socialist sect. I may now add that another effect will be—indeed, has been—to set up and endow the Booth dynasty with unlimited control of the physical, moral, and financial resources of the sect. Mr. Booth is already a printer and publisher, who, it is plainly declared, utilizes the officers of the Army as agents for advertising and selling his publications;

and some of them are so strongly impressed with the belief that active pushing of Mr. Booth's business is the best road to their master's favor, that when the public obstinately refuse to purchase his papers they buy them themselves and send the proceeds to headquarters. Mr. Booth is also a retail trader on a large scale, and the Dean of Wells has, most seasonably, drawn attention to the very notable banking project which he is trying to float. Anyone who follows Dean Plumptre's clear exposition of the principles of this financial operation can have little doubt that, whether they are, or are not, adequate to the attainment of the first and second of Mr. Booth's ostensible objects, they may be trusted to effect a wide extension of any kingdom in which worldly possessions are of no value. We are, in fact, in sight of a financial catastrophe like that of Law a century ago. Only it is the poor who will suffer.

I have already occupied too much of your space, and yet I have drawn upon only one of the sources of information about the inner working of the Salvation Army at my disposition. Far graver charges than any here dealt with are publicly brought in the others.

I am, Sir, your obedient servant,

T. H. Huxley

P.S. I have just read Mr. Buchanan's letter in the Times *of today. Mr. Buchanan is, I believe, an imaginative writer. I am not acquainted with his works, but nothing in the way of fiction he has yet achieved can well surpass his account of my opinions and of the purport of my writings.*

IV

The Times, *December 20ᵗʰ, 1890*
Sir—In discussing Mr. Booth's projects I have hitherto left in the background a distinction which must be kept well in sight by those who wish to form a fair judgment of the influence, for good or evil, of the Salvation Army. Salvationism, the work of

"saving souls" by revivalist methods, is one thing; Boothism, the utilization of the workers for the furtherance of Mr. Booth's peculiar projects, is another. Mr. Booth has captured, and harnessed with sharp bits and effectual blinkers, a multitude of ultra-Evangelical missionaries of the revivalist school who were wandering at large. It is this skillfully, if somewhat mercilessly, driven team which has dragged the "General's" coach-load of projects into their present position.

Looking, then, at the host of Salvationists proper, from the "captains" downwards (to whom, in my judgment, the family hierarchy stands in the relation of The Old Man of the Sea *to* Sinbad*), as an independent entity, I desire to say that the evidence before me, whether hostile or friendly to the General and his schemes, is distinctly favorable to them. It exhibits them as, in the main, poor, uninstructed, not unfrequently fanatical, enthusiasts, the purity of whose lives, the sincerity of whose belief, and the cheerfulness of whose endurance of privation and rough usage, in what they consider a just cause, command sincere respect. For my part, though I conceive the corybantic method of soul-saving to be full of dangers, and though the theological speculations of these good people are to me wholly unacceptable, yet I believe that the evils which must follow in the track of such errors, as of all other errors, will be largely outweighed by the moral and social improvement of the people whom they convert. I would no more raise my voice against them (so long as they abstain from annoying their neighbors) than I would quarrel with a man, vigorously sweeping out a stye, on account of the shape of his broom, or because he made a great noise over his work. I have always had a strong faith in the principle of the injunction, "Thou shalt not muzzle the ox that treadeth out the corn." If a kingdom is worth a Mass, as a great ruler said, surely the reign of clean living, industry, and thrift is worth any quantity of tambourines and eccentric doctrinal hypotheses. All that I have hitherto said, and propose further to say, is directed against Mr. Booth's extremely clever, audacious, and hitherto successful* *attempt to utilize the credit won by all this honest devotion and self-sacrifice for the purposes of his socialistic autocracy.*

I now propose to bring forward a little more evidence as to how things really stand where Mr. Booth's system has had a fair trial. I obtain it, mainly, from a curious pamphlet, the title of which runs: The New Papacy. Behind the Scenes in the Salvation Array, *by an ex-Staff Officer. "Make not my Father's house a house of merchandise" (John ii. 16). 1889. Published at Toronto, by A. Britnell. On the cover it is stated that "This is the book which was burned by the authorities of the Salvation Army." I remind the reader, once more, that the statements which I shall cite must be regarded as* ex parte; *all I can vouch for is that, on grounds of internal evidence and from other concurrent testimony respecting the ways of the Booth hierarchy, I feel justified in using them.*

This is the picture the writer draws of the army in the early days of its invasion of the Dominion of Canada:

Then, it will be remembered, it professed to be the humble handmaid of the existing churches; its professed object was the evangelization of the masses. It repudiated the idea of building up a separate religious body, and it denounced the practice of gathering together wealth and the accumulation of property. Men and women other than its own converts gathered around it and threw themselves heart and soul into the work, for the simple reason that it offered, as they supposed, a more extended and widely open field for evangelical effort. Ministers everywhere were invited and welcomed to its platforms, majors and colonels were few and far between, and the supremacy and power of the General were things unknown. . . . Care was taken to avoid anything like proselytism; its converts were never coerced into joining its ranks. . . . In a word, the organization occupied the position of an auxiliary mission and recruiting agency for the various religious bodies. . . . The meetings were crowded, people professed conversion by the score, the public liberally supplied the means to carry on the work in their respective communities; therefore every corps was wholly self-supporting, its officers were properly, if not luxuriously, cared for, the local expenditure was amply provided, and, under the supervision of the secretary, a local member, and the officer in charge, the funds were disbursed in the towns where they were collected, and the spirit of satisfaction and confidence was mutual all around (p. 3).

Such was the army as the green tree. Now for the dry:

Those who have been daily conversant with the army's machinery are well aware how entirely and radically the whole system has changed, and how, from a band of devoted and disinterested workers, united in the bonds of zeal and charity for the good of their fellows, it has developed into a colossal and aggressive agency for the building up of a system and a sect, bound by rules and regulations altogether subversive of religious liberty and antagonistic to every (other?) branch of Christian endeavor, and bound hand and foot to the will of one supreme head and ruler. . . . As the work has spread through the country, and as the area of its endeavors has enlarged, each leading position has been filled, one after the other, by individuals strangers to the country, totally ignorant of the sentiments and idiosyncrasies of the Canadian people, trained in one school under the teachings and dominance of a member of the Booth family, and out of whom every idea has been crushed, except that of unquestioning obedience to the General, and the absolute necessity of going forward to his bidding without hesitation or question (p. 4).

What is the result of all this? In the first place, whilst material prosperity has undoubtedly been attained, spirituality has been quenched, and, as an evangelical agency, the army has become almost a dead letter. . . . In seventy-five percent of its stations its officers suffer need and privation, chiefly on account of the heavy taxation that is placed upon them to maintain an imposing headquarters and a large ornamental staff. The whole financial arrangements are carried on by a system of inflation and a hand-to-mouth extravagance and blindness as to future contingencies. Nearly all of its original workers and members have disappeared (p. 4). "In reference to the religious bodies at large the army has become entirely antagonistic. Soldiers are forbidden by its rules to attend other places of worship without the permission of their officers. . . . Officers or soldiers who may conscientiously leave the service or the ranks are looked upon and often denounced publicly as backsliders. . . . Means of the most despicable description have been resorted to in order to starve them back to the service" (p. 5). "In its inner workings the army system is identical with Jesuitism. . . . That 'the end justifies the means,' if not openly taught, is as tacitly agreed as in that celebrated order (p. 5).

Surely a bitter, overcharged, anonymous libel, is the reflection which will occur to many who read these passages, especially the last. Well, I turn to other evidence which, at any rate, is not anonymous. It is contained in a pamphlet entitled General Booth, the Family, and the Salvation Army, showing its Rise, Progress, and Moral and Spiritual Decline, *by S. H. Hodges, LL.B., late Major in the Army, and formerly private secretary to General Booth (Manchester, 1890). I recommend potential contributors to Mr. Booth's wealth to study this little work also. I have learned a great deal from it. Among other interesting novelties, it tells me that Mr. Booth has discovered* "the necessity of a third step or blessing, in the work of Salvation. He said to me one day, 'Hodges, you have only two barrels to your gun; I have three'" *(p. 18). And if Mr. Hodges' description of this third barrel is correct—*"giving up your conscience" *and,* "for God and the army, stooping to do things which even honorable worldly men would not consent to do" *(p. 19)—it is surely calculated to bring down a good many things, the first principles of morality among them.*

Mr. Hodges gives some remarkable examples of the army practice with the "General's" new rifle. But I must refer the curious to his instructive pamphlet. The position I am about to take up is a serious one; and I prefer to fortify it by the help of evidence which, though some of it may be anonymous, cannot be sneered away. And I shall be believed, when I say that nothing but a sense of the great social danger of the spread of Boothism could induce me to revive a scandal, even though it is barely entitled to the benefit of the Statute of Limitations.

On the 7ᵗʰ of July, 1883, you, Sir, did the public a great service by writing a leading article on the notorious "Eagle" case, from which I take the following extract:

Mr. Justice Kay refused the application, but he was induced to refuse it by means which, as Mr. Justice Stephen justly remarked, were highly discreditable to Mr. Booth. Mr. Booth filed an affidavit which appears totally to have misled Mr. Justice Kay, as it would have misled anyone who regarded it as a frank and honest statement by a professed teacher of religion.

When I addressed my first letter to you I had never so much as heard of the "Eagle" scandal. But I am thankful that my perception of the inevitable tendency of all religious autocracies towards evil was clear enough to bring about a provisional condemnation of Mr. Booth's schemes in my mind. Supposing that I had decided the other way, with what sort of feeling should I have faced my friend, when I had to confess that the money had passed into the absolute control of a person about the character of whose administration this concurrence of damnatory evidence was already extant?

I have nothing to say about Mr. Booth personally, for I know nothing. On that subject, as on several others, I profess myself an agnostic. But, if he is, as he may be, a saint actuated by the purest of motives, he is not the first saint who, as you have said, has shown himself "in the ardor of prosecuting a well-meant object" to be capable of overlooking "the plain maxims of everyday morality." If I were a Salvationist soldier, I should cry with Othello, "Cassio, I love thee; but never more be officer of mine."

I am, Sir, your obedient servant,

T. H. Huxley

V

The Times, *December 24ᵗʰ, 1890*

Sir—If I have any strong points, finance is certainly not one of them. But the financial, or rather fiscal, operations of the General of the Salvation Army, as they are set forth and exemplified in The New Papacy, *possess that grand simplicity which is the mark of genius; and even I can comprehend them—or, to be more modest, I can portray them in such a manner that every lineament, however harsh, and every shade, however dark, can be verified by published evidence.*

Suppose there is a thriving, expanding colonial town, and that, scattered among its artizans and laborers, there is a sprinkling of Methodists, or other such ultra-evangelical good people, doing their best, in a quiet way, to "save souls." Clearly, this is an outpost which it is desirable to capture. "We," therefore, take measures to get up a Salvation "boom" of the ordinary pattern. Enthusiasm is roused. A score or two of soldiers are enlisted into the ranks of the Salvation Army. "We" select the man who promises to serve our purposes best, make a "captain" of him, and put him in command of the "corps." He is very pleased and grateful; and indeed he ought to be. All he has done is that he has given up his trade; that he has promised to work at least nine hours a day in our service (none of your eight-hour nonsense for us) as collector, bookseller, general agent, and anything else we may order him to be. "We," on the other hand, guarantee him nothing whatever; to do so might weaken his faith and substitute worldly for spiritual ties between us. Knowing that, if he exerts himself in a right spirit, his labors will surely be blessed, we content ourselves with telling him that if, after all expenses are paid and our demands are satisfied each week, 25s. remains, he may take it. And, if nothing remains, he may take that, and stay his stomach with what the faithful may give him. With a certain grim playfulness, we add that the value of these contributions will be reckoned as so much salary. So long as our "captain" is successful, therefore, a beneficent spring of cash trickles unseen into our treasury; when it begins to dry up we say, "God bless you, dear boy," turn him adrift (with or without 2s. 4d. in his pocket), and put some other willing horse in the shafts.

The "General," I believe, proposes, among other things, to do away with "sweating." May he not as well set a good example by beginning at home?

My little sketch, however, looks so like a monstrous caricature that, after all, I must produce the original from the pages of my Canadian authority. He says that a "captain" "has to pay 10 percent of all collections and donations to the divisional fund for the support of his divisional officer, who has also the privilege of arranging for such special meetings as he shall think fit, the proceeds of which he takes away for the general needs of the division. Headquarters, too, has the right to hold such special meetings at the corps and send around such special attractions as its wisdom sees fit, and to take away the proceeds for the purposes it decides upon. . . . He has to pay the rent of his building, either to headquarters or a private individual; he has to send the whole collection of the afternoon meeting of the first Sunday in the month to the 'Extension Fund' at headquarters; he has to pay for the heating, lighting, and cleaning of his hall, together with such necessary repairs as may be needed; he has to provide the food, lodging, and clothing of his cadet, if he has one; headquarters taxes him with so many copies of the army papers each week, for which he has to *pay, sold or unsold; and when he has done this, he may take $6 (or $5, being a woman), or such proportion of it as may be left, with which to clothe and feed himself and to pay the rent and provide for the heating and lighting of his quarters. If he has a lieutenant he has to pay him $6 per week, or such proportion of it as he himself gets, and share the house expenses with him. Now, it will be easily understood that at least 60 percent of the stations in Canada the officer gets no money at all, and he has to beg specially amongst his people for his house-rent and food. There are few places in the Dominion in which the soldiers do not find their officers in all the food they need; but it must be remembered that the value of the food so received has to be accounted for at headquarters and entered upon the books of the corps as cash received, the amount being deducted from any moneys that the officer is able to take from the week's collections. So that, no matter how much may be specially given, the officer cannot receive more than the value of $6 per week. The officer cannot collect any arrears of salary, as each week has to pay its own expenses; and if there is any surplus cash after all demands are met it must be sent to the 'war chest' at headquarters."*—The New Papacy *(pp. 33, 36).*

Evidently, Sir, "headquarters" has taken to heart the injunction about casting your bread upon the waters. It casts the crumb of a day or two's work of an emissary, and gets back any quantity of loaves of cash, so long as "captains" present themselves to be used up and replaced by new victims. What can be said of these devoted poor fellows except, O sancta simplicitas!

But it would be a great mistake to suppose that the money-gathering efficacy of Mr. Booth's fiscal agencies is exhausted by the foregoing enumeration of their regular operations. Consider the following edifying history of the "Rescue Home" in Toronto:

It is a fine building in the heart of the city; the lot cost $7,000, and a building was put up at a cost of $7,000 more, and there is a mortgage on it amounting to half the cost of the whole. The land today would probably fetch double its original price, and every year enhances its value. . . . In the first five months of its existence this institution received from the public an income of $1,812 70c.; out of this $600 was paid to headquarters for rent, $590 52c. was spent upon the building in various ways, and the balance of $622 18c. paid the salaries of the staff and supported the inmates (pp. 14, 15).

Said I not truly that Mr. Booth's fisc bears the stamp of genius? Who else could have got the public to buy him a "corner lot," put a building upon it, pay all its working expenses: and then, not content with paying him a heavy rent for the use of the handsome present they had made him, they say not a word against his mortgaging it to half its value? And, so far as anyone knows, there is nothing to stop headquarters from selling the whole estate tomorrow, and using the money as the "General" may direct.

Once more listen to the author of The New Papacy, *who affirms that "out of the funds given by the Dominion for the evangelization of the people by means of the Salvation Army, one sixth had been spent in the extension of the Kingdom of God, and the other five sixths had been invested in valuable property, all handed over to Mr. Booth and his heirs and assigns, as we have already stated" (p. 15).*

And this brings me to the last point upon which I wish to touch. The answer to all inquiries as to what has become of the enormous personal and real estate which has been given over to Mr. Booth is that it is held "in trust." The supporters of Mr. Booth may feel justified in taking that statement "on trust." I do not. Anyhow, the more completely satisfactory this "trust" is, the less can any man who asks the public to put blind faith in his integrity and his wisdom object to acquaint them exactly with its provisions. Is the trust drawn up in favor of the Salvation Army? But what is the legal status *of the Salvation Army? Have the soldiers any claim? Certainly not. Have the officers*

*any legal interest in the "trust"? Surely not. The "General"
has taken good care to insist on their renouncing all claims
as a condition of their appointment. Thus, to all appearance,
the army as a legal person, is identical with Mr. Booth. And,
in that case, any "trust" ostensibly for the benefit of the army
is—what shall we say that is at once accurate and polite?*

*I conclude with these plain questions—Will Mr. Booth take
counsel's opinion as to whether there is anything in such legal
arrangements as he has at present made which prevents him
from disposing of the wealth he has accumulated at his own
will and pleasure? Will anybody be in a position to set either the
civil or the criminal law in motion against him or his successors if he or they choose to spend every farthing in ways very
different from those contemplated by the donors?*

*I may add that a careful study of the terms of a "Declaration
of Trust by William Booth in favor of the Christian Mission,"
made in 1878, has not enabled persons of much greater compe-
tence than myself to answer these questions satisfactorily.[3]*

I am, Sir, your obedient servant,

T. H. Huxley

On December 24th a letter appeared in the *Times* signed "J. S.
Trotter," in which the following passages appear:

*It seems a pity to put a damper on the spirits of those who agree
with Professor Huxley in his denunciation of General Booth
and all his works. May I give a few particulars as to the "book"
which was published in Canada? I had the pleasure of an interview with the author of a book written in Canada. The book
was printed at Toronto, and two copies only struck off by the
printers; one of these copies was stolen from the printer, and
the quotation sent to you by Professor Huxley was inserted
in the book, and is consequently a forgery. The book was published
lished without the consent and against the will of the author.*

*So the quotation is not only "a bitter, overcharged anony-
mous libel," as Professor Huxley intimates, but a forgery as*

well. As to Mr. Hodges, it seems to me to be simply trifling with your readers to bring him in as an authority. He was turned out of the army, out of kindness taken on again, and again dismissed. If this had happened to one of your staff, would his opinion of the Times *as a newspaper be taken for gospel?*

But in the *Times* of December 29th Mr. J. S. Trotter writes:

I find I was mistaken in saying, in my letter of Wednesday, to the Times *that Mr. Hodges was dismissed from the service of General Booth, and regret any inconvenience the statement may have caused to Mr. Hodges.*

And on December 30th the *Times* published a letter from Mr. Hodges in which he says that Mr. Trotter's statements as they regard himself "are the very reverse of truth. I was never turned out of the Salvation Army. Nor, so far as I was made acquainted with General Booth's motives, was I taken on again out of kindness. In order to rejoin the Salvation Army, I resigned the position of manager in a mill where I was in receipt of a salary of £250 per annum, with house-rent and one third of the profits. Instead of this Mr. Booth allowed me £2 per week and house-rent."

VI

The Times, *December 26th, 1890*
Sir—I am much obliged to Mr. J. S. Trotter for the letter which you published this morning. It furnishes evidence, which I much desired to possess on the following points:

1. The author of The New Papacy *is a responsible, trustworthy person; otherwise Mr. Trotter would not speak of having had "the pleasure of an interview" with him.*

2. After this responsible person had taken the trouble to write a pamphlet of sixty-four closely printed pages, some influence was brought to bear upon him, the effect of which was that he refused his consent to its publication. Mr. Trotter's excellent information will surely enable him to tell us what influence that was.

3. How does Mr. Trotter know that any passage I have quoted is an interpolation? Does he possess that other copy of the "two" which alone, as he affirms, were printed?

4. If so, he will be able to say which of the passages I have cited is genuine and which is not; and whether the tenor of the whole uninterpolated copy differs in any important respect from that of the copy I have quoted.

It will be interesting to hear what Mr. J. S. Trotter has to say upon these points. But the really important thing which he has done is that he has testified, of his own knowledge, that the anonymous author of The New Papacy *is no mere irresponsible libeller, but a person of whom even an ardent Salvationist has to speak with respect.*

I am, Sir, your obedient servant,
T. H. Huxley

[I may add that the unfortunate Mr. Trotter did me the further service of eliciting the letter from Mr. Hodges referred to on p. 173—which sufficiently establishes that gentleman's credit, and leads me to attach full weight to his evidence about the "third barrel."]

January 1891

VII

The Times, *December 27ᵗʰ, 1890*
Sir—In making use of the only evidence of the actual working of Mr. Booth's autocratic government accessible to me, I was fully aware of the slippery nature of the ground upon which I was treading. For, as I pointed out in my first letter, "no personal habit more surely degrades the conscience and the intellect than blind and unhesitating obedience to unlimited authority." Now we have it, on Mr. Booth's own showing, that every officer of

*his has undertaken to "obey without questioning or gainsay-
ing the orders from headquarters." And the possible relations
of such orders to honor and veracity are demonstrated not
only by the judicial deliverance on Mr. Booth's affidavit in
the "Eagle" case, which I have already cited; not only by Mr.
Bramwell Booth's admission before Mr. Justice Lopes that
he had stated what was "not quite correct" because he had
"promised Mr. Stead not to divulge" the facts of the case (the*
Times, *November 4ᵗʰ, 1885); but by the following passage in
Mr. Hodges's account of the reasons of his withdrawal from
the Salvation Army:*

The General and Chief did not and could not deny
doing these things; the only question was this, Was
it right to practice this deception? These points of
difference were fully discussed between, myself and
the Chief of the Staff on my withdrawal, especially the
Leamington incident, which was the one that finally
drove me to decision. I had come to the conclusion,
from the first, that they had acted as they supposed
with a single eye to the good of God's cause, and had
persuaded myself that the things were, as against the
devil, right to be done, that as in battle one party
captured and turned the enemy's own guns upon them,
so, as they were fighting against the devil, it would be
fair to use against him his weapons. And I wrote to this
effect to the General (p. 63):

*Now, I do not wish to say anything needlessly harsh, but I
ask any prudent man these questions. Could I, under these
circumstances, trust any uncorroborated statement emanat-
ing from headquarters, or made by the General's order? Had I
any reason to doubt the truth of Mr. Hodges' naïve confession
of the corrupting influence or Mr. Booth's system? And did it
not behove me to pick my way carefully through the mass or
statements before me, many of them due to people whose moral*

sense might, by possibility, have been as much blunted by the army discipline in the use of the weapons of the devil as Mr. Hodges affirms that his was?

Therefore, in my third letter, I commenced my illustrations of the practical working of Boothism with the evidence of Mr. Redstone, fortified and supplemented by that of a non-Salvationist, Dr. Cunningham Geikie. That testimony has not been challenged, and, until it is, I shall assume that it cannot be. In my fourth letter, I cited a definite statement by Mr. Hodges in evidence of the Jesuitical principles of headquarters. What sort of answer is it to tell us that Mr. Hodges was dismissed the army? A child might expect that some such red herring would be drawn across the trail; and, in anticipation of the stale trick, I added the strong primâ facie *evidence of the trustworthiness of my witness, in this particular, which is afforded by the "Eagle" case. It was not until I wrote my fourth letter to you, Sir—until the exploitation of the "captains" and the Jesuitry of headquarters could be proved up to the hilt—that I ventured to have recourse to* The New Papacy. *So far as the pamphlet itself goes, this is an anonymous work; and, for sufficient reasons, I did not choose to go beyond what was to be found between its covers. To anyone accustomed to deal with the facts of evolution, the Boothism of* The New Papacy *was merely the natural and necessary development of the Boothism of Mr. Redstone's case and of the "Eagle" case. Therefore, I felt fully justified in using it, at the same time carefully warning my readers that it must be taken with due caution.*

Mr. Trotter's useful letter admits that such a book was written by a person with whom he had the "pleasure of an interview," and that a version of it (interpolated, according to his assertion) was published against the will of the author. Hence I am justified in believing that there is a foundation of truth in certain statements, some of which have long been in my possession, but which for lack of Mr. Trotter's valuable corroboration I have refrained from using. The time is come when I can set forth some of the heads of this information, with the request that

Mr. Trotter, who knows all about the business, will be so good as to point out any error that there may be in them. I am bound to suppose that his sole object, like mine, is the elucidation of the truth, and to assume his willingness to help me therein to the best of his ability.

1. The author of The New Papacy *is a Mr. Sumner, a person of perfect respectability, and greatly esteemed in Toronto, who held a high position in the Army. When he left, a large public meeting, presided over by a popular Methodist minister, passed a vote of sympathy with him.*

Is this true or false?

2. On Saturday last, about noon, Mr. Sumner, the author of the book, and Mr. Fred Perry, the Salvation Army printer, accompanied by a lawyer, went down to Messrs. Imrie and Graham's establishment, and asked for all the manuscript, stereotype plates, &c., of the book. Mr. Sumner explained that the book had been sold to the Army, and, on a cheque for the amount due being given, the printing material was delivered up.

Did these paragraphs appear in the Toronto Telegram *of April 24th, 1889, or did they not? Are the statements they contain true or false?*

3. Public interest in the fate or probable outcome of that mysterious book called The New Papacy; or, Behind the Scenes in the Salvation Army, *continues unabated, though the line of proceedings by the publisher and his solicitor, Mr. Smoke, of Watson, Thorne, Smoke, and Masten, has not been altered since yesterday. The book, no doubt, will be issued in some form. So far as known, only one complete copy remains, and the whereabouts of this is a secret which will be profoundly kept. It is safe to say that if the Commissioner kept on guessing until the next anniversary, he would not strike the secluded location of the one volume among five thousand which escaped, when he and his assistant, Mr. Fred Perry, believed they had cast every vestige of the forbidden work into the fiery furnace. On Tuesday last, when the discovery was made that a copy of* The New Papacy *was in existence, Publisher Britnell, of Yonge*

Street, was at once the suspected holder, and in a short time his book-store was the resort of army agents sent to reconnoitre (Toronto News, *April 28th, 1889*).

Is this a forgery, or is it not? Is it in substance true or false? When Mr. Trotter has answered these inquiries categorically, we may proceed to discuss the question of interpolations in Mr. Sumner's book.

I am, Sir, your obedient servant,
T. H. Huxley

[On the 26th of December a letter, signed J. T. Cunningham, late Fellow of University College, Oxford, called forth the following commentary.]

VIII

The Times, *December 29th, 1890*

Sir—If Mr. Cunningham doubts the efficacy of the struggle for existence, as a factor in social conditions, he should find fault with Mr. Booth and not with me.

*I am laboring under no delusion as to the possibility of inaugurating the millennium by my social specific. In the struggle of life the weakest will go to the wall, and there are so many weak. The fittest in tooth and claw will survive. All that we can do is to soften the lot of the unfit, and make their suffering less horrible than it is at present (*In Darkest England, *p. 44).*

That is what Mr. Cunningham would have found if he had read Mr. Booth's book with attention. And, if he will bestow equal pains on my second letter, he will discover that he has interpolated the word "wilfully" in his statement of my "argument," which runs thus: "Shutting his eyes to the necessary consequences of the struggle for life, the existence of which he admits as fully as any Darwinian, Mr. Booth tells men whose evil case is one of those consequences that envy is a corner-stone of our competitive system." Mr. Cunningham's physiological

studies will have informed him that the process of "shutting
the eyes," in the literal sense of the words, is not always wilful;
and I propose to illustrate, by the crucial instance his own
letter furnishes, that the "shutting of the eyes" of the mind to
the obvious consequences of accepted propositions may also be
involuntary. At least, I hope so.

1. "Sooner or later," says Mr. Cunningham, "the popula-
tion problem will block the way once more." What does this
mean, except that multiplication, excessive in relation to the
contemporaneous means of support, will create a severe compe-
tition for those means? And this seems to me to be a pretty
accurate "reflection of the conceptions of Malthus" and the
other poor benighted folks of a past generation at whom Mr.
Cunningham sneers.

2. By way of leaving no doubt upon this subject, Mr.
Cunningham further tells us, "The struggle for existence is
always going on, of course; let us thank Darwin for making us
realize it." It is pleasant to meet with a little gratitude to Darwin
among the epigoni *who are squabbling over the heritage he*
conquered for them, but Mr. Cunningham's personal expression
of that feeling is hasty. For it is obvious that he has not "real-
ized" the significance of Darwin's teaching—indeed, I fail to
discover in Mr. Cunningham's letter any sign that he has even
"realized" what he would be at. If the "struggle for existence is
always going on"; and if, as I suppose will be granted, indus-
trial competition is one phase of that struggle, I fail to see how
my conclusion that it is sheer wickedness to tell ignorant men
that "envy" is a corner-stone of competition can be disputed.

Mr. Cunningham has followed the lead of that polished
and instructed person, Mr. Ben Tillett, in rebuking me for (as
the associates say) attacking Mr. Booth's personal character.
Of course, when I was writing, I did not doubt that this very
handy, though not too clean, weapon would be used by one
or other of Mr. Booth's supporters. And my action was finally
decided by the following considerations: I happen to be a member
of one of the largest life insurance societies. There is a vacancy

in the directory at present, for which half a dozen gentlemen are candidates. Now, I said to myself, supposing that one of these gentlemen (whose pardon I humbly beg for starting the hypothesis), say Mr. A., in his administrative capacity and as a man of business, has been the subject of such observations as a Judge on the Bench bestowed upon Mr. Booth, is he a person for whom I can properly vote? And, if I find, when I go to the meeting of the policy-holders, that most of them know nothing of this and other evidences of what, by the mildest judgment, must be termed Mr. A.'s unfitness for administrative responsibilities, am I to let them remain in their ignorance? I leave the answer and its application to men of sense and integrity.

The mention of Mr. Cunningham's ally reminds me that I have omitted to thank Mr. Tillett for his very useful and instructive letter; and I hasten to repair a neglect which I assure Mr. Tillett was more apparent than real. Mr. Tillett's letter is dated December 20th. On the 21st the following pregnant (however unconscious) commentary upon it appeared in Reynolds's Newspaper:

I have always maintained that the Salvation Army is one of the mightiest Socialistic agencies in the country; and now Professor Huxley comes in to confirm that view. How could it be otherwise? The fantastic religious side of Salvationism will disappear in the course of time, and what will be left? A large number of men and women who have been organized, disciplined, and taught to look for something better than their present condition, and who have become public speakers and not afraid of ridicule. There you have the raw materials for a Socialist army.

Mr. Ben Tillett evidently knows Latin enough to construe proximus ardet.

I trust that the public will not allow themselves to be led away by the false issues which are dangled before them. A man

really may love his fellow-men; cherish any form of Christianity
he pleases; and hold not only that Darwinism is "tottering to
its fall," but, if he pleases, the equally sane belief that it never
existed; and yet may feel it his duty to oppose, to the best of his
capacity, despotic Socialism in all its forms, and, more particu-
larly, in its Boothian disguise.

I am, Sir, your obedient servant,
T. H. Huxley

[Persons who have not had the advantage of a classical education
might fairly complain of my use of the word *epigoni*. To say truth,
I had been reading Droysen's *Geschichte des Hellenismus,* and the
familiar historical title slipped out unawares. In replying to me,
however, the late "Fellow of University College," Oxford, declares he
had to look the word out in a Lexicon. I commend the fact to the
notice of the combatants over the desirability of retaining the present
compulsory modicum of Greek in our Universities.]

IX

The Times, *December 30th, 1890*
Sir—I am much obliged to Messrs. Ranger, Burton, and
Matthews for their prompt answer to my questions. I presume
it applies to all money collected by the agency of the Salvation
Army, though not specifically given for the purposes of the
"Christian Mission" named in the deed of 1878; to all sums
raised by mortgage upon houses and land so given; and,
further, to funds subscribed for Mr. Booth's various projects,
which have no apparent reference to the objects of the "Christian
Mission," as defined in the deed. Otherwise, to use a phrase
which has become classical, "it does not assist us much." But I
must leave these points to persons learned in the law.

And, indeed, with many thanks to you, Sir, for the amount
of valuable space which you have allowed me to occupy, I now
propose to leave the whole subject. My sole purpose in embarking

upon an enterprise which was extremely distasteful to me was to prevent the skillful "General," or rather "Generals," who devised the plan of campaign from sweeping all before them with a rush. I found the pass already held by such stout defenders as Mr. Loch and the Dean of Wells, and, with your powerful help, we have given time for the reinforcements, sure to be sent by the abundant, though somewhat slowly acting, commonsense of our countrymen, to come up.

I can no longer be useful, and I return to more congenial occupations.

I am, Sir, your obedient servant
T. H. Huxley

The following letter appeared in the *Times* of January 2nd, 1891:

Dear Mr. Tillett—I have not had patience to read Professor Huxley's letters. The existence of hunger, nakedness, misery, "death from insufficient food," even of starvation, is certain, and no agency as yet reaches it. How can any man hinder or discourage the giving of food or help? Why is the house called a workhouse? Because it is for those who cannot work? No, because it was the house to give work or bread. The very name is an argument. I am very sure what Our Lord and His Apostles would do if they were in London. Let us be thankful even to have a will to do the same.

Yours faithfully,
Henry E. Card. Manning

X

The Times, *January 3rd, 1891*
Sir—In my old favorite, The Arabian Nights, *the motive of the whole series of delightful narratives is that the sultan, who refuses to attend to reason, can be got to listen to a story.*

May I try whether Cardinal Manning is to be reached in the same way? When I was attending the meeting of the British Association in Belfast nearly forty years ago, I had promised to breakfast with the eminent scholar Dr. Hincks. Having been up very late the previous night, I was behind time; so, hailing an outside car, I said to the driver as I jumped on, "Now drive fast, I am in a hurry." Whereupon he whipped up his horse and set off at a hand-gallop. Nearly jerked off my seat, I shouted, "My good friend, do you know where I want to go?" "No, yer honner," said the driver, "but, anyway, I am driving fast." I have never forgotten this object-lesson in the dangers of ill-regulated enthusiasm. We are all invited to jump on to the Salvation Army car, which Mr. Booth is undoubtedly driving very fast. Some of us have a firm conviction, not only that he is taking a very different direction from that in which we wish to go, but that, before long, car and driver will come to grief. Are we to accept the invitation, even at the bidding of the eminent person who appears to think himself entitled to pledge the credit of "Our Lord and His Apostles" in favor of Boothism?

I am, Sir, your obedient servant,

T. H. Huxley

XI

The Times, *January 13th, 1891*

Sir—A letter from Mr. Booth-Clibborn, dated January 3rd, appeared in the Times *of yesterday. This elaborate document occupies three columns of small print—space enough, assuredly, for an effectual reply to the seven letters of mine to which the writer refers, if any such were forthcoming. Mr. Booth-Clibborn signs himself "Commissioner of the Salvation Army for France and Switzerland," but he says that he accepts my "challenge" without the knowledge of his chiefs. Considering the self-damaging character of his letter, it was, perhaps, hardly necessary to make that statement.*

Mr. "Commissioner" Booth-Clibborn speaks of my "chal-
lenge." I presume that he refers to my request for information
about the authorship and fate of The New Papacy, *in the*
letter published in the Times *on December 27ᵗʰ, 1890.*
The "Commissioner" deals with this matter in paragraph No.
4 of his letter; and I observe, with no little satisfaction, that
he does not venture to controvert anyone of the statements of
my witnesses. He tacitly admits that the author of The New
Papacy *was a person "greatly esteemed in Toronto," and that he*
held "a high position in the army"; further, that the Canadian
"Commissioner" thought it worth while to pay the printer's bill,
in order that the copies already printed off might be destroyed
and the pamphlet effectually suppressed. Thus the essential facts
of the case are admitted and established beyond question.

How does Mr. Booth-Clibborn try to explain them away?

Mr. Sumner, who wrote the little book in a hot fit, soon
regretted it (as any man would do whose conscience
showed him in a calmer moment, when his "respectability" returned with his repentance, that he had grossly
misrepresented), and just before it appeared offered
to order its suppression if the army would pay the costs
already incurred, and which he was unable to bear.

The New Papacy fills sixty closely printed duodecimo
pages. It is carefully written, and for the most part in
studiously moderate language; moreover, it contains
many precise details and figures, the ascertainment
of which must have taken much time and trouble. Yet,
forsooth, it was written in "a hot fit."

I sincerely hope, for the sake of his own credit, that Mr.
"Commissioner" Booth-Clibborn does not know as much about
this melancholy business as I do. My hands are unfortunately
tied, and I am not at liberty to use all the information in my
possession. I must content myself with quoting the following
passage from the preface to The New Papacy:

It has not been without considerable thought and a good deal of urging that the following pages have been given to the public. But though we would have shrunk from a labor so distasteful, and have gladly avoided a notoriety anything but pleasant to the feelings, or conducive to our material welfare, we have felt that in the interests of the benevolent public, in the interests of religion, in the interests of a band of devoted men and women whose personal ends are being defeated, and the fruit of whose labor is being destroyed, and, above all, in the interests of that future which lies before the Salvation Army itself, if purged and purified in its executive and returned to its original position in the ranks of Canadian Christian effort, it is no more than our duty to throw such light as we are able upon its true inwardness, and with that object and for the furtherance of those ends we offer our pages to the public view.

The preface is dated April 1889. According to the statement in the Toronto Telegram, *which Mr. "Commissioner" Booth-Clibborn does not dare to dispute, his Canadian fellow-"Commissioner" bought and destroyed the whole edition of* The New Papacy *about the end of the third week in April. It is clear that the writer of the paragraph quoted from the preface was well out of a "hot fit," if he had ever been in one, while he had not entered on the stage of repentance within three weeks of that time. Mr. "Commissioner" Booth-Clibborn's scandalous insinuations that Mr. Sumner was bribed by "a few sovereigns," and that he was "bought off," in the face of his own admission that Mr. Sumner "offered to order its suppression if the army would pay the costs already incurred, and which he was unable to bear," is a crucial example of that Jesuitry with which the officials of the army have been so frequently charged.*

Mr. "Commissioner" Booth-Clibborn says that when "London headquarters heard of the affair, it disapproved of the action of the Commissioner." That circumstance indicates that headquarters is not wholly devoid of intelligence; but it has nothing to do with the value of Mr. Sumner's evidence, which is all I am concerned about. Very likely London headquarters will disapprove of its French "Commissioner's" present action. But what then? The upshot of all this is that Mr. Booth-Clibborn has made as great a blunder as simple Mr. Trotter did. The pair of Balaams greatly desired to curse, but have been compelled to bless. They have, between them, completely justified my reliance on Mr. Sumner as a perfectly trustworthy witness; and neither of them has dared to challenge the accuracy of one solitary statement made by that worthy gentleman, whose full story I hope some day or other to see set before the public. Then the true causes of his action will be made known.

Paragraph 2 of the "Commissioner's" letter says many things, but not much about Mr. Hodges. The columns of the Times *recently showed that Mr. Hodges was able to compel an apology from Mr. Trotter. I leave it to him to deal with the "Commissioner."*

As to the "Eagle" case, treated of in paragraph No. 3, a gentleman well versed in the law, who was in court during the hearing of the appeal, has assured me that the argument was purely technical; that the facts were very slightly gone into; and that, so far as he knows, no dissenting comment was made on the strictures of the Judge before whom the case first came. Moreover, in the judgment of the Master of the Rolls, fully recorded in the Times *of February 14th, 1884, the following passages occur:*

The case had been heard by a learned Judge, who had exercised his discretion upon it, and the Court would not interfere with his discretion unless they could see that he was wrong. The learned Judge had taken a strong view of the conduct of the defendant, but nevertheless had said that he would have given relief if he could have seen how far protection and compensation could be given. And if this Court differed from him in that view, and could give relief without forfeiture, they would be acting on his own principle in doing so. Certain suggestions had been made with that view, and the Court had to consider the case under all the circumstances. . . . He himself (the Master of the Rolls) considered that it was probable the defendant, with his principles, had intended to destroy the property as a public-house, and that it was not right thus to take property under a covenant to keep it up as a public-house, intending to destroy it as such. He did not, however, think this was enough to deprive him of all relief. . . . The defendant could only expect severe terms.

Yet, Sir, Mr. "Commissioner" Booth-Clibborn, this high official of the Salvation Army, has the audacity to tell the public that if I had made inquiries I should have found that "in the Court of Appeal the Judge reversed the decision of his predecessor as regards seven eighths of the property, and the General was declared to have acted all along with straightforwardness and good faith."

But the nature of Mr. "Commissioner" Booth-Clibborn's conceptions of straightforwardness and good faith is so marvelously illustrated by the portions of his letter with which I have dealt that I doubt not his statements are quite up to the level of the "Army" Regulations and Instructions in regard to those cardinal virtues. As I pointed out must be the case, the slave is subdued to that he works in.

For myself, I must confess that the process of wading through Mr. "Commissioner's" verbose and clumsy pleadings has given me a "hot fit," which, I undertake to say, will be followed by not so much as a passing shiver of repentance. And it is under the influence of the genial warmth diffused through the frame, on one of those rare occasions when one may be "angry and sin not," that I infringe my resolution to trouble you with no more letters. On reflection, I am convinced that it is undesirable that the public should be misled, for even a few days, by misrepresentations so serious.

I am copiously abused for speaking of the Jesuitical methods of the superior officials of the Salvation Army. But the following facts have not been, and, I believe, cannot be, denied:

1. Mr. Booth's conduct in the "Eagle" case has been censured by two of the Judges.

2. Mr. Bramwell Booth admitted before Mr. Justice Lopes that he had made an untrue statement because of a promise he had made to Mr. Stead.[4]

And I have just proved that Mr. "Commissioner" Booth-Clibborn asserts the exact contrary of that which your report of the judgment of the Master of the Rolls tells us that distinguished judge said.

Under these circumstances, I think that my politeness in applying no harder adjective than "Jesuitical" to these proceedings is not properly appreciated.

I am, Sir, your obedient servant,

T. H. Huxley

XII

The Times, *January 22nd, 1891*

Sir—I think that your readers will be interested in the accompanying opinion, written in consultation with an eminent Chancery Queen's Counsel, with which I have been favored. It will be observed that this important legal deliverance justifies much stronger language than any which I have applied to the only security (?) for the proper administration of the funds in Mr. Booth's hands which appears to be in existence.

I am, Sir, your obedient servant,

T. H. Huxley

1, DR. JOHNSON'S BUILDINGS, TEMPLE, E. C.,
January 14, 1891.

MR. BOOTH'S DECLARATION OF TRUST DEED, 1878

I am of opinion, subject to the question whether there may be any provision in the Charitable Trusts Acts which can be made available for enforcing some scheme for the appropriation of the property, and with regard to the real and leasehold properties whether the conveyances and leases are not altogether void, as frauds on the Mortmain Acts, that nothing can be done to control or to interfere with Booth in the disposition or application of the properties or moneys purported to be affected by the deed.

As to the properties vested in Booth himself, it appears to me that such are placed absolutely under his power and control both as to the disposal and application thereof, and that there are no trusts for any specific purposes declared which could be enforced, and that there are no defined persons nor classes of persons who can claim to be entitled to the benefit of them, or at whose instance they could be enforced by any legal process.

As to the properties (if any) vested in trustees appointed by Booth, it appears to me that the only person who has a *locus standi to* enforce these trusts is Booth himself, and that he would have absolute power over the trusts and the property, and might deal with the property as he pleased, and that, as in the former case, nothing could be done in the way of enforcing any trusts against him.

As to the moneys contributed or raised by mortgage for the general purposes of the mission, it appears to me that Booth may expend them as he pleases, without being subject to any legal control, and that he cannot even be compelled to publish any balance-sheets.

Whether there are any provisions in the Charitable Trusts Acts which could be made available for enforcing some scheme for the application of the property or funds is a question to which I should require to give a closer consideration should it become necessary to go into it; but at present, after perusing these Acts, and especially 16 and 17 Vict. c. 137 and 18 and 19 Vict. c. 124, I cannot see how they could be made applicable to the trusts as declared in this deed.

As to the Mortmain Acts, the matter is clearly charitable, and unless in the conveyances and leases to Booth, or to the trustees (if any) named by him, all the provisions of the Acts have been complied with, and the deeds have been enrolled under the Acts, they would be void. It is probable, however, that every conveyance and lease has been taken without disclosing any charitable trust, for the purpose of preventing it from being void on the face of it. It is to be noted that the deed is a mere deed poll by Booth himself, without any other party to it, who, as a contracting party, would have a right to enforce it.

Whether there are any objects of the trust I cannot say. If there is, as the recital indicates, a society of enrolled members called "The Christian Mission," those members would be objects of the trust, but then, it appears to me, Booth has entire control and determination of the application. And, as to the trusts enuring for the benefit of the "Salvation Army," I am not aware what is the constitution of the "Salvation Army," but there is no reference whatever to any such body in the deed. I have understood the army as being merely the missionaries, and not the society of worshippers.

If there is no Christian Mission Society of enrolled members, then there are no objects of the trust. The trusts are purely religious, and trading is entirely beyond its purposes. Booth can "give away" the property, simply because there is no one who has any right to prevent his doing so.

ERNEST HATTON

It is probably my want of legal knowledge which prevents me from appreciating the value of the professed corrections of Mr. Hatton's opinion contained in the letters of Messrs. Ranger, Burton, and Matthews, *Times,* January 28th and 29th, 1891.

The note on page 216 refers to a correspondence, incomplete at the time fixed for the publication of my pamphlet, the nature of which is sufficiently indicated by the subjoined extracts from Mr. Stead's letter in the *Times* of January 20th, and from my reply in the *Times* of January 24th. Referring to the paragraphs numbered 1, 2, at the end of my letter XI., Mr. Stead says:

> On reading this, I at once wrote to Professor Huxley, stating that, as he had mentioned my name, I was justified in intervening to explain that, so far as the second count in his indictment went—for the Eagle dispute is no concern of mine—he had been misled by an error in the reports of the case which appeared in the daily papers of November 4, 1885. I have his reply today, saying that I had better write to you direct. May I ask you, then, seeing that my name has been brought into the affair, to state that, as I was in the dock when Mr. Bramwell Booth was in the witness-box, I am in a position to give the most unqualified denial to the statement as to the alleged admission on his part of falsehood? Nothing was heard in Court of any such admission. Neither the prosecuting counsel nor the Judge who tried the case ever referred to it, although it would obviously have had a direct bearing on the credit of the witness; and the jury, by acquitting Mr. Bramwell Booth, showed that they believed him to be a witness of truth. But fortunately the facts can be verified beyond all gainsaying by a reference to the official shorthand-writer's report of the evidence. During the hearing of the case for the prosecution, Inspector Borner was interrupted by the Judge, who said:

"I want to ask you a question. During the whole of that conversation, did Booth in any way suggest that that child had been sold?" Borner replied:

"Not at that interview, my Lord."

It was to this that Mr. Bramwell Booth referred when, after examination, cross-examination, and re-examination, during which no suggestion had been made that he had ever made the untrue statement now alleged against him, he asked and received leave from the Judge to make the following explanation, which I quote from the official report:

"Will you allow me to explain a matter mentioned yesterday in reference to a question asked by your Lordship some days ago with respect to one matter connected with my conduct? Your Lordship asked, I think it was Inspector Borner, whether I had said to him at either of our interviews that the child was sold by her parents, and he replied 'No.' That is quite correct; I did not say so to him, and what I wish to say now is that I had been specially requested by Mr. Stead, and had given him a promise, that I would not under any circumstances divulge the fact of that sale to any person which would make it at all probable that any trouble would be brought upon the persons who had taken part in this investigation." (*Central Criminal Court Reports*, Vol. CII., part 612, pp. 1,035–6.)

In the daily papers of the following day this statement was misreported as follows:

I wish to explain, in regard to your Lordship's condemnation of my having said "No" to Inspector Borner when he asked me whether the child had been sold by her parents—the reason why I stated what was not correct was that I had promised Mr. Stead not to divulge the fact of the sale to any person which would make it probable that any trouble should be brought on persons taking part in this proceeding.

Hence the mistake into which Professor Huxley has unwittingly fallen.

I may add that, so far from the statement never having been challenged for five years, it was denounced as "a remarkably striking lie" in the "War Cry" of November 14th, and again the same official organ of the Salvation Army of November 18th specifically adduced this mis-report as an instance of "the most disgraceful way" in which the reports of the trial were garbled by some of the papers. What, then, becomes of one of the two main pillars of Professor Huxley's argument?"

In my reply, I point out that, on the 10th of January, Mr. Stead addressed to me a letter, which commences thus: "I see in the *Times* of this morning that you are about to republish your letters on Booth's book."

I replied to this letter on the 12th of January:

> *Dear Mr. Stead—I charge Mr. Bramwell Booth with nothing. I simply quote the* Times *report, the accuracy of which, so far as I know, has never been challenged by Mr. Booth. I say I quote the* Times *and not Mr. Hodges,[5] because I took some pains about the verification of Mr. Hodges's citation.*
>
> *I should have thought it rather appertained to Mr. Bramwell Booth to contradict a statement which refers, not to what you heard, but to what he said. However, I am the last person to wish to give circulation to a story which may not be quite correct; and I will take care, if you have no objection (your letter is marked "private"), to make public as much of your letter as relates to the point to which you have called my attention.*
>
> *I am, yours very faithfully,*
> *T. H. Huxley*

To this Mr. Stead answered, under date of January 13th, 1891:

> *Dear Professor Huxley—I thank you for your letter of the 12th inst. I am quite sure you would not wish to do any injustice in this matter. But, instead of publishing any extract from my*

letter, might I ask you to read the passage as it appears in the verbatim report of the trial which was printed day by day, and used by counsel on both sides, and by the Judge during the case? I had hoped to have got you a copy today, but find that I was too late. I shall have it first thing tomorrow morning. You will find that it is quite clear, and conclusively disposes of the alleged admission of untruthfulness. Again thanking you for your courtesy,

I am, yours faithfully,
W. T. Stead

Thus it appears that the letter which Mr. Stead wrote to me on the 13th of January does not contain one word of that which he says it contains, in the statement which appears in the *Times* today. Moreover, the letter of mine to which Mr. Stead refers in his first communication to me is not the letter which appeared on the 13th, as he states, but that which you published on December 27th, 1890. Therefore, it is not true that Mr. Stead wrote "at once." On the contrary, he allowed nearly a fortnight to elapse before he addressed me on the 10th of January 1891. Furthermore, Mr. Stead suppresses the fact that, since the 13th of January, he has had in his possession my offer to publish his version of the story; and he leads the reader to suppose that my only answer was that he "had better write to you direct." All the while, Mr. Stead knows perfectly well that I was withheld from making public use of his letter of the 10th by nothing but my scruples about using a document which was marked "private"; and that he did not give me leave to quote his letter of the 10th of January until after he had written that which appeared yesterday.

And I add:

As to the subject-matter of Mr. Stead's letter, the point which he wishes to prove appears to be this—that Mr. Bramwell Booth did not make a false statement, but that he withheld from the officers of justice, pursuing a most serious criminal inquiry, a fact of grave importance, which lay within his own knowledge. And this because he had promised Mr. Stead to keep the fact secret. In short, Mr. Bramwell Booth did not say what was wrong; but he did what was wrong.

I will take care to give every weight to the correction. Most people, I think, will consider that one of the "main pillars of my argument," as Mr. Stead is pleased to call them, has become very much strengthened.

Legal Opinions Respecting "General" Booth's Acts

In referring to the course of action adopted by "General" Booth and Mr. Bramwell Booth in respect of their legal obligations to other persons, or to the criminal and civil law, I have been as careful as I was bound to be, to put any difficulties suggested by mere lay commonsense in an interrogative or merely doubtful form; and to confine myself, for any positive expressions, to citations from published declarations of the judges before whom the acts of "General" Booth came; from reports of the Law Courts; and from the deliberate opinions of legal experts. I have now some further remarks to make on these topics.

1. The observations at p. 191 express, with due reserve, the impression which the counsel's opinions, quoted by "General" Booth's solicitors, made on my mind. They were written and sent to the printer before I saw the letter from a "Barrister *not* Practising on the Common Law Side," and those from Messrs. Clarke and Calkin and Mr. George Kebbell, which appeared in the *Times* of February 3rd and 4th.

These letters fully bear out the conclusion which I had formed, but which it would have been presumptuous on my part to express, that the opinions cited by "General" Booth's solicitors were like the famous broken tea-cups "wisely ranged for show"; and that, as Messrs. Clarke and Calkin say, they "do not at all meet the main points on which Mr. Hatton advised." I do not think that anyone who reads attentively the able letter of "A Barrister *not* Practising on the Common Law Side" will arrive at any other conclusion; or who will not share the very natural desire of Mr. Kebbell to be provided with clear and intelligible answers to the following inquiries:

1. Does the trust deed by its operation empower anyone legally to call upon Mr. Booth to account for the application of the funds?
2. In the event of the funds not being properly accounted for, is anyone, and, if so, who, in a position to institute civil or criminal proceedings against anyone, and whom, in respect of such refusal or neglect to account?
3. In the event of the proceedings, civil or criminal, failing to obtain restitution of misapplied funds, is or are any other person or persons liable to make good the loss?

On December 24th, 1890, a letter of mine appeared in the *Times* (No. V. above) in which I put questions of the same import, and asked Mr. Booth if he would not be so good as to take counsel's opinion on the "trusts" of which so much has been heard and so little seen, not as they stood in 1878, or in 1888, but as they stand now? Six weeks have elapsed, and I wait for a reply.

It is true that Dr. Greenwood has been authorized by Mr. Booth to publish what he calls a "Rough outline of the intended Trust Deed" (*General Booth and His Critics*, p. 120), but unfortunately we are especially told that it "*does not profess to be an absolutely accurate analysis.*" Under these circumstances I am afraid that neither lawyers nor laymen of moderate intelligence will pay much attention to the assertion, that "*it gives a fair idea of the general effect of the draft,*" even although "*the words in quotation marks are taken from it verbatim.*"

These words, which I give in italics, (1) define the purposes of the scheme to be "*for the social and moral regeneration and improvement of persons needy, destitute, degraded, or criminal, in some manner indicated, implied, or suggested in the book called* In Darkest England." Whence I apprehend that, if the whole funds collected are applied to "mothering society" by the help of speculative attorney "tribunes of the people," the purposes of the trust will be unassailably fulfilled. (2) The name is to be *Darkest England Scheme*, (3) the General of the

Salvation Army is to be *"Director of the Scheme."* Truly valuable information all this! But taking it for what it is worth, the public must not be misled into supposing that it has the least bearing upon the questions to which neither I, nor anybody else, has yet been able to obtain an intelligible answer, and that is, where are the vast funds which have been obtained, in one way or another, during the last dozen years in the name of the Salvation Army? Where is the presumably amended Trust Deed of 1888? I ask once more: Will Mr. Booth submit to competent and impartial legal scrutiny the arrangements by which he and his successors are prevented from dealing with the funds of the so-called "army chest" exactly as he or they may please?

II. With respect to the "Eagle" case, I am advised that Dr. Greenwood, whose good faith I do not question, has been misled into misrepresenting it in the appendix to his pamphlet. And certainly, the evidence of authoritative records which I have had the opportunity of perusing, appears to my non-legal mind to be utterly at variance with the statement to which Dr. Greenwood stands committed. I may observe, further, that the excuse alleged on behalf of Mr. Booth, that he signed the affidavit set before him by his solicitors without duly considering its contents, is one which I should not like to have put forward were the case my own. It may be, and often is, necessary for a person to sign an affidavit without being able fully to appreciate the technical language in which it is couched. But his solicitor will always instruct him as to the effect of these terms. And, in this particular case, where the whole matter turns on Mr. Booth's personal intentions, it was his plainest duty to inquire, very seriously, whether the legal phraseology employed would convey neither more nor less than such intentions to those who would act on the affidavit, before he put his name to it.

III. With respect to Mr. Bramwell Booth's case, I refer the reader to p. 194.

IV. As to Mr. Booth-Clibborn's misrepresentations, see above, pp. 186, 187.

This much for the legal questions which have been raised by various persons since the first edition of the pamphlet was published.

DR. GREENWOOD'S "GENERAL BOOTH AND HIS CRITICS"

So far as I am concerned, there is little or nothing in this *brochure* beyond a reproduction of the vituperative stuff which has been going the round of those newspapers which favor "General" Booth for some weeks. Those who do not want to see the real worth of it all will not read the preceding pages; and those who do will need no help from me.

I fear, however, that in justice to other people I must put one of Dr. Greenwood's paragraphs in the pillory. He says that I have "built up, on the flimsy foundation of stories told by three or four deserters from the Army" (p. 71), a sweeping indictment against General Booth. This is the sort of thing to which I am well accustomed at the hands of anonymous newspaper writers. But in view of the following easily verifiable statements, I do not think that an educated and, I have no doubt, highly respectable gentleman like Dr. Greenwood can, in cold blood, contemplate that assertion with satisfaction.

The persons here alluded to as "three or four deserters from the army" are:

1. Mr. Redstone, for whose character Dr. Cunningham Geikie is guarantee, and whom it has been left to Dr. Greenwood to attempt to besmirch.
2. Mr. Sumner, who is a gentleman quite as worthy of respect as Dr. Greenwood, and whose published evidence not one of the champions of the Salvation Army has yet ventured to impugn.
3. Mr. Hodges, similarly libelled by that unhappy meddler Mr. Trotter, who was compelled to the prompt confession of his error (see p. 172).
4. Notwithstanding this evidence of Mr. Trotter's claims to attention, Dr. Greenwood quotes a statement of his as evidence that a statement quoted by me from. Mr. Sumner's work is a "forgery." But Dr.

Greenwood unfortunately forgets to mention that on the 27th of December 1890 (Letter No. VII. above) Mr. Trotter was publicly required to produce proof of his assertion; and that he has not thought fit to produce that proof.

If I were disposed to use to Dr. Greenwood language of the sort he so freely employs to me, I think that he could not complain of a handsome scolding. For what is the real state of the case? Simply this— that having come to the conclusion, from the perusal of *In Darkest England*, that "General" Booth's colossal scheme (as apart from the local action of Salvationists) was bad in principle and must produce certain evil consequences, and having warned the public to that effect, I quite unexpectedly found my hands full of evidence that the exact evils predicted had, in fact, already shown themselves on a great scale; and, carefully warning the public to criticize this evidence, I produced a small part of it. When Dr. Greenwood talks about my want of "regard to the opinion of the nine thousand odd who still remain among the faithful" (p. 71), he commits an imprudence. He would obviously be surprised to learn the extent of the support, encouragement, and information which I have received from active and sincere members of the Salvation Army—but of which I can make no use, because of the terroristic discipline and systematic espionage which my correspondents tell me is enforced by its chief. Some of these days, when nobody can be damaged by their use, a curious light may be thrown upon the inner workings of the organization which we are bidden to regard as a happy family, by these documents.

THE SALVATION ARMY

Articles of war

To be signed by all who wish to be entered on the roll as soldiers

HAVING RECEIVED WITH ALL MY HEART THE SALVATION OFFERED to me by the tender mercy of Jehovah, I do here and now publicly acknowledge God to be my Father and King, Jesus Christ to be my Savior, and the Holy Spirit to be my Guide, Comforter, and Strength; and that I will, by His help, love, serve, worship, and obey this glorious God through all time and through all eternity.

Believing solemnly that The Salvation Army has been raised up by God, and is sustained and directed by Him, I do here declare my full determination, by God's help, to be a true soldier of the Army till I die.

I am thoroughly convinced of the truth of the Army's teaching.

I believe that repentance towards God, faith in our Lord Jesus Christ, and conversion by the Holy Spirit, are necessary to Salvation, and that all men may be saved.

I believe that we are saved by grace, through faith in our Lord Jesus Christ, and he that believeth hath the witness of it in himself. I have got it. Thank God!

I believe that the Scriptures were given by inspiration of God, and that they teach that not only does continuance in the favor of God depend upon continued faith in, and obedience to, Christ, but that it is possible for those who have been truly converted to fall away and be eternally lost.

I believe that it is the privilege of all God's people to be "wholly sanctified," and that "their whole spirit and soul and body" may "be preserved blameless unto the coming of our Lord Jesus Christ." That is to say, I believe that after conversion there remain in the heart of the believer inclinations to evil, or roots of bitterness, which, unless overpowered by Divine grace, produce actual sin; but these evil tendencies can be entirely taken away by the Spirit of God, and the whole heart thus cleansed from anything contrary to the will of God, or entirely sanctified, will then produce the fruit of the Spirit only. And I believe that persons thus entirely sanctified may, by the power of God, be kept unblamable and unreprovable before Him.

I believe in the immortality of the soul; in the resurrection of the body; in the general judgment at the end of the world; in the eternal happiness of the righteous; and in the everlasting punishment of the wicked.

Therefore, I do here, and now, and forever, renounce the world with all its sinful pleasures, companionships, treasures, and objects, and declare my full determination boldly to show myself a Soldier of Jesus Christ in all places and companies, no matter what I may have to suffer, do, or lose, by so doing.

I do here and now declare that I will abstain from the use of all intoxicating liquors, and also from the habitual use of opium, laudanum, morphia, and all other baneful drugs, except when in illness such drugs shall be ordered for me by a doctor.

I do here and now declare that I will abstain from the use of all low or profane language; from the taking of the name of God in vain; and from all impurity, or from taking part in any unclean conversation or the reading of any obscene book or paper at anytime, in any company, or in any place.

I do here declare that I will not allow myself in any falsehood, deceit, misrepresentation, or dishonesty; neither will I practice any fraudulent conduct, either in my business, my home, or in any other relation in which I may stand to my fellow men, but that I will deal truthfully, fairly, honorably, and kindly with all those who may employ me or whom I may myself employ.

I do here declare that I will never treat any woman, child, or other person, whose life, comfort, or happiness may be placed within my power, in an oppressive, cruel, or cowardly manner, but that I will protect such from evil and danger so far as I can, and promote, to the utmost of my ability, their present welfare and eternal salvation.

I do here declare that I will spend all the time, strength, money, and influence I can in supporting and carrying on this War, and that I will endeavor to lead my family, friends, neighbors, and all others whom I can influence, to do the same, believing that the sure and only way to remedy all the evils in the world is by bringing men to submit themselves to the government of the Lord Jesus Christ.

I do here declare that I will always obey the lawful orders of my Officers, and that I will carry out to the utmost of my power all the Orders and Regulations of The Army; and further, that I will be an example of faithfulness to its principles, advance to the utmost of my ability its operations, and never allow, where I can prevent it, any injury to its interests or hindrance to its success.

And I do here and now call upon all present to witness that I enter into this undertaking and sign these Articles of War of my own free will, feeling that the love of Christ who died to save me requires from me this devotion of my life to His service for the Salvation of the whole world, and therefore wish now to be enrolled as a Soldier of the Salvation Army.

_____

_____ CORPS _____   18

.... *Corps.*

.... *Division.*

.... 18

(SINGLE)

FORM OF APPLICATION FOR AN APPOINTMENT AS AN

OFFICER IN THE SALVATION ARMY

Name ....

Address ....

1. What was your AGE last birthday? .... What is the date of your birthday? ....

2. What is your height? ....

3. Are you free from bodily defect or disease? ....

4. What serious illnesses have you had, and when? ....

5. Have you ever had fits of any kind? .... If so how long ago, and what kind? ....

6. Do you consider your health good, and that you are strong enough for the work of an Officer? .... If not, or if you are doubtful, write a letter and explain the matter. ....

7. Is your doctor's certificate a full and correct statement so far as you know? ....

8. Are you, or have you ever been married? ....

9. When and where CONVERTED? ....

10. What other Religious Societies have you belonged to? ....

11. Were you ever a Junior Soldier?............... If so, how long? ....

12. How long have you been enrolled as a SOLDIER? .... and signed Articles of War? ....

13. If you hold any office in your Corps, say what, and how long held? ....

14. Do you intend to live and die in the ranks of the Salvation Army? ....

_____

15. Have you ever been an open BACKSLIDER? .... If so, how long? ....

16. Why? .... Date of your Restoration? ....

17. Are you in DEBT? .... If so, how much? ....
Why? ....

18. How long owing? .... What for? ....

19. Did you ever use Intoxicating Drink? .... If so, how long is it since you entirely gave up its use? ....

20. Did you ever use Tobacco or Snuff? .... If so, how long is it since you gave up using either? ....

---

21. What UNIFORM do you wear? ....

22. How long have you worn it? ....

23. Do you agree to dress in accordance with the direction of Headquarters? ....

24. Can you provide your own uniform and "List of Necessaries" before entering the Service? ....

---

25. Are you in a Situation? .... If so, how long? ....

26. Nature of duties, and salary ....

27. Name and address of employer? ....

28. If out, date of leaving last situation? .... How long there? ....

29. Why did you leave? ....

30. Name and address of last employer? ....

---

31. Can you start the SINGING? ....

32. Can you play any musical instrument? .... If so, what? ....

33. Is this form filled up by you? .... Can you read well at first sight? ....

34. Can you write SHORTHAND? .... If so, what speed and system? ....

35. Can you speak any language other than English? .... If so, what? ....

36. Have you had any experience and success in the JUNIOR SOLDIERS' WAR? ....

37. If so, what? ....

_____

38. Are you willing to sell the "WAR CRY" on Sundays? ....

39. Do you engage not to publish any books, songs, or music except for the benefit of the Salvation Army, and then only with the consent of Headquarters? ....

40. Do you promise not to engage in any trade, profession, or other money-making occupation, except for the benefit of the Salvation Army, and then only with the consent of Headquarters? ....

41. Would you be willing to go ABROAD if required? ....

42. Do you promise to do your utmost to help forward the Junior Soldiers' work if accepted? ....

43. Do you pledge yourself to spend not less than nine hours every-day in the active service of the Army, of which not less than three hours of each week-day shall be spent in VISITATION? ....

44. Do you pledge yourself to fill up and send to Headquarters forms as to how your day is spent? ....

_____

45. Have you read, and do you believe, the DOCTRINES printed on the other side? ....

46. Have you read the "Orders and Regulations for Field Officers" of the Army? ....

    If you have not got a copy of "Orders and Regulations," get one from Candidates' Department at once. The price to Candidates is 2_s._ 6_d._

47. Do you pledge yourself to study and carry out and to endeavor to train others to carry out all Orders and Regulations of the Army? ....

48. Have you read the Order on page 3 of this Form as to PRESENTS and TESTIMONIALS, and do you engage to carry it out? ....

49. Do you pledge yourself never to receive any sum in the form of pay beyond the amount of allowances granted under the scale which follows? ....

    ALLOWANCES—From the day of arrival at his station, each officer is entitled to draw the following allowances, provided the amount remains in hand after meeting all local expenses, namely: For Single Men: Lieutenants, 16s. weekly, and Captains, 18s.; for Single Women: Lieutenants, 12s. weekly, and Captains, 15s. weekly; Married Men, 27s. per week, and 1s. per week for each child under 14 years of age; in all cases without house-rent.

50. Do you perfectly understand that no salary or allowance is guaranteed to you, and that you will have no claim against the Salvation Army, or against anyone connected therewith, on account of salary or allowances not received by you? ....

51. Have you ever APPLIED BEFORE? .... If so, when?.................

52. With what result? ....

53. If you have ever been in the service of the Salvation Army in any position, say what? ....

54. Why did you leave?...

55. Are you willing to come into TRAINING that we may see whether you have the necessary goodness and ability for an Officer in the Salvation Army, and should we conclude that you have not the necessary qualifications, do you pledge yourself to return home and work in your Corps without creating any dissatisfaction? ....

56. Will you pay your own traveling expenses if we decide to receive you in Training? ....

57. How much can you pay for your maintenance while in Training? ....

58. Can you deposit £1 so that we can provide you with a suit of Uniform when you are Commissioned?...................................

59. What is the shortest NOTICE you require should we want you? ....

60. Are your PARENTS willing that you should become an Officer? ....

61. Does anyone depend upon you for support? .... If so, who? ....

62. To what extent? ....

63. Give your parents', or nearest living reslatives', full address ....
....

---

64. Are you COURTING? .... If so, give name and address of the person ....

65. How long have you been engaged? .... What is the person's age? ....

66. What is the date of Birthday? .... How long enrolled as a SOLDIER? ....

67. What Uniform does the person wear? .... How long worn? ....

68. What does the person do in the Corps? ....

69. Has the person applied for the work? ....

70. If not, when does the person intend doing so? ....

71. Do the parents agree to the person coming into Training? ....

---

72. Do you understand that you may not be allowed to marry until three years after your appointment as an Officer, and do you engage to abide by this? ....

73. If you are not courting, do you pledge yourself to abstain from anything of the kind during Training and for at least twelve months after your appointment as a Commissioned Field Officer? ....

74. Do you pledge yourself not to carry on courtship with anyone at the station to which you are at the time appointed? ....

76. Do you pledge yourself never to marry anyone marriage with whom would take you out of the Army altogether? ....

77. Have you read, and do you agree to carry out, the following Regulations as to Courtship and Marriage? ....

(*a*) Officers must inform their Divisional Officer or Headquarters of their desire to enter into or break off any engagement, and no Officer is permitted to enter into or break off an engagement without the consent of his or her D.O.

(*b*) Officers will not be allowed to carry on any courtship in the Town in which they are appointed; nor until twelve months after the date of their Commission.

(c) Headquarters cannot consent to the engagement of Male Lieutenants, until then Divisional Officer is prepared to recommend them for command of a Station as Captain.

(d) Before Headquarters can consent to the marriage of any Officer, the Divisional Officer must be prepared to give him three stations as a married man.

(e) No Officer accepted will be allowed to marry until he or she has been at least three years in the field, except in cases of long-standing engagements before application for the work.

(f) No Male Officer will, under any circumstances, be allowed to marry before he is twenty-two years of age, unless requited by Headquarters for special service.

(g) Headquarters will not agree to the Marriage of any Male Officer (except under extraordinary circumstances) until twelve months after consenting to his engagement.

(h) Consent will not be given to the engagement of any male Officer unless the young woman is likely to make a suitable wife for an Officer, and (if not already an Officer) is prepared to come into Training at once.

(i) Consent will be given to engagements between Female Officers and Soldiers, on condition that the latter are suitable for Officers, and are willing to come into Training if called upon.

(j) Consent will never be given to any engagement or marriage which would take an Officer out of the Army.

(k) Every Officer must sign before marriage the Articles of Marriage, contained in the Orders and Regulations for Field Officers.

PRESENTS AND TESTIMONIALS

1. Officers are expected to refuse utterly, and to prevent, if possible, even the proposal of any present or testimonial to them.

2. Of course, an Officer who is receiving no salary, or only part salary, may accept food or other gifts, such as are needed to meet his wants; but it is dishonorable for anyone who is receiving their salary to accept gifts of food also.

THE DOCTRINES OF THE SALVATION ARMY

The principal Doctrines taught in the Army are as follows:

1. We believe that the Scriptures of the Old and New Testament were given by inspiration of God, and that they only constitute the Divine rule of Christian faith and practice.

2. We believe there is only one God, who is infinitely perfect, the Creator, Preserver, and Governor of all things.

3. We believe that there are three persons in the Godhead—the Father, the Son, and the Holy Ghost, undivided in essence, coequal in power and glory, and the only proper object of religious worship.

4. We believe that, in the person of Jesus Christ, the Divine and human natures are united, so that He is truly and properly God, and truly and properly man.

5. We believe that our first parents were created in a state of innocency, but by their disobedience they lost their purity and happiness; and that, in consequence of their fall, all men have become sinners, totally depraved, and as such are justly exposed to the wrath of God.

6. We believe that the Lord Jesus Christ has, by His suffering and death, made an atonement for the whole world, so that whosoever will may be saved.

7. We believe that repentance towards God, faith in our Lord Jesus Christ, and regeneration by the Holy Spirit, are necessary to Salvation.

8. We believe that we are justified by grace, through faith in our Lord Jesus Christ, and that he that believeth hath the witness in himself.

9. We believe the Scriptures teach that not only does continuance in the favor of God depend upon continued faith in, and obedience to, Christ, but that it is possible for those who have been truly converted to fall away and be eternally lost.

10. We believe that it is the privilege of all believers to be "wholly sanctified," and that "the whole spirit and soul and body" may "be preserved blameless unto the coming of our Lord Jesus Christ."

That is to say, we believe that after conversion there remain in the heart of the believer inclinations to evil, or roots of bitterness, which, unless overpowered by Divine grace, produce actual sin; but that these evil tendencies can be entirely taken away by the Spirit of God, and the whole heart, thus cleansed from everything contrary to the will of God, or entirely sanctified, will then produce the fruit of the Spirit only. And we believe that persons thus entirely sanctified may, by the power of God, be kept unblamable and unreprovable before Him.

11. We believe in the immortality of the soul; in the resurrection of the body; in the general judgment at the end of the world; in the eternal happiness of the righteous; and in the everlasting punishment of the wicked.

DECLARATION

I HEREBY DECLARE that I will never, on any consideration, do anything calculated to injure The Salvation Army, and especially, that I will never, without first having obtained the consent of The General, take any part in any religious services or in carrying on services held in opposition to the Army.

I PLEDGE MYSELF to make true records, daily, on the forms supplied to me, of what I do, and to confess, as far as I am concerned, and to report, as far as I may see in others, any neglect or variation from the orders or directions of The General.

I FULLY UNDERSTAND that he does not undertake to employ or to retain in the service of The Army anyone who does not appear to him to be fitted for the work, or faithful and successful in it; and I solemnly pledge myself quietly to leave any Army Station to which I may be sent, without making any attempt to disturb or annoy The Army in any way, should The General desire me to do so. And I hereby discharge The Army and The General from all liability, and pledge myself to make no claim on account of any situation, property, or interest I may give up in order to secure an engagement in The Army.

I understand that The General will not be responsible in any way for any loss I may suffer in consequence of being dismissed from

Training; as I am aware that the Cadets are received into Training for the very purpose of testing their suitability for the work of Salvation Army Officers.

I hereby declare that the foregoing answers appear to me to fully express the truth as to the questions put to me, and that I know of no other facts which would prevent my engagement by The General, if they were known to him.

Candidate to sign here...

NOTICE TO CANDIDATES

1. All Candidates are expected to fill up and sign this form themselves, if they can write at all.
2. You are expected to have obtained and read "Orders and Regulations for Field Officers" before you make this application.
3. Making this application does NOT imply that we can receive you as an officer, and you are, therefore, NOT to leave your home, or give notice to leave your situation, until you hear again from us.
4. If you are appointed as an Officer, or received into Training, and it is afterwards discovered that any of the questions in this form have not been truthfully answered, you will be instantly dismissed.
5. If you do not understand any question in this form, or if you do not agree to any of the requirements stated upon it, return it to Headquarters, and say so in a straightforward manner.
6. Make the question for this appointment a matter of earnest prayer, as it is the most important step you have taken since your conversion.

We must have your Photo. Please enclose it with your forms, and address them "Candidate Department," 101, Queen Victoria Street, London, E. C.

THE END.

ENDNOTES

INTRODUCTION

[1] S. Tilghman, Dec. 1, 2005. *http://www.princeton.edu/president/speeches/20051201/index.xml.*

[2] T. Huxley, 1860, quoted by John Green in a letter to Boyd Dawkins. *Life and Letters of Thomas Henry Huxley (LLTHH)*, 2 vols., Leonard Huxley, ed. (1900, New York: D. Appleton & Co.), 1: 199.

[3] T. Huxley, 1868, "A Liberal Education and Where to Find It," *Science and Education, Collected Essays*, vol. 3, (New York: D. Appleton & Co., 1898), pp. 82–83.

[4] See a series of twelve letters by Spencer, "The Proper Sphere of Government," published in the *Nonconformist*, June 1842–November 1842.

[5] W. Sumner, *The Challenge of Facts and Other Essays*, A. S. Kelle, ed. (1914, New Haven: Yale University Press), 293.

[6] T. Huxley, 1859, "On the Persistent Types of Animal Life," *Proc. Royal Institute Great Britain*, 3, 151–153, in *Scientific Manuscripts of T. H. Huxley*, vol. 1–4, M. Foster and E. Ray Lancaster, eds. (1898–1902, London: Macmillan & Co.), vol. 2, 91.

[7] P. Kropotkin, 1902, *Mutual Aid: A Factor of Evolution* (1955, Boston: Extending Horizon Books), 58, 50.

[8] T. Huxley, 1863, *Man's Place in Nature* (1898, New York: D. Appleton & Co.), 152–154.

[9] T. Huxley to Charles Kingsley, September 23, 1860, *LLTHH* 1, 235.

CHAPTER I

[1] See "On a piece of Chalk" in the preceding volume of these Essays (vol. viii. p. 1).

[2] That every theory of evolution must be consistent not merely with progressive development, but with indefinite persistence in the same condition and with retrogressive modification, is a point which I have insisted upon repeatedly from the year 1862 till now. *See Collected Essays*, vol. ii. pp. 461-89; vol. iii. p. 33; vol. viii. p. 304. In the address on "Geological

Contemporaneity and Persistent Types" (1862), the paleontological proofs of this proposition were, I believe, first set forth.

3 "On the Border Territory between the Animal and the Vegetable Kingdoms," *Essays*, vol. viii. p. 162.

4 See "Evolution in Biology," *Essays*, vol. ii. p. 187.

5 *Collected Essays*, vol. ii. *passim*.

6 *Ibid.*, vol. iv. p. 138; vol. v. pp. 71–73.

7 *Ibid.*, vol. viii. p. 321.

8 The sense of the term "Art" is becoming narrowed; "work of Art" to most people means a picture, a statue, or a piece of *bijouterie*; by way of compensation "artist" has included in its wide embrace cooks and ballet girls, no less than painters and sculpt

9 See "Man's Place in Nature," *Collected Essays,* vol. vii., and "On the Struggle for Existence in Human Society" (1888), below.

10 Or to put the case still more simply. When a man lays hold of the two end of a piece of string and pulls them, with intent to break it, the right arm is certainly exerted in antagonism to the left arm; yet both arms derive their energy from the same original source.

11 Not that the conception of such a society is necessarily based upon the idea of evolution. The Platonic state testifies to the contrary.

12 *Collected Essays*, vol. i., "Animal Automatism"; vol. v., "Prologue," pp. 45 *et seq.*

13 *Collected Essays*, vol. v., Prologue, pp. 50–54.

14 See below. "Romanes Lecture," note 7.

15 Adam Smith makes the pithy observation that the man who sympathizes with a woman in childbed, cannot be said to put himself in her place. (*The Theory of the Moral Sentiments*, Part vii. sec. iii. chap. i.) Perhaps there is more humor than force in the example; and, in spite of this and other observations of the same tenor, I think that the one defect of the remarkable work in which it occurs is that it lays too much stress on conscious substitution, too little on purely reflex sympathy.

16 Esther v. 9–13. ". . . but when Haman saw Mordecai in the king's gate, that he stood not up, nor moved for him, he was full of indignation against Mordecai. . . . And Haman told them of the glory of his riches. . . . and all the things wherein the king had promoted him. . . . Yet all this availeth me nothing, so long as I see Mordecai the Jew sitting at the king's gate." What a shrewd exposure of human weakness it is!

17 *Theory of the Moral Sentiments* Part iii. chap. 3. *On the influence and authority of conscience.*

18 Worked out, in its essential features, chiefly by Hartley and Adam Smith, long before the modern doctrine of evolution was thought of. See *Note* below, p. 26.

19 See the essay "On the Struggle for Existence in Human Society" below: and *Collected Essays*, vol. i. p. 276, for Kant's recognition of these facts.

[20] *Collected Essays,* vol. v., Prologue, p. 52.

[21] Whether the struggle for existence with the state of nature and with other societies, so far as they stand in the relation of the state of nature with it, exerts a selective influence upon modern society, and in what direction, are questions not easy to answer. The problem of the effect of military and industrial warfare upon those who wage it is very complicated.

[22] Those who read the last Essay in this volume will not accuse me of wishing to attenuate the evil of the existence of this group, whether great or small.

[23] I have elsewhere lamented the absence from society of a machinery for facilitating the descent of incapacity. "Administrative Nihilism." *Collected Essays,* vol. i. p. 54.

CHAPTER III

[1] See the famous *Collection of Papers,* published by Clarke in 1717. Leibnitz says: "'Tis also a supernatural thing that bodies should *attract* one another at a distance without any intermediate means." And Clarke, on behalf of Newton, caps this as follows: Newton, caps this as follows: "That one body should attract another without any intermediate means is, indeed, not a miracle, but a contradiction; for 'tis supposing something to act where it is not."

[2] I may cite, in support of this obvious conclusion of sound reasoning, two authorities who will certainly not be regarded lightly by Mr. Lilly. These are Augustine and Thomas Aquinas. The former declares that "Fate" is only an ill-chosen name for Providence.

"Prorsus divina providentia regna constituuntur humana. Quæ si propterea quisquam fato tribuit, quia ipsam Dei voluntatem vel potestatem fati nomine appellat, sententiam teneat, linguam corrigat." (Augustinus *De Civitate Dei,* V. c. i.)

The other great doctor of the Catholic Church, "Divus Thomas," as Suarez calls him, whose marvelous grasp and subtlety of intellect seem to me to be almost without a parallel, puts the whole case into a nutshell, when he says that the ground for doing a thing in the mind of the doer is as it were the pre-existence of the thing done:

"Ratio autem alicujus fiendi in mente actoris existens est quædam præ-existentia rei fiendæ in eo." (*Summa,* Qu. xxiii. Art. i.)

If this is not enough, I may further ask what "Materialist" has ever given a better statement of the case for determinism, on theistic grounds, than is to be found in the following passage of the *Summa,* Qu. xiv. Art. xiii.

"Omnia quæ sunt in tempore, sunt Deo ab æterno præsentia, non solum ea ex ratione quâ habet rationes rerum apud se presentes, ut quidam dicunt, sed quia ejus intuitus fertur ab æterno supra omnia, prout sunt in sua præsentialitate. Unde manifestum est quo.

[As I have not said that Thomas Aquinas is professedly a determinist, I do not see the bearing of citations from him which may be more or less inconsistent with the foregoing.]

CHAPTER IV

[1] It remains to be seen whether the plants which have no chlorophyll, and flourish in darkness, such as the *Fungi,* can live upon purely mineral food.

[2] In some remarkable passages of the *Botany* of Sir James Ross' Antarctic voyage, which toot place half a century ago, Sir Joseph Hooker demonstrated the dependence of the animal life of the sea upon the minute, indeed microscopic, plants which float in it: a marvelous example of what may be done by water-culture. One might indulge in dreams of cultivating and imploring diatoms, until the domesticated bore the same relation to the wild forms, as cauliflowers to the primitive Brassica oleracea, without passing beyond the limits of fair scientific speculation.

[3] It is a pity that we have no word that signifies plant-culture exclusively. But for the present purpose I may restrict agriculture to that sense.

[4] I do not forget electric lighting, greenhouses and hothouses, and the various modes of affording shelter against violent winds: but in regard to production of food-stuffs on the large scale they may be neglected. Even if synthetic chemistry should effect the construction of proteids, the Laboratory will hardly enter into competition with the Farm within any time which the present generation need trouble itself about.

[5] See the discussion of this subject further on.

[6] *Collected Essays,* vol. i. pp. 359–382.

[7] The italics are the author's.

[8] Not merely on the grounds stated below, but on the strength of Mr. George's own definition. Does the gatherer of eggs, or berries, *produce* them by his labor? If so, what do the hens and the bushes do?

CHAPTER V

[1] *See Collected Essays,* vol. i. p. 290 to end; and this volume, p. 147.

[2] See *Letter VIII.*

[3] See *Letter II.*

INTRODUCTORY ESSAY

[1] [The reader will observe that this is the argument of the "Romanes Lecture," in brief. 1894.]

[2] The late Sir W. Gull.

³ These numbers are only approximately accurate. In 1881, our population amounted to 35,241,482, exceeding the number in 1871 by 3,396,103. The average annual increase in the decennial period 1871–1881 is therefore 339,610. The number of minutes in a calendar year is 525,600.

⁴ [It is hard to say whether the increase of the unemployed poor, or that of the unemployed rich, is the greater social evil. 1894.]

⁵ Training in the use of simple tools is no doubt very desirable, on all grounds. From the point of view of "culture," the man whose "fingers are all thumbs" is but a stunted creature. But the practical difficulties in the way of introducing handiwork of this kind into elementary schools appear to me to be considerable.

⁶ In what follows I am only repeating and emphasizing opinions which I expressed seventeen years ago, in an Address to the members of the Midland Institute (republished in *Critiques and Addresses* in 1873, and in Vol. i. of these *Essays*). I have seen no reason to modify them, notwithstanding high authority on the other side.

LETTERS ON THE *TIMES*
ON THE
DARKEST ENGLAND SCHEME

¹ See note pp. 152–53.

² See p. 61.

³ See preface to this volume pp. xix—xxii.

⁴ This statement has been disputed, but not yet publicly. (See p. 191.)

⁵ This is a slip of the pen. Mr. Hodges had nothing to do with the citation of which I made use.

SUGGESTED READING

DAMASIO, ANATONIO. *Descartes' Error.* New York: Avon Books, 1994.

DARWIN, CHARLES. 1859. *The Origin of Species.* London: John Murray; 1976.

———. 1871. *The Descent of Man.* New York: Barnes & Noble, 2005.

DE WAAL, FRANZ. *Good Natured.* Cambridge: Harvard University Press, 1996.

GREENE, JOHN. *Science, Ideology, and World View.* Berkeley: University of California Press, 1981.

HUXLEY, THOMAS. 1863. *Evidence As to Man's Place in Nature.* New York: Barnes & Noble, 2006.

IRVINE, WILLIAM. *Apes, Angels, and Victorians.* New York: Time, 1955.

LYONS, SHERRIE. *Thomas Henry Huxley, The Evolution of a Scientist.* Amherst, New York: Prometheus Books, 1999.

RICHARDS, ROBERT. *Darwin and Emergence of Evolutionary Theories of Mind and Behavior.* Chicago: University of Chicago Press, 1987.

SOBER, ELLIOT, AND DAVID SLOAN WILSON. *Unto Others.* Cambridge: Harvard University Press, 1998.